Lord Atkin

Lord Atkin

by Geoffrey Lewis

London
Butterworths
1983

England	Butterworth & Co (Publishers) Ltd, 88 Kingsway, LONDON WC2B 6AB
Australia	Butterworth Pty Ltd, SYDNEY, MELBOURNE, BRISBANE, ADELAIDE and PERTH
Canada	Butterworth & Co (Canada) Ltd, TORONTO Butterworth & Co (Western Canda) Ltd, VANCOUVER
New Zealand	Butterworths of New Zealand Ltd, WELLINGTON
Singapore	Butterworth & Co (Asia) Pte Ltd, SINGAPORE
South Africa	Butterworth Publishers (Pty) Ltd, DURBAN
U.S.A.	Mason Publishing Co, St PAUL, Minnesota Butterworth Legal Publishers, SEATTLE, Washington; BOSTON, Massachusetts; and AUSTIN, Texas D & S Publishers, CLEARWATER, Florida

British Library Cataloguing in Publication Data

Lewis, Geoffrey
  Lord Atkin.
  1. Atkin, James Richard, *Baron Atkin*
  2. Judges — England — Biography
  I. Title
  344.207'14'0924   KD632.A/

  ISBN 0 406 27210 7

£15·95

U28046

340·0924

Printed and bound in Great Britain
by Billings & Sons Limited, Worcester.

PREFACE

The life of an English judge is traditionally private to the point of seclusion; and Lord Atkin was in any case naturally inclined to be a private person, hating the glare of publicity of the sort that came from the disturbance caused by his dissent in *Liversidge v Anderson*, and preferring above everything the company of his own family. These considerations deprive the biographer of any real volume of personal material on Lord Atkin's life, and so it seemed from the first that a conventional biography in the narrative style would be impossible. Another approach was called for. I have therefore attempted a discussion of the more important aspects of Atkin's pervasive contribution to the development of English law. As Lord Wright pointed out in his obituary notice in the *Law Quarterly Review*, Atkin's work was animated by a liberal spirit, and I have come to believe that that was the single most important strand in his thinking. I thought I should discover as much as possible about Lord Atkin's personality, and the chief influences on his life and thought, because of the light these circumstances would shed on his legal thinking. In this I have been greatly helped by personal reminiscences which, through the kindness of many, I have been able to collect and draw upon. These illumine the man in a way which nothing else can. I have also been permitted to include as an appendix the interesting autobiographical fragment which Atkin left, and which deals with his early life up to the time of his call.

If there is a theme, it is that the personality of the individual judge is of profound importance. I do not mean this in the now unhappily fashionable sociological sense. It seems to me to matter little whether a judge went to this school or that, or whether he has had actual experience of the factory floor. The significance of his achievement lies more in the force and tendency of his individual mind. Most cases can be decided in more than one way, and the preferred decision is the product of that individual mind. In face of Lord Denning's remarkable career, this is perhaps now little more than a truism.

Few members of the legal profession would dispute an assessment of Lord Atkin as one of the greatest common lawyers of this century. But it is not my purpose to establish a precise position for him in the pantheon. I have been more concerned to try to discover the nature of Atkin's greatness, and how it was that, notwithstanding the confines of the doctrine of precedent and literal interpretation of statute, he could still give his own impetus to the unfolding development of the law. I also wished to know how it could be that a judge of Lord Atkin's stature, individually responsible in *Donoghue v Stevenson* for one of the most profound shifts in legal thinking during this century, and whose name is a byword among practitioners and law students everywhere in the common law world, is virtually unknown outside that circle. To some extent the answers to these questions remain mysterious, but perhaps some glimmers of light on them will be found in this book.

I acknowledge my gratitude for the help I have received from many quarters. First and foremost, Mrs Elizabeth Robson, Lord Atkin's daughter and custodian of his papers, has throughout been unfailingly kind and quick to help. I could have done little without her friendship. William Atkin, Lord Atkin's son, Richard Youard, Rachel Gibbs, John Hope, Lord Aldington, Patience Martin and Thomas Morison, his grandchildren, Mrs Hamer and Mrs Trench, his cousins, and Harold Morison, his son-in-law, all gave me help and encouragement, and in many cases personal recollections. Mr Andrew Ruck unearthed the splendid piece which Atkin wrote about his remarkable grandmother and Mrs Hamer made available to me his grandmother's own memoirs. Lord Denning, Lord Gardiner, Lord Morris, Lord Wilberforce, Sir John Foster and Mr Frank Heyworth Talbot all generously gave time to pass on their own memories of Atkin; as did Mr D. E. M. Glynne Jones. Professor Stephen Scott of McGill University patiently and hospitably explained to me the significance of the Canadian constitutional cases; and I owe a debt to Professor R. F. V. Heuston for the research which he did into the background of *Liversidge v Anderson*, published in the *Law Quarterly Review*, and in relation to which I have not been able to do much more than trace his footsteps. Bernard Barringer and the late Mr P. C. Beddingham, both accomplished librarians, have answered, always comprehensively, a host of enquiries. Miss Linda McGough produced an immaculate typescript from daunting material.

I wish also to express thanks to the Librarian of The Flinders University of South Australia for permission to reproduce the letter from Lord Atkin to Sir Herbert Evatt on p 221; the National Library of Wales and the Secretary of the Governing Body of the Church in Wales for their help and permission to publish the correspondence between Lord Atkin and Archbishop Green reproduced on pp 231–4; the Public Record Office and the Cabinet Office for permission to reproduce part of Lord Sankey's memorandum to the Cabinet on p 19; Lord Hailsham and the Lord Chancellor's Department for permission to reproduce the letters from the elder Lord Hailsham and Sir Claud Schuster on pp 213–217; Miss Joyce Gutteridge for permission to reproduce the correspondence between her father and Lord Atkin on pp 225–228; the Public Record Office and the Labour Party for permission to refer to the letter from Sir Henry Slessor to Mr Ramsay MacDonald dated 3 January 1923 p 18; Mr N. C. Cairncross and his colleagues at The Home Office for making available the papers relating to *Liversidge v Anderson* referred to on pp 149–151; and Miss Sian Fellows for permitting me to draw on her unpublished dissertation on Lord Atkin's contribution to the subjects of crime and insanity, and legal education.

Finally, I thank Francis Mann, mentor and friend, for his constant and perceptive encouragement.

October 1983   Geoffrey Lewis

CONTENTS

ILLUSTRATIONS

Between pages 132 – 133

James Richard Atkin

James Richard Atkin was born in Queensland on 28 November 1867, son of an Irish father and Welsh mother, a celtic origin of much significance. Robert Travers Atkin, his father, came from 'Fernhill', Kilgariff, County Cork where the family had landed interests, and there were lawyers on that side. Robert's father, Walter Atkin, died when Robert was an infant and left his property in trust. It seems that the trustees were careless or worse and the estate dwindled. His mother took Robert to France where he received part at least of his education. Robert Travers and his mother returned to Ireland at some unknown time and then met Mary Elizabeth Ruck of Merioneth, whom he married. The two are said to have met in Dublin 'doing the season'. Little else can be discovered about his father's family, save for what Lord Atkin himself wrote in the autobiographical fragment that he left.

By contrast with the scantiness of the information about Atkin's Irish forbears, there is a great amount of detail on the Welsh side. As events turned out, the land and people of Merioneth came to become one of the abiding influences and passions of his life.

Within months of their marriage in July of 1864, Atkin's parents sailed for Australia to establish their home and make their way on a sheep-farming station in Queensland. Perhaps the enterprise and courage which had to be summoned up to embark on a voyage into the unknown far side of the world was unremarkable in the mid-nineteenth century. But now it must provoke a sense of envious admiration.

The Atkins sailed from London on 11 November 1864 in a small sailing vessel, the 'Wansfell', taking with them a Welsh maid and an iron cooking stove. They were not to get out of the English Channel for a month, and during that time Robert Atkin reported that they 'were not for twelve hours without reefed topsails. That is to say, it blew a gale of wind the whole time. We were dreadfully knocked about . . .' By 8 December, Robert's sister Kate, who with his other sister Grace and his mother were accompanying the newly married couple, had died, 'worn out with tossing about'. Then shortly after her burial at sea, when the vessel was in Biscay, the gale increased

1

to a hurricane, and 'a tremendous sea struck the ship, making a complete wreck of her deck, and throwing her on her beam ends'. The ship nearly foundered, and the Captain had a narrow escape. Atkin's mother wrote that 'he was carried over the spanker boom, and tossed into the mizen rigging, by clinging to which he was saved. He says, he never saw such a heavy sea, and had another struck her before she had recovered, she must have gone down . . .'

Gales and high winds continued almost to the line, but thereabouts the vessel picked up the south-east trades, and eventually landed at Brisbane by the end of March 1865 where the ship was greeted with relief because it was so long overdue that it was thought to have foundered. Mary Atkin was curious to see the ship from the coastal steamer. 'Although all that was possible had been done to repair damages still she looked woefully battered, and weather beaten. I was very sorry to leave the poor old thing, she seemed the last link with England.'

The party took the steamer to Rockhampton and from there Robert went up country to apply for land for sheep farming. He found land at a place called Herberts Creek, some sixty miles from Rockhampton, and built a house and established himself there. Later he was joined by the women. 'Mary will ride up (60 miles). I shall drive the others. I have a white arab pony for her to ride, very handsome and very strong although small. It took me 60 miles in ten hours the other day and it was not at all knocked up.'

But the farming venture did not succeed. By the Spring of 1866 Robert had begun to interest himself in Queensland politics, and Mary wrote to her mother that her husband had made quite a sensation in an election speech. She reported that 'he is quite buried at Herberts Creek' and in any case 'business of all kinds is very dull in Queensland just now. People prophesy a grand smash, squatters and all. The Colony was pushed on too rapidly and now comes the reaction'. Moreover, both Robert and Mary found the Queensland summer heat intolerable and both were ill, Robert from a fall when riding and in Mary's case seriously so. She began to think of returning home, longing for her mother and her family. By May they had decided to move back to Rockhampton and to let the station at Herberts Creek.

There are no letters remaining which bear a date later than the early part of 1867, but Mary kept the collection which had been handed down to her and in 1915 wrote a little postscript to them. The railway scheme, which was to have linked the Herberts Creek area with Brisbane, failed, the Atkins sold the property, and moved back to Dalgarvan on the Fitzroy River, near Rockhampton. There Robert 'went in for buying mobs of fat cattle up country and then selling them at a profit to the Rockhampton butchers'. He also brought racehorses and rode himself. For Mary this was the happiest time in Queensland. But 'in the course of our three years the life rather palled on Robert, who wished for a more literary and cultivated life. He was made Editor of a Brisbane newspaper and later on with a friend started a newspaper of his own in Brisbane and went into Parliament. So once more we migrated, this time to Brisbane where three sons were born'.

Of these boys, James Richard was the eldest, born in November, 1867. Walter Stewart was born in May 1869 and Robert Laurence in September 1870. But none of them was to know anything of Australia, for their father's new and promising career as a journalist and Member of the Queensland legislature was cut down in 1872, within a year or so of its start, and he died at the appallingly early age of 30 in that year in Brisbane, after much ill health.

Before he died he developed a friendship with a Mr. William Hemmant, a merchant, fellow member of the Queensland Parliament, and a minister of the State Government. Their friendship was to have important consequences for Robert's eldest son, for when Hemmant later on returned to England, he made the young Dick Atkin warmly welcome in his Sevenoaks home, a warmth which was repaid by Atkin's marriage in 1893 to Hemmant's daughter, Lucy Elizabeth.

The exceptional regard in which Robert Atkin was held by his fellow Queenslanders and especially those of the Hibernian Society was shown by a monument erected to his memory in Sandgate, just outside Brisbane. It took the form of a broken column to symbolise 'the irreparable loss of a man who well represented some of the finest characteristics of the Celtic race — its rich humour and subtle wit, its fervid passion and genial warmth of heart'. The monument bears on its East face the simple inscription: 'His days were few but his labours and attainments bore the stamp of a wise maturity'.

Sixty years later Lord Atkin arranged for the restoration of the monument and gave carved lunettes to St. Margaret's Church, Sandgate. A contemporary report speaks of the little church filled to overflowing for the ceremony with many making use of the seats outside on the green. 'There were several people present who could recall Brisbane of the very early days and also had known Robert Travers Atkin.'[1]

More than a year before Robert's death, Mary (or 'Tilly' as she was called by her family), had returned home with the boys to Merioneth. The youngest child was in such poor health that she was advised she must return. The eldest boy, Dick, remembered nothing of the voyage except for the livestock with which they sailed, penned behind bars, and including a goat to provide milk for the children. Of that voyage, undertaken in a sailing ship of only 800 tons, no record remains, but for Tilly, although she could not know it then,

1 Sandgate Church Notes, March 1934.

it was to be a permanent homecoming, and for her eldest son, the beginning of one of the most potent influences on his life.

The three boys and their mother returned to a small slate-roofed country house with a powerful atmosphere, set in a wooded cleft above the Dovey river. This was 'Pantlludw', described affectionately in Lord Atkin's own memoir and by his cousin Bernard Darwin, in *The World that Fred Made*.[2] The name means either 'the valley or hollow of the ashes' or 'the hollow where the water widens'. The house belonged to Tilly's parents, Laurence Ruck, an Englishman from Kent who had run through the better part of his own and his wife's fortunes laying out the grounds of the house; and his wife 'Nain' (the Welsh word for grandmother). Another cousin, Berta Ruck, has devoted a whole chapter of *A Storyteller Tells the Truth*[3] to this remarkable woman, who left so clearly etched a picture of herself in the memory of all who knew her.

Fascinated by genealogy herself she claimed to trace her descent from Owen Glendower, and on her mother's side to have gypsy blood. Of all the written pictures of Nain, the best are Lord Atkin's own memoir and her own reminiscences which she wrote out for her favourite grandson, Bernard Darwin, who could hold her spellbound by his singing of Gilbert and Sullivan lyrics. In her own notes appear most clearly her literary gift and her thirst for life. Here is her description of Christmas in Wales when she was a child:

'At Christmas time the London friends send down barrels of oysters which became the nucleus of hospitable gatherings. Everyone then brewed at home and little groups assembled to test the goodness of the new tap in long narrow ale glasses which are never seen now. Sunday fetes of a semi-ecclesiastical character have also passed out of fashion. On 12th Night there was placed in Servants' Hall or kitchen as the case might be a large tub of water into which were thrown 6d pieces or apples to be ducked for. Sometimes an apple hung from the ceiling surrounded by many candles. This was to be devoured by snatch bites. On Christmas morning there was a Service in Church called Plygain supposed to be the remnant of midnight mass. I can recall the desperate effort to stay awake, the cold walk by starlight through the frosty air, and the smell of the Church, a mixture of holly and Cyfleth, for everyone took with them this kind of Christmas toffee made the night before of treacle, sugar and caraway seeds. The Church decorations were then restricted to sprigs of holly stuck promiscuously about. A goose was generally the Christmas dinner, eaten with grosty pudding. This was prepared by boiling groats a long time with a mixture of treacle and currants, and it was usual to take a liquor glass of brandy with the goose.'

2   Chatto & Windus, 1955.
3   Hutchinson, 1935.

And here is part of her 'Impressions of the Merionethshire Election of December 1st, 1885, from an Aberdovey point of view':

'The day was a brilliant one with a clear sky and bright sunshine. The chrysanthemums spread their petals to enjoy the glow. The sea birds floated lazily on the water and the little waves came rippling in under the gentle influence of a West wind. All nature seemed quietly happy, not so the human portion of the little village. Everyone walked with a quickened step and the new Miller with hat well tilted back swung his coat tails from side to side with unwonted animation. Presently vehicles of many kinds arrived, bearing their captive voters, who were heralded by a body of small boys shouting their different war cries of Morgan Lloyd ar Dgn, Wynne for ever, and Robertson for me. An oily sly Preacher appeared from Pennal, whose face in repose looked solemn and heavy, but when spoken to it lighted up with a false smile. He took his stand on the Terrace in full command of his Pennal flock who had gathered in groups on the road all oily and sly too. From none of these gentry or from their leader could anyone extract a confession as to whom they voted for. To their account I place the 43 neutrals returned at the close of the Poll, every man of whom was no doubt a Robertsonian. The only outspoken voter from Pennal that I saw was Hugh Price of Ty Bricks, who did not hesitate to say that he came to vote for Mr. Wynne. Later in the day the train brought its additions. Amongst these were zealous Conservatives who came from East and West to vote and to vanish. Amongst them were Mr. Robertson from Rhyl, Pearson Griffiths and Robert Anwyl from London. No one was to be found in any of the shops, business having been adjourned to the different Committee rooms.'

The impression of Nain which emerges is almost tangible. She was a very strong character but far from being a bully; well-educated, well-informed and exceptionally well-read, emancipated according to the fashion of her day, fierce in loyalty, immediate in her affection, hating above everything sanctimoniousness and meanness, energetic and gay. She must have left a deep, beneficent, mark on the consciousness of the small Dick Atkin who lived in her house in the impressionable years between five and twelve.

The children with their nurse were in the cottage, while their mother was with her parents in Pantlludw which was not big enough for them all. From the cottage the boys could step out on to the cropped turf of the North Welsh uplands and look into the valley of the Dovey, or plunge down into the woods where the house lay hidden. This landscape, its people and its way of life fixed 'in every fibre the feelings that culminate in that passionate love of hill and gorge and trees and brooks and bracken that fills the heart of every Welshman', as Lord Atkin described it himself.

Dick Atkin went away to school in 1876 at the age of eight to the Friars School, Bangor. From Bangor the Headmaster, Mr Lloyd, wrote to Atkin's mother: 'I think he goes on well — and might have a chance for Winchester Scholarship when about 13 years of age.

We are all very fond of him and he is always a good boy'. But in 1878 Lloyd moved to Christ College, Brecon, and both he and Mrs Atkin wanted the boy to go with him. This old school with a high academic tradition established a permanent place in Atkin's affections. Lloyd was an outstanding teacher and headmaster. The school was in a poor condition when Lloyd arrived with only a single form of 10 or 11 boys, but within a few years it had 100 boys and was regularly taking open scholarships at Oxford and Cambridge. When Atkin returned in 1913, shortly after his appointment to the Bench, to distribute prizes, he described his old headmaster as 'one of the greatest Welshmen of the last century'.

'There was a definition', he said, 'of a philanthropist as someone who made two blades of grass grow where one grew before, and if that was a proper definition of a philanthropist, did it not apply to a man who created three great schools in his career?'

Then, in going on to give general advice to the boys, he spoke of moral courage:

'There was one thing the boys ought to learn when at school, which was in the domain of language . . . If they learnt while at school how and when to say 'no' they would have learnt one of the greatest lessons of their life.'[4]

Atkin's own time at Brecon was happy and fruitful, ending by his winning a classical demyship to Magdalen College, Oxford. While he was at Brecon his mother married again, Lt Col Thomas Ruddiman Steuart. Although the colonel was thirty years older than his wife, the marriage was an exceptionally happy one, and Atkin came to respect and love his step-father with an extreme of devotion. He had gone out to India in 1827 as a cadet of infantry on graduating from Edinburgh University, and spent his entire career there. In 1842 he served in the second Afghan war and later as a Collector and Magistrate of the Lower Scinde and Shikapoor. He retired from the service in 1859. By the time of his death in 1895 at the age of 87 he was one of the oldest surviving officers of the East India Company's service, described in an obituary notice as 'a genial and kindly gentleman', whose 'soldierly bearing and "old school" manners will be much missed'.

In 1856 Colonel Steuart wrote a confidential note to his wife which Lord Atkin later transcribed so that it could be left with his own papers. The Colonel thanked Tilly for her great kindness to him and for her love and affection, and of the three boys he wrote:

---

4   *The Brecon County Times*, 2 October 1913.

'We have endeavoured to give your dear boys a good education so as to send them into the world in a creditable way and it is due to them to say that they have availed themselves of this help and that they have invariably been dutiful and loving to you. They will remember that it has not been without difficulty and self denial on your part and that it has considerably lessened the provision I am able to make for you.'

From Brecon, Atkin went up to Magdalen in 1885 at the age of seventeen. Oxford was not the happiest period of his life. As he conceded, he was too young and the college too full of the well-to-do for him to gain confidence quickly. The indifferent health which dogged his later life first became apparent and he was disappointed to miss by the narrowest margin firsts in Classical Moderations and Greats.

He played a great deal of tennis, a game at which he continued to excel until well into his sixties, and again by a narrow margin just missed a blue in his final year. Although he did not experience that unalloyed pleasure which university life sometimes brings, few honours gave him more satisfaction than the fellowship which he was awarded by Magdalen in 1924, and the giving of his name to the College Law Society in 1936.

Lord Atkin's memoir does not record how he came to choose the Bar as his profession, but he selected Gray's Inn because his grandfather's cousin, who had a prosperous practice and was a Bencher of the Inn, undertook to help him. When he went to eat his dinners, the Inn was in low water. Speaking at a dinner in 1938 in honour of Lord Atkin's completion of twenty-five years of judicial office and referring to a time shortly before Atkin's own call, Sir Miles Mattinson described the then condition of the Inn as to be 'judged by the empty Hall, by the meagre Bench and by the straitened finance. I think you will agree', he said, 'that that time in the history of Gray's Inn marked "the darkest hour before dawn" '. That the Inn was restored to its former prestige, originally made glorious in Tudor times by the names of Bacon, Burghley and Philip Sidney, was due more than anyone else to Lords Atkin and Birkenhead. Each of the two, as Atkin himself said of Birkenhead, loved Gray's Inn from the depths of his soul. Atkin was three times Treasurer and for many years Master of the Library, and as Mattinson said in his speech he 'neglected none of the common tasks of the House, whether in Hall, in Chapel or in Pension'. One event which gave him a special pleasure was when, as Treasurer, he called his youngest daughter Mrs Rose Youard in Gray's Inn Hall in Trinity Term, 1937. Another was his editing and publication in 1924 of *The Moot Book of Gray's Inn,* when he was Master of the Moots. In his foreward he recalled that the custom of mooting in the Inn went back at least to the time of Henry VIII but had fallen into disuse until revived in

1875, and he described the procedure as being that of the Court of Appeal 'by which the irreverent chiefly understood that counsel are subject to interruption from the Bench'. He explained that the judge is not bound even by a decision of the House of Lords, so that he 'has opportunities of expressing himself as to decisions in which as counsel or judge he had taken a different view, opportunities which have not been neglected'.

Atkin set about finding chambers for his pupillage by walking the courts to discover the advocates of greatest ability. His choice was Thomas Scrutton, then enjoying an outstanding practice at the Commercial Bar which was rivalled only by that of John Hamilton. 'I chose for myself soon after I was called', Atkin wrote. 'I went into the courts one afternoon and saw a tall, bearded junior waving his arms at a judge who was listening benevolently to an address in which it was obvious the speaker was complete master of the facts and the law. I found out who he was and induced him to let me read with him'.[5] There began a lifelong friendship with that remarkable man. Scrutton's character and habits have been described elsewhere, but it will be sufficient here to say that he carried on his practice in aggressively unattractive chambers in Temple Gardens under conditions of austerity. He himself worked at a table which came out of one of his father's ships, while in another two rooms his pupils or 'devils' toiled at his papers. These included not only Atkin but also the future Lord Wright and Lord Justice Mackinnon. After the courts rose in the afternoon Scrutton would meet his pupils for tea, but then, far from discussing sets of papers with them, he, 'silently absorbed in thinking about his work, would stride about the room until, almost daily, the top of his head crashed into the knob of the chandelier that hung from the ceiling'.[6] Scrutton's legendary irascibility may have been due to shyness, and it does not seem that relations between himself and Atkin were ever strained. In any event, Atkin admired all his life Scrutton's unique ability as a commercial lawyer and the passion for justice which he disguised beneath his rough manner.

On completing his pupillage in 1891, Atkin took chambers at 3 Pump Court. The period which then ensued was hard to endure. Neither he nor his family knew any solicitors except one or two in North Wales, and a single member of the profession 'esconced among his deed boxes somewhere in Bedford Row'. Work did not come and there was no reason why it should. At this time he was living in rooms in London with Arthur Hughes, who later married Molly Hughes, the author of *A London Family 1870–1900*, which contains some reference to the young Dick Atkin and his family in Wales.

5   III Graya 9 at 10 (1982).
6   *Dictionary of National Biography 1931–1940* p 800.

Then his luck turned. He had been brought into touch with his father's friend from Queensland days, William Hemmant, and visited him at 'Bulimba', his house in Sevenoaks. There he was introduced to two men who were largely responsible for getting his practice under way. The first was Norman Herbert Smith, a city solicitor and old friend of Hemmant. Herbert Smith promised him work and was quickly as good as his word. In March 1891 Atkin received his first set of papers, and wrote immediately to his mother:

Thursday [March 1891]

Dearest Mother,

Norman Smith sent the first brief yesterday. It was an opinion as to how a Scotch firm who had obtained judgment in Constantinople against an Italian trading there could get hold of some of the Italian's property over here. It was a very complicated case and I think I earned my guinea. He sent another case today but that was for an informal kind of opinion and I don't expect a fee. The first opinion was wanted by 12 o'clock this morning so I was in chambers last night till 11 looking out points. It is very good of him I think to keep his promise so promptly. I am going down to Sandown tomorrow and shall be back on Wednesday. I am looking forward very much of course to spending Easter with Lucy. I expect she will be very glad to hear of the first opinion. The fee came with it so that I have earned my first money. I hope you and Father are quite well as this leaves me at present. Best love to you both and Walter.

Always your affectionate son.

Dick

The other introduction, a little later, was to a Mr Grant, the Official Assignee of the Stock Exchange. The last decade of the nineteenth century was one of hectic speculation and several brokers were left exposed by the failure of their clients. The Assignee's duty was to administer the affairs of broking firms which had failed, and many difficult points of Stock Exchange law were thrown up. Atkin had made a study of this subject and had gone some way to preparing a textbook on it. In any event, he made a favourable impression on the Assignee, as he had on Norman Herbert Smith, and both ensured that he had a steady supply of work. In a letter to his grandmother dated November 1897, he speaks of 'a very big Stock Exchange case likely to come on in a few weeks in which Sir. Ed. Clarke has been retained to lead me'. By that date at any rate his practice was on a sound footing. In 1900, he was able to take over his own set of chambers at 1 Hare Court 'lock stock and barrel', as he told his grandmother, 'but I don't think I shall lose by it'. His practice had now broadened. As well as commercial cases, he was undertaking

work of a 'fashionable' character and Sir George Lewis and Charles
Russell were among his professional clients. 'I have got a delightful
case', he told his grandmother, so often his confidante, 'in which a
Lieut. Roe, an Indian Officer, is suing Herbert Compton the novelist
for libel because, in the *Inimitable Mrs. Massingham* the scene of
which is laid over 100 years ago, Compton introduces at Botany Bay
a Lieutenant Roe who beats his convict servant to death with other
disparaging details. I am for Compton and the publishers and we
expect to win.'

No kindness which William Hemmant did for the young Dick
Atkin bore comparison with his bringing him to meet his own
daughter, Lucy Elizabeth, whom Atkin married at Whitsuntide in
1893 after an engagement lasting five years. The long period of
waiting was irksome to both, but Atkin wanted to be sure he could
support his wife. In the event, Hemmant generously gave the couple
an allowance to tide them over the first four years. Atkin had first
met the Hemmants while at Oxford and he wrote to his grandmother
just before going up for his viva of 'a grand dinner party at the
Hemmants' which he and his mother had attended, giving details of
the menu. 'You can't think how kind the Hemmants are. Mr.
Hemmant introduces me as the son of his dearest friend in Brisbane,
and has several times told me to consider his house a second home
when I am in London: and really it is just like being at home.'

Lucy Elizabeth Hemmant, like Atkin's mother and grandmother,
was a girl and woman of strong, vivid character, great warmth and
the habit of outspoken opinions. She gave her husband support
which never faltered in his uniquely demanding profession, surviving
with happiness the difficult early years of the Bar, and later, often
effacing her own inclination and talent for brilliant entertaining when
his work or poor health intervened. Their son William has given this
recollection of her:

> 'Lizzie Atkin was born in Brisbane, Australia, within 12 days and 100
> yards of her future husband. Their fathers were friends though William
> Hemmant had emigrated to Australia some time before Robert Atkin.
> History has it that Hemmant, the younger son of a Peterborough
> farmer, decided when he was 18 years old that the future of the
> younger son of a farmer was not hopeful enough for him. He and a
> young friend bought cheap assisted passages to Australia with the
> atural intention of making fortunes on the goldfields. Fortunately for
> them they attracted the attention of an older passenger who advised
> them strongly to go to the goldfields but not to look for gold. This
> could more readily be obtained by opening a trading store. He even
> volunteered to lend the two young men £100 to start them off. This
> advice proved to be good and William Hemmant in time came to
> own one of the biggest department stores in Brisbane. He also became
> a shareholder and director of one of the principal Australian banks
> and in course of time came home to England with his twelve children

— the youngest, the 13th, died young — to represent his interests in Britain and to build himself a big house in the outskirts of Sevenoaks.

So both husband and wife had seen something of life outside England and were children of very enterprising highly intelligent parents. Their long happy life together was perhaps a natural result of their early history. Theirs was indeed a happy life. Early recollections of their children indicate that once the difficult days of low finances and early babies had been successfully survived Lizzie Atkin began to show the kind of person she was. She was a brilliant pianist and a magnificent hostess. The legal profession has always enjoyed entertaining and being entertained. All the big men of law came to the Atkins' dinner parties where the food and wine were excellent and the talk lively and interesting.

Lizzie liked to dress well but never wore a new dress or hat until it had been approved by her husband: if it was not approved back it went. She bought before the First World War a Unic car, the same model as a London taxi, in which she went shopping and, taxi-wise, could skip easily from one shop to another a hundred yards back. In later years she patronised the Army and Navy Stores into which she would enter majestically leading her bulldog and smoking her cigarette knowing confidently that none of the staff would think of reminding her that both dogs and cigarettes were forbidden in the Stores. She often went on circuit and when she could not she wrote to her husband every day. Dick Atkin's health was a constant worry and she fought hard and successfully to save him from the worst effects of overwork and too many official dinners.

And then the War came and the death of their son Dickie in action, the apple of their eyes, it took them both a long time to recover from that tragedy. In one particular way his mother never recovered. She never played another note of the classical music she loved. But as her younger daughters grew up she organised small dances for them both in London and Aberdovey, the dance music always played, brilliantly by their mother. But she never really recovered and in the end her health and nerves suffered irreparably.'

Lizzie Atkin's generous spirit speaks from a letter which she wrote to her husband after fifteen years of marriage — although their life together was to continue for another thirty-one.

'If I should die while you are still a young man', she wrote, 'you know I would not wish you to lead a solitary life and should be glad that you should marry again, but hope that you would not rush into a second marriage through loneliness but that you would greatly consider your future wife's suitability as a sympathetic kindly woman to look after your children as well as yourself.'

There were eight children of the marriage, six girls and two boys. The elder boy, Dickie, with a career full of promise at Winchester, was killed among the flower of his generation in France in 1917 at the age of twenty. Lady Atkin never shook off the sorrow of that loss. Nancy, the fourth girl, had a dramatic talent which gave her father a particular pleasure. Her first professional appearance was at the Repertory Theatre, Liverpool at the age of 17, where she was 'discovered' by A. A. Milne and Charles Hawtrey, and brought to London to play Anne in 'The Dover Road' at the Haymarket. The cast included Allan Aynesworth, Henry Ainley, Nicholas Hannen, Athene Seyler and John Deverell. Hawtrey, who was the producer, wrote to Atkin after the first night: 'it was a great pleasure to do the play and it is an especial joy to me that Nancy has done so well. I have heard nothing but praise about her performance which I also thought most charming and delightful'. Later she appeared in West End productions of 'The Gay Lord Quex' and 'The Importance of Being Earnest'. Nancy's success on the stage appealed to a side of Atkin which can have been known only to his family and closest friends — his addiction to drama and low humour, if you can call George Robey and Marie Lloyd 'low humour'. He loved the music halls all his life, and had, after all, been the close friend and companion of his debonair first cousin, Bernard Darwin.

As the family increased, they moved to larger and larger late-Victorian houses in Kensington. Before Atkin was made a judge, the entertainments and musical evenings at home were on a large scale, although only two of his daughters were old enough to be present. After the First War, by which time the three eldest daughters were married, there was still a lot of entertaining at home, with small dances and regular tea-time 'At Homes' on Sunday afternoons, at which anybody might turn up — fellow-judges and their wives, barristers, relations and, regularly, Maurice Healy of whom the Atkins were very fond.

Atkin enjoyed the role of host and took pleasure also in the societies to which he belonged. These were not only of an exclusively legal character, and perhaps the most abiding interest was The Medico-Legal Society. Formed in 1901 by R. Henslowe Wellington to discuss matters of interest to both professions, the Society had a diverse, and sometimes colourful, membership. In 1908 George Bernard Shaw spoke on 'The Socialist Criticism of the Medical Profession', and in 1926 Marie Stopes delivered a paper on abortion. She is reported also as having observed to the Society at the time of the women's suffrage campaign: 'I am thankful that we are no longer solely to be ruled by the sex which so egregiously fails to understand us . . .'.[7] Atkin was President for a record number of years between 1920 and 1927 and spoke frequently, especially on the subjects of compensation for industrial accident and disease, and crime and insanity. When he was appointed in 1922 by his friend, Lord Birkenhead, to chair the Committee on the criminal responsibility of the insane, he acknowledged with possibly undue modesty that the invitation was due to his connection with the Society. He was responsible also for

7   Transactions of the Medico-Legal Society XXIV p 19.

arranging for Bernard Spilsbury, the Home Office Pathologist, to give a course of lectures to practising barristers on the subject of medical jurisprudence. The reports of the annual dinners at the Holborn Restaurant in the Transactions of the Society make pleasurable reading, and were evidently animated affairs.

In 1912 Atkin was able to realise a wish he had for long nourished, the purchase of a house in Aberdovey. The solicitor's bill records that 'Craig-y-Don' was acquired at a price of £1,725. It was a comfortable, capacious holiday home set into the hillside with a tennis court above and croquet lawn and within walking distance of the golf-course. There, every summer until the end of his life, Atkin's increasingly numerous family and their friends would repair, for holidays abroad were then almost unknown, and in any case no alternative was ever given serious consideration. Atkin's pleasures were tennis, golf, bridge, the works of Edgar Wallace, and above all the company of his family. These were all available in abundance at Aberdovey.

Craig-y-Don also brought him back regularly to the land of his childhood, his attachment to which was reciprocated by the residents of Aberdovey. When in 1913 he was appointed to the High Court Bench, there were fire crackers on the railway line into the village and he was drawn in a cab with men between the shafts. The inhabitants inscribed an address to him which read, in the grave third person style of the day:

> 'They have watched his career with the greatest admiration; proud to remember that he is by immemorial ancestry their fellow Countryman; justly proud in that he has won for himself in the highest possible degree the reputation for conscientious justice and integrity combined with a considerate and genial courtesy; qualities whereof is fashioned the noblest fame of the British race.'

Considerate and genial courtesy was the quality for which he was remembered by Lord Morris of Borth-y-Gest:

> 'To have had the privilege of knowing Lord Atkin leaves one with memories of a very learned kindly and human person. Great lawyer and judge as he undoubtedly was he was never remote. The young barrister did not endure a state of alarm at the prospect of appearing in any court in which he was sitting though perhaps that prospect would act as a spur to encourage preparation of a well-based and supportable argument.
>
> I probably appeared a few times in the years before 1928 in that division of the Court of Appeal (there were only the two divisions in those days) where Bankes, Scrutton and Atkin LJJ sat together — a remarkable trio. The profession would be well warranted in assessing it is a 'strong Court'. Practitioners looked back to it with legitimate pride. I appeared before him in the House of Lords though not during the years of the last war for I was engaged during the main part of

that period in war work which took me entirely away from practice and Lord Atkin unhappily died in June 1944.

I recall many social occasions when I had the pleasure of seeing Lord Atkin. He was always very attentive to the affairs of any Welsh body with which he was concerned. I remember that he was President one day when the Welsh National Eisteddfod was held at Machynlleth. I heard his speech and chatted with him afterwards. His speech was performed in English. That would not be allowed today but the occasion I speak of was before the 'All Welsh' rule was introduced and enforced at the Eisteddfod. I recall also an occasion when we were both guests in London at the Dinner of the London Welsh Golfing Society. I think that he enjoyed his golf at Aberdovey when he was spending his vacations there. During such interludes he presided when he could at sittings of the Magistrates' Court. That gave much pleasure locally and I understand that he presided with real modesty and with a kindly understanding of the ways and the problems of the humblest of folk.

In London he frequently dined at the Reform Club. In that period very many members of the higher judiciary belonged. He became a Trustee and in due course the senior Trustee. If a young member of the Bar was present he would ask questions showing not only a genuine interest but a most friendly concern as to how the young member was faring. I had many chats with him and nearly always they were about the Bar.

I remember one occasion when I was quite junior. He asked me had I been in Court? (There were not many days at that time when I or my contemporaries were in Court: it so happened however that I had been in Court and very secretly I had been quite pleased with the day's outcome. I had had what was a reasonably good win.) To his question I replied Yes (uttering the word with as much nonchalance as I could command). He wanted to know more. Had I been for the Plaintiff or the Defendant? For the Plaintiff. Who was the Plaintiff? A widowed lady. Whom had she been suing? A Bank. Who was the Judge? Horridge. Had there been a Jury? Yes. What kind? A common jury. What was the result of the case? Well we won (replying with as much reluctant diffidence as I could effect). Did you get damages? Yes. How much? £100. There was a merry twinkle in his eye which after all these years I can still conjure up. He said: What! You tell me that you appeared *for* a widow and *against* a Bank and that the case was before Horridge and a common jury and you only got £100 — I think that you did very badly!

I enjoyed his remark hugely — as I did every occasion when I met him or was in his presence. I am very proud to have know so exalted a lawyer and to have had opportunities of admiring his modesty and his humanity.'

When he was at Aberdovey, Atkin always sat when he could as a magistrate at Towyn or Machynlleth, eventually becoming Chairman of the Merionethshire Quarter Sessions. Although he once described himself (in 1939) as 'an elderly magistrate and therefore one having the taint of sentimentality about me', he not only thought that the

Bench was one of the most important of all public offices, but also that age should not be a bar to sitting. When at the end of his life the question arose whether members of the juvenile court should compulsorily retire at the age of seventy, he wrote to *The Times*:

> Some of the writers on the subject appear to think that the farther a man is removed from his own youth the less he is disposed to appreciate the difficulties of present youth: so that a man with children of his own will have more sympathy with youth than a man with children and grandchildren. That is not in the least my experience of grandparents. But the question is not so much that of understanding one's children as of understanding the children who are juvenile offenders and their conditions of life.[8]

He certainly understood and sympathised with the conditions of life of people of every background in Merioneth; and recognised that as an important qualification for the Bench. He once initiated the appointment as a magistrate of a sheep farmer who had given expert evidence in a sheep stealing case. Atkin publicly congratulated him for his clear and fearless evidence and a friendship developed between the two men, which led directly to the farmer's appointment.

From about the turn of the century Atkin's practice had grown steadily. While still a junior he had appeared before Mr H. H. Asquith sitting as an arbitrator, and had made so favourable an impression on the future Prime Minister that he had arranged for his own son, Raymond, to read in Atkin's chambers. When he took silk in 1906, he was, according to the judgment of *The Times*, probably the busiest junior at the Bar;[9] and when Hamilton was appointed to the Bench in 1909 and his rival Scrutton followed the next year, Atkin was left in more or less undisputed possession of the commercial field.

Of Atkin's style as an advocate all accounts agree that it was restrained and understated, avoiding always the histrionic or showy. *The Times* put it that 'there was nothing on the surface to show what grip, learning and real force he possessed'.[9] As a junior, he excelled in the procedural niceties of interlocutory work which so often are the necessary preliminary for an advantageous position at the opening of the trial. 'Above all things master your procedure', he advised students reading for the Bar, and commended brevity to them. 'Do not make too many points. You will be lucky if you have two good ones. Counsel during the war opened a *habeas corpus* case before a Court of which I was a member by saying that he had 15 points. He was a very experienced counsel, and needless to say they were all bad.'[10] In his own view, most cross-examinations were much too long, and more cases were won by good examination-in-chief than by good cross-examination.

8   *The Times*, 31 August 1943.
9   *The Times*, 26 June 1944.
10 (1928) III Graya 9 at 13.

When Sir John Hamilton wrote to acknowledge Atkin's congratulations on his promotion to the Court of Appeal in 1912, he added revealingly: 'I shall always look back with cordial recollection to trying cases in the Commercial Court, and feeling the responsive twitch, when you threw a dextrous fly over me in a touch and go case — may the Lord forgive me, as Lord Westbury (you remember) used to say'. More conventionally, Sir Richard Henn Collins wrote in 1907 on his own appointment as a Lord of Appeal: 'I am sure to see more and more of your work in my new sphere and if you can only manage to husband your strength there is nothing you may not hope to reach in your profession'.

Atkin's own opinion was that oratory was very rare at the Bar and that it was seldom that sentences were properly finished by the ordinary, or for that matter the extraordinary, silk. His own list of the best advocate speakers of his day was T. R. Kemp, Sir Robert McCall, Sir Edward Clarke, 'one of the greatest speakers it has been my good fortune to hear, and a man who studied oratory from all the great authorities from Quintilian onwards'; and Lord Carson. To those he added Sir Alexander Cockburn, remarking that Cockburn's opening speech in the trial of William Palmer was the most wonderful effect of forensic ability that he knew. 'I often think', he said, 'that one of the best equipments for a man in these days, whether at the Bar or politics, is that he should enrich his ordinary vocabulary by three or four hundred words, and I believe that would be quite sufficient.'[11]

Atkin took silk in 1906, and his practice became almost exclusively concerned with heavy commercial cases. He rarely appeared in jury cases because his style as an advocate was not that which is traditionally associated with juries. But whether the distinction is as sharp as tradition would have it may be open to doubt; and style perhaps should not absolutely disable a man from certain types of case. Among Lord Atkin's papers is an undated letter from Edward Marshall Hall, considered by many to be the jury advocate par excellence. Atkin had apparently written him a note of congratulation on some forensic success and Marshall Hall replied: 'It seems to be my fate to deal with really interesting and difficult scientific questions only when they arise in the defence of some great criminal, and that rather galls me — only a little while ago, a manufacturer in one of the big trades had a heavy case consisting of facts, figures and detail — His solicitors advised him to brief me, but his reply was, "Good God, they will think I have committed a murder" — comment is needless'.

It was only seven years after his taking silk that Lord Haldane appointed Atkin to the Bench in 1913 at the age of forty-five and assigned him to the King's Bench Division. He was an immediate success, having ready-made the temperamental qualities required of a judge. Patient, courteous and quick, he asked few questions, but those, according to Sir John Foster who appeared before him later in Atkin's career, were the most incisive of any judge of whom he had ever had experience. Mr F. Heyworth Talbot QC appeared in a number of tax cases in the House of Lords in which Lord Atkin sat and his impression was similar.

> 'To appear before Lord Atkin was an experience that no one who had enjoyed the privilege would be likely ever to forget. The range and acuity of his mind distinguished him even when he sat with such intellectual giants as Lord Thankerton, Lord Russell of Killowen, Lord Macmillan and Lord Maugham. He listened to argument with generous indulgence; his interjections were few and in tone almost apologetic; but his observations were as pointed as a needle.'

Lord Wilberforce argued a few appeals in the Privy Council when Atkin was sitting.

> 'He impressed me as a superb judge: great intellectual power, displayed with courtesy and elegance, and never divorced from common sense. It was advisable to present a coherent and thought out argument, otherwise one risked fairly quick demolition: but he was in no way a judicial bully, and, in my experience was always kind to the young advocate.'

It would be difficult to give higher praise.
Lord Denning also recollects his judicial style.

> 'But again he was precise in his speech, a quiet voice, but always much to the point. He never dozed or missed anything. He was always courteous. If he was on your side, you had no need to worry — he would put the points in your favour. If he was against you, you could never get him round.'

Lord Gardiner, as a junior whose client could no longer afford a leader, found himself against the formidable Sir Stafford Cripps in a breach of contract and slander appeal in the House of Lords. He won the case by four to one, Atkin leading the majority. 'I shall never forget Atkin's personal kindness and encouragement when I got up', Lord Gardiner wrote.

Atkin became a criminal judge of very high reputation, and in his obituary notice, Professor Gutteridge wrote that to his own knowledge, 'at least two of the most experienced Clerks of Assize of this period regarded him as one of the best criminal judges of his generation'. 'It is curious and interesting', remarked Gutteridge, 'that two of the most successful criminal judges of the twentieth century, Scrutton and Atkin, should have been commercial lawyers without previous experience of crime.'[12]

12   60 LQR 334 at 337.

The six years during which Atkin sat as a King's Bench judge were the years of his professional career that he enjoyed most, and the nine which followed in the Court of Appeal were paradoxically those that he enjoyed least. From the point of view of the development of commercial law, the years in the Court of Appeal as a member of that remarkable court with Lords Justices Bankes and Scrutton, were perhaps more fruitful even than the long period of sixteen years during which he sat in the House of Lords and the Privy Council. Although there is little permanent material in the Reports of his work at first instance, that would have been of small concern to him. He was then master in his own court, and a substantial part of his time was taken up with criminal work on assize, work that with its unique responsibility was also uniquely satisfying.

Judge Bensley Wells who accompanied Atkin on assize as his Marshall in 1914 has left a picture of the judge of that time:

> 'What impressed me more than anything . . . was his gentle and quiet manner and his equanimity. He always seemed to be calm and quite imperturbable . . . When he was on Circuit he would never accept an invitation to dine out, nor would he entertain at all at the Judge's Lodgings while he was engaged in trying a case of murder. Normally, when he and Lady Atkin and I were alone we would play Bridge or, sometimes, Patience after dinner. But while he was trying a murder case he would never take part in any such game, but would retire to his own room to be alone.'

In July 1919, shortly after Atkin's promotion to the Court of Appeal, Birkenhead who was then Lord Chancellor, invited him to become President of the Probate, Divorce and Admiralty Division. The offer was politely but firmly declined. 'I have spent all my professional life in the kind of work that I am now doing', Atkin wrote, 'while I cannot profess to be familiar with the work of the other Division, I am happy where I am and hope to be able in time to do useful work there: I am doubtful as to both points if I were to make the change. I cannot think it my duty to make what would be to me a heavy sacrifice, even in view of the prospects of return which you so kindly and so generously held out to me.' The appointment clearly held no attraction for Atkin, and he would have been wasted in it.

There has been some speculation about whether Atkin was ever offered the Lord Chancellorship, but if he was, no record of the invitation survives. The nearest the evidence goes is a letter of 3 January 1923 from Sir Henry Slesser to Ramsay MacDonald[13] in which, after saying that he understood that there was some difficulty about the Lord Chancellorship, Slesser suggested the names of Sankey, Atkin and McCardie. In the event, Haldane became Lord Chancellor in the first Labour Government, having been urged to do so by Cave 'to save the state', and being with Henderson one of the only two members of that administration who had previously sat in Cabinet. Slesser described all his nominees as 'personal friends of mine who have, I believe, pronounced Labour sympathies'. In that he was wrong, at least so far as Atkin was concerned, for, although he sat on the Liberal benches in the House of Lords, he had little or no political affiliation, and Sir Miles Mattinson was accurate when he said, in 1938, 'Lord Atkin owes nothing to politics'. His membership of the Reform Club was hardly more conclusive than it would be today of Liberal sympathies, and it seems fairest to think of him as a political agnostic. If he never received an invitation to occupy the Woolsack, the explanation may be that he had no sufficient identification with any political party and no evident appetite for politics.

For almost the whole of his career Atkin was troubled by anxiety about money. He began at the Bar without any resources behind him and the fee books record his slow start. By the time he was established as a leading commercial silk he was earning some £11,000 a year, but this relative affluence was short-lived, and as has always been the case in England, his appointment to the High Court Bench brought with it a sharp reduction in income. He returned more than once to the idea of leaving the profession in order to earn more, first as a teacher, later for a post in the City, and even when a judge, to return to the Bar. In 1924, in the middle of his time in the Court of Appeal, he went so far as to compose a letter to the Lord Chancellor who had appointed him (Haldane) to say that he was seriously considering the step of submitting his resignation and returning to the Bar. He hoped that he might be granted a patent of precedence which would give him his old place, and he wrote: 'I am approaching a position in which no Judge ought to be: and I do not think that I can endure it'. He never sent the letter. But the anxiety which prompted it was recurrent.

The judges' salaries had been fixed at £5,000 in 1832 and remained unchanged until 1931 when a 20 per cent cut was proposed as part of the Government's policy to meet the economic crisis. Sankey, the Lord Chancellor, prepared a memorandum for the Cabinet protesting about the cut, saying that taxation would reduce net judicial salaries to about £2,600 a year.

> 'I must . . . point out that their [the Judges'] prestige will be lowered. They will be addressed in Court by Leaders of the Bar who sometimes make in two or three days as much as a Judge makes in a year. There are obvious reasons why it should not be in the power of any Government to decrease the salary of a Judge. His independence must be secured. There is an express provision in the American Constitution to this effect. Speaking with many years' experience both as a Judge, as a Lord Justice of Appeal, and now as Lord Chancellor, I must give it as my considered opinion that unless some alteration is made, it

will not be possible to obtain the services of the best men at the Bar, if the salary of the Judges remains at its present figure.'[14]

By this time Atkin was a Lord of Appeal, but there is a melancholy familiarity about Sankey's arguments. It is painful to reflect how close Atkin came to becoming a victim of these conditions.

Lord Atkin's Christian faith was a strong constant in his life. He was a regular, indeed invariable, Churchgoer, and his long association with the Church in Wales was an activity of high importance to him.

In 1914, the disestablishment of the Welsh Church at last attained the statute book. The question which had been live since at least the 1840s had had a national importance for Wales which John Morley compared with Irish Home Rule. Disestablishment and disendowment were the twin weapons with which radical non-conformity attacked the Church which had come to be thought of by Welsh dissenters as alien. By the late 1880s, the established Church 'had ceased to be a religious issue and was now in essence a nationalist campaign expressed in terms of the class struggle'.[15] But by 1912, when a Disestablishment Bill finally passed the Commons, many of the old arguments had become stale. In the debate on the second reading, F. E. Smith had asked whether the miners of South Wales were 'really palpitating with the desire to transfer £170,000 from curates to museums?'[16] Nevertheless, the Bill was thrown out by the Lords and had in the next two years to be forced on them through the procedures laid down in the new Parliament Act. Because of the War the implementation of the Act, together with that relating to Irish Home Rule, was suspended. The Welsh Bishops continued to canvass for repeal but gradually hope faded and they eventually reconciled themselves to reality and to the work of designing constitutional machinery for the new separate Church.

In this they were fortunate in their legal advisers. 'Their deliberations', wrote a historian of the Welsh Church, 'owed much to the work of two judges, John Sankey and John Bankes, and to the critical acumen of a third judge, J. R. Atkin.'[17] The crucial event was a four-day Convention of the Welsh Church in Cardiff in October 1917, held to settle the means by which the Church should be governed and administered upon the assumption that disestablishment had become an accomplished fact. The Convention was attended by Sankey and Bankes, through whose efforts the

---

14   Public Record Office ref CAB/24/225: reproduced by permission of the Controller of Her Majesty's Stationery Office.

15   K. O. Morgan 'Liberals, Nationalists and Mr. Gladstone' *Transactions of the Honourable Society of Cymmrodorion* (1960) p 46.

16   38 HC Official Report col 803. Far from treating disendowment as a sterile issue, Smith attacked it as offensive to the Christian conscience, and so provoked G. K. Chesterton's celebrated poem 'Anti-Christ', ending with the refrain 'Chuck it! Smith'.

17   D. Walker *Disestablishment and Independence* (Penarth, 1976). The Historical Society of the Church in Wales.

delegates' 'labours had been eased and their perplexity dissipated',[18] but Atkin was unable to be there because of the death of his elder son in France.

The work of the Convention and of the following years brought the Church more into consonance with the national aspirations of Wales than ever before, and gave it a more democratic constitution. The years between 1916 and 1920 when the Welsh Church was finally and formally disestablished also brought a more generous financial settlement than had been feared. In all of this Atkin played a prominent part and he became an original member of the Governing Body, and the Representative Body of bishops, clergy and laity, the two chief organs of the Church. There is no direct evidence of what were his own views on disestablishment, but it seems reasonable to presume that by 1914, when he first became active in the work of preparing a constitution, he would have accepted it as the only realistic course.[19]

At the 1917 Convention, Sir John Bankes said: 'here in Wales the Church has been compulsorily set free . . . if the occasion is wisely used, it affords a great opportunity'.[18] Had Atkin been there, he must have applauded that sentiment. But there is another reason for thinking that the balance of the Church settlement was to his liking. His position was low church and opposed to unchecked authority in the bishops. That emerged clearly in his dispute with the Archbishop in 1938 over the power of the episcopate to issue a universal ban on the remarriage of divorced persons in Church. It was a question, he said then, that arises 'between his parishioner and the individual incumbent'.[20] The charge of Erastianism which was made at the time was extravagant,[21] but the important role which the laity was given by the Church's constitution was entirely consistent with his viewpoint.

Atkin held office as a member of the Governing Body until his death, as a member of the Representative Body until 1922, and as a judge of the Provincial Court of the Church between 1922 and 1938.

Mr D. E. M. Glynne Jones, who was a young curate in Aberdovey and later Archdeacon of Montgomery, has given an impression of Lord Atkin as one of his parishioners in the early 30s:

---

18 *Western Mail*, 3 October 1917.
19 Among the Atkin papers is an undated handwritten note, apparently intended for use in a speech, headed 'The Question of Disestablishment'. It argues the case for disestablishment and begins: 'Question is at hand though to be treated with tenderness and care'. The general thesis seems to be that the trend of history is against establishment so as to ensure government neutrality in matters of opinion and belief; religious equality is incompatible with establishment.
20 See appendix 6.
21 The charge has been persisted in: see '50 Years After' by the Archbishop of Wales, *Church Times* of 9 January 1970, in which the Archbishop wrote: '. . . Atkin in particular tended to see the Church, even as disestablished, as a department of State, and was suspicious of episcopal authority'.

'My knowledge of Lord Atkin dates from 1930–1934 when I was curate of Aberdovey. My Vicar (Canon J. D. Jones) had died a few months only after I was ordained and an inexperienced young deacon had to preside at meetings of the Parochial Church Council of which Lord Atkin was a member. It was quite widely known that the Constitution of the Church in Wales had been largely drawn up by three eminent lawyers with close Welsh connections — Lords Sankey, Bankes and Atkin. The first is said to have written the frame-work of the Constitution in long-hand and then the three were believed to have "gone into retreat" for a week to alter and amend each clause as was thought necessary. My impression is that once the amending act was passed, in which the blow of total disendowment was softened, Lord Atkin with the others saw a great future for the Church in Wales with her new-found independence.

His interest in me began when he knew that one of the papers set for my Priest's examination was on the Constitution and on one occasion he came up to me with that kind amused expression to "quiz" me on certain aspects of the new set up — one question was on the Electoral College and the other on methods of patronage and this was on the golf course on a fine summer's evening! When on vacation in Aberdovey he always read the lessons on Sunday mornings and we were always careful to choose hymns sung to well-known Welsh tunes such as Cym Rhondda and Aberystwyth. His reading was an example to all — clear, incisive and devout. I would describe him as a "low" Church-man with a great love of the Prayer Book; he was a regular monthly Communicant. The request he made to me was that I should learn by heart the Exhortation before Matins and Evensong in the 1662 Prayer Book and not read it. He argued that the opening sentences from Holy Scripture should be read and then the Exhortation recited — facing the congregation. This may seem a detail but is typical of his thoughtfulness.

He was an expert player of tennis and Bridge and a steady golfer. I always found him the kindest of people and I know that many of the villagers went to him with their troubles; he always found time, even on vacation, to talk with them. This very inadequate tribute is gladly paid to a man who made a deep impression on me in the early years of my ministry. I thank God that I knew him.'

Lord Atkin died at Aberdovey on 25 June 1944 at the age of 77 after a prolonged attack of bronchitis (his old enemy). He was buried at the church in the little seaside town to which he had given so much of himself.

These were some of the principal influences on the life and thought of Lord Atkin, and some of the principal events and preoccupations of his life. Of the man himself, the real person standing behind the great judgments, his daughter Mrs Elizabeth Robson should speak.

'I have been trying to think of my father as a lawyer in a detached way but have found it quite impossible because to all his children he was first a very beloved father of a large family and second only a public man. What I remember then is personal; and memories of him at home in Wales and in London, from the time when we asked why we hadn't seen Daddy that morning and were told he had gone to Chambers to the day that I went with him to the House of Lords in 1941 to hear him deliver his judgment in *Liversidge v Anderson*. For most of the time before he went to the House of Lords I only saw him in vacations — his and mine from boarding-school.

So my earliest memories are of him at Aberdovey; but I do remember that in London, when I must have been about six years old, and my younger sister five, he used to sit on the sofa with us in his library and read to us before we went to bed. His favourite poem — and ours — was "Llewellyn and his Dog" (The Hon W. R. Spencer) which reduced us all to tears; and "The Inchape Rock" (Robert Southey). At Aberdovey I can remember him riding his old green bicycle very fast along the roads, dressed in a very old and disreputable suit. He was very proud that one of the suits he wore regularly was thirty years old and he would turn his pocket over so that we could see the tailor's label. He was very athletic, in spite of having a delicate chest, he played tennis for Magdalen and had his golf handicap reduced from 14 to 12 when he was sixty, much to his pride. We went to Church with him every Sunday; and when I was young we were not allowed to play tennis or golf or bathe on Sundays. Later on, when Daddy was President of the Aberdovey Golf Club, he supported a movement to play golf on Sundays (though I don't remember his ever playing himself); and following the decision a large number of greens were cut up with "A" all over them.

After my older sisters were married, Daddy and I used to go to tennis parties all over the neighbourhood — he was much in demand because he still played better than most of the younger men when he was sixty. We didn't have a motor after the first War and we used to hire the village taxi which, in taking us to some houses, very alarmingly had to go up the drive backwards, because the lowest forward gear couldn't manage the hills.

Daddy was called to the Bar when he was twenty-four and married when he was twenty-five. He had met my mother some years before when her parents, who had befriended his parents in Brisbane, invited him to their house. He told us that Mother and he had fallen in love and became engaged five years before they were married — in those days it was usual to wait to marry until there was some prospect of the husband being able to support a wife. Mother was a very good pianist — she had been taught by Clara Schumann — but according to her most of the music she provided for their parties before they married was the playing of ballads — sentimental we would think now — and music hall songs, which Daddy sang with gusto. In those days, when you went to an evening party with your music, you expected to be asked to play or sing. Daddy's role was that of a low comedian and a taste for low comedy lasted all his life — he saw the 'Lambeth Walk' at least twelve times — sometimes by himself and sometimes with me. He was a great admirer of George Robey and of Gordon Harker.

Daddy was born in Brisbane and his mother was widowed when he was six and had two younger brothers.

After her husband died she returned to her parents in Wales, where she had taken the children three years before; and he was brought up by her and his grand-parents in a remote valley in Merionethshire. He went to a Welsh preparatory school — Friars School, Bangor — and from there won a scholarship to Brecon and from Brecon a demyship at Magdalen College, Oxford, and from Magdalen the Arden Scholarship at Gray's Inn so that from the earliest age he largely supported himself.

He was never very strong physically when he was young — his father had died of consumption when he was thirty-one — and Mother had to take great care of him. When his practice grew they had very little social life because he could not manage late hours and the work that a large practice entails. He never worked late at night but Mother gave him breakfast at 6.30 am and he would work at his morning's Brief before he went off to Chambers.

When he was thirty-nine he took silk; and was made a Judge when he was forty-five in 1913. He enjoyed his work as a Judge of first instance more than anything else he did, although, as he said, it is a very lonely life after the comradeship of the Bar. When he was a small boy he had decided he was going to be Lord Chief Justice of England and was disappointed that he did not achieve that ambition. His work in the Court of Appeal he did not enjoy — he was neither dealing direct with problems of law nor with the individual but with other people's opinion of the law; and he felt himself merely an intermediary between one Court and the next. His usual answer to the usual question from the family "Any interesting cases?" was in those days "No, very dull". He was in the Court of Appeal for nine years — from 1919 to 1928 — and was then appointed a Lord of Appeal in Ordinary at the age of sixty.

He was very pleased when he was invited to sit on the local Bench of Magistrates in Merioneth and never missed a sitting when he was at home in the vacations. He was also a Juvenile Court Magistrate until he resigned because he said he was too old, though I don't know that youth *qua* youth is the most important qualification for dealing with troublesome children. A wise and compassionate grandfather may be as sensible as any young magistrate. He did not like many of the children being brought before the Court at all — he was of the opinion that for some of the offences which he regarded as natural mischief — such as robbing an orchard — the right punishment was a whacking from the father or even from the owner of the orchard. He thought that corporal punishment for the child's first offence — was probably the right treatment and very great care and probation if the offender ever came before the Court again.

He was Chairman of the Committee on Crime and Insanity that was appointed in 1924 and whose Report was shelved. He was in favour of capital punishment and also of corporal punishment for some offences, his view being that people forgot the victim in their benevolence towards the criminal. The sanctions of the law were to protect the innocent as well as to reform the guilty. Although all his life he took no part in politics, when he took part in debates in the House of Lords he spoke from the Liberal Benches, for he was truly liberal in his respect for the individual, although he had absolute convictions about the place of law in English society.

I understand that his strength as an advocate lay not in his powers of oratory but in the reasoning and persuasiveness of the arguments by which he tried to bring the Court to his point of view. He continued to use his powers of persuasion when he was sitting as a Lord of Appeal and would come home and say that he thought he had won his "brothers" over to his side or "so-and-so is still not convinced but I think he may be tomorrow". He certainly persuaded his family that he was right. When he gave us the facts of a case and asked us what we thought about it, his way of presenting the problem was such that there never was any suggestion in our minds that the other side could have a leg to stand on. I remember his asking us whom we thought was our "neighbour" and he listened to us before he gave his opinion, which eventually became part of his judgment in *Donoghue v Stevenson*. He told us that he was making law by that judgment. It amazes me now to think with what patience he listened to the dogmas laid down by his children. He was tolerant of almost everybody; and he liked us to argue with him.

All his letters and judgments were written in his own hand because he never had a secretary. In the legal profession the higher you advance and the older you get, the more work you have to do, unlike the rest of the world where you are expected to stop work at sixty-five. Though the hours of work in Court of a Judge are short, they are very exhausting concentrated hours and the judgments that are reserved and have to be written afterwards need much research. When Daddy was a Lord of Appeal he spent almost every Saturday morning working in his room at the House of Lords and when he went to Wales in the vacations he took with him judgments that had still to be written. He would shut himself up in his library morning after morning until he had finished — much against my mother's wishes, who thought he ought to have a holiday.

At the House of Lords he kept his own very large library of law books but at home a library of other books. Apart from the English classics and a lot of poetry, which he had mainly collected when he was at Oxford, these were chiefly "thrillers"; and he had a complete set of Edgar Wallace both in London and in Wales. His children thought he was very "low-brow" in his tastes and we tried hard to educate him into better ways. We told him he never "read" anything but somehow he always seemed to have read everything we wanted to talk about. He found that thrillers were the relaxation he needed — they occupied his mind without making him think. It was a very difficult job to keep him supplied, as he read very quickly and was fussy about his authors — for instance he would not read any detective story written by a woman. His other relaxation was playing bridge — fortunately there were usually enough of us at home to make up a four. I think he liked it because it prevented people talking — he had probably had enough of that in Court.

My knowledge of Judges is fairly limited but nothing that I have read or seen on the stage approximates in any way to the Judge I knew. He was, I suppose, an extraordinarily modest and simple man and at home was treated with great disrespect by his family and apparently did not mind. He went everywhere by bus and I remember him coming home from the Law Courts one day very shaken because he had fallen when running for a No. 11 bus, and it had started before he was completely on board. That was when he was in the Court of Appeal. In the summer he went to watch cricket whenever he could, paying his way like everyone else.

I once enjoyed reflected glory from a judgment of his when, just after the House of Lords' decision in *Waterlow v. Bank of Portugal*, we were in a train in Portugal and happened to share a carriage with a Portuguese lawyer. He had been tremendously impressed and could not speak highly enough of British justice.

Until quite late in his life he suffered from very bad migraine headaches and his doctor had told him he was not to drink port. He was not much of a drinker anyway — at home he had Graves and soda water with his meals, he never drank spirits and at home, of course, never port. However, I gather that when he dined at the Reform or elsewhere he always had a glass of port.

A bomb fell near his flat in Morpeth Terrace (near Victoria Station) in 1940. When I went to see if he was all right in the morning, I found him sitting in his dressing-gown surrounded by rubble, with no windows, but quite cheerful. He emigrated to Roehampton, where we were living, and eventually took over our flat there while we moved to another across the road. He hired a car to take him backwards and forwards to the House of Lords or Privy Council, which was a change from walking from his flat in Morpeth Mansions or taking a bus. I used to go and see him every evening on my way home from work — he was very well looked after by his housekeeper who had been with him before Mother died. One evening when I arrived he was looking quite grey — he had driven as usual from the Privy Council where he had been sitting, to Gray's Inn for lunch and had found it no longer existed. It was a victim of the fire blitz when the bombing the night before had destroyed the water system and despite heroic efforts by everyone concerned there was not enough available to put out the fire. It was a dreadful shock for him because Gray's Inn was a major part of his life — he was Treasurer three times, always attended Pensions and took an interest in everything that was going on. When he was Treasurer in 1937 his youngest daughter, Rosaline, was called by him to the Bar. Naturally he kissed her whereupon I am told that the other women waiting call winced, in case he should do the same.

I planted some runner beans in his little garden in Roehampton, which he thought was miraculous — he was not a gardener himself. In spite of having been brought up within a few yards of the River Dovey with very good fishing, he never fished or shot, but he used to walk miles over the mountains. When I went to a Boxing Day Meet in Machynlleth in 1938 (all the followers were on foot and the fox always disappeared over the top of the hills) I met a farmer who had run up the hills with Daddy when they were boys.

There wasn't much going out at night during the bombing but we used to play bridge with him when we could. I took him out to lunch and a Matinee on his last birthday. He wanted to see Gordon Harker, whom he admired very much. When we sat comfortably in our seats, we found that the ticket agency had given us the wrong theatre — no more seats available — a dreadful disappointment for us both. He spent all his vacations at Craig-y-don with his daughter Nancy and her four children, whom he found very amusing. While her husband was away in the Army, Nancy had started to educate the children herself — aged from 7 downwards and soon became so popular that she had twenty children from evacuated families. Daddy was very interested in all that was going on and also encouraged her in her work as a District Councillor.

Apart from going to the Isle of Wight for their honeymoon, neither of my parents ever went in a boat. However, after my mother died in 1938, he decided to go out to visit my brother in Rio de Janeiro in the summer vacation of 1939. While there, war broke out, so he took the first ship home and was much impressed by the captain, who issued all the passengers (of whom there were very few) with a tin of food and a nail with which to open it if they had to take to the sea. Daddy said that when they had dodged their way across the Atlantic (not in convoy) and arrived in the Solent at the end of September, they were met by a small naval boat, whose officer told them they could not come in. The Captain replied "I have brought my ship and passengers safely across the Atlantic — get out of my way because I am coming in". I met him at Waterloo station in the blackout. Very emotional for us all — he said he had come back to look after "his girls".'

Liberal Philosophy

Every law student knows that when Lord Atkin came to make his great statement about legal responsibility for carelessness, he chose to express it as an analogy to the lawyer's gospel question, who is my neighbour? The unity which he made from the wilderness of precedent was the concern which each man ought to accept for others for what he does or leaves undone. The lawyer would have to concede that his own answer to the question was a restricted one, for legal obligation could never go as far as Christian philosophy, but as he said, 'I do not think so ill of our jurisprudence as to suppose that its principles are so remote from the ordinary needs of civilised society and the ordinary claims it makes on its members as to deny a legal remedy where there is so obviously a social wrong'.[1]

That was a remark which reveals much about the springs of Lord Atkin's thinking. Again and again, in the decisions to which he was party, his judgment, often alone, reveals an uncommon perception of the commerce of daily life underlying a dispute. Such an understanding was essential for a humane law and ensured that it would run consistently with the needs of those whose ordinary lives it, sometimes involuntarily, touched. If the law were to detach itself from that every day world it would lose its use, just as surely as would commercial law if it removed itself from the needs and intentions of businessmen. Lord Atkin's preoccupation was to see that neither should happen. If the law supposed that a man's wife acted in accordance with his directions, then Mr Bumble gave it as his opinion that the law was ass, idiot and bachelor, and most of all that it wanted experience.[2]

The understanding of ordinary life was perhaps the most important facet of Atkin's compassion. Another was a complete absence of

---

1 *Donoghue v Stevenson* [1932] AC 562 at 583.
2 Lord Atkin himself explained in the debates on the Trial of Peers that Mr Bumble's own matrimonial experience was quite contrary to the alleged legal presumption that when a woman committed a crime she acted under the coercion of her husband, and that Bumble's outburst had been so often quoted as a general reflection on the law — see 100 HL Official Report col 406, 4 February 1936.

sentimentality. 'We have had one of the too prevalent cases of bigamy', he wrote to his son Bill about Quarter Sessions in Towyn during the war, 'where a sergeant in the RA of 25-years' standing away from his wife got a girl into trouble and then married her to enable her to preserve appearances. It is rather a strain on a man to refuse in those circumstances. The child was born two days after the wedding. We had only to commit, but I don't suppose he will get anything very severe, perhaps nothing'. Equally practical was a decision twenty years earlier that a wife, living apart from her husband but who wished him to return, was entitled to a decree for the restitution of conjugal rights, although if he disobeyed the order to return, she might take proceedings for divorce. Atkin thought her attitude both fair and sensible. 'She might well say: "If he obeys I shall go back to my husband and make him happy; if he does not I may be compelled to sue for a divorce".'[3]

His humanity did not spring from a rigid moral code which would not yield to social needs. That was why he staunchly supported A. P. Herbert's Marriage Bill in 1937 and did not side with those who thought it would bring with it a new Sodom. He was a devout and committed Christian but he had no time for 'churchiness' or sanctimony. Like his grandmother he detested pretence in rank or religion, and the opinionated puritan was one of his pet aversions.[4] So when the question of Sunday golf arose in Aberdovey in the Autumn of 1927, he opposed the Sabbatarians and published an exchange of letters between himself and the Secretary of the West Merioneth Presbytery in *The County Times*. He wrote:

> 'I can only state my regret that gentlemen for whom I have the highest esteem can have expressed themselves with such intolerance of the opinions and rights of others. You must be aware that thousands of your fellow Christians entertain the considered opinion that to take reasonable recreation on Sunday including playing games is not to violate any divine commandment and it is consistent with a religious life.'[5]

The drama played out in the town and on the links is worth a small digression. A meeting one Saturday between the golfers and their opponents, led by the Vicar, was inconclusive: it was decided regrettably that the issue would have to be fought to a finish.

> 'A vote of thanks to the Vicar for presiding and the whole-hearted singing of "Hen Wlad fy Nhadan" brought the meeting to a close. Animated groups of ˆn   in the square further discussed the matter and plans were formed for the morrow.'[6]

3   *Palmer v Palmer* [1923] P 180 at 184, CA.
4   See Lord Atkin's memoir of his grandmother: appendix 2
5   *The County Times* (Merioneth), 22 October 1927.
6   *The Cambrian News and Welsh Farmers, Gazette,* 21 October 1927.

The morrow, a Sunday, brought the trial of strength. A large crowd on the first tee prevented the would-be golfers from driving off. The protesters claimed rights of common as well as desecration of the Sabbath, and a certain 'Mr David Jones, of Trefeddian Farm who by virtue of freehold ownership, claims common rights and is a strong upholder of the public rights of access, brought down to the 17th green an immense horned Welsh mountain ram which grazed on the green at the end of a long rope'.[7] Having previously informed Lord Atkin in a letter marked 'without prejudice' that she intended to do so, a Miss Budig Pughe pitched her easel on the 18th green and began painting, later sending a message to the 'Commons Defence Committee' reading, 'We do not sell our souls in Aberdovey. Cymru am Byth'.

Confronted by such exhilarated opponents, the golfers wisely retired and in due course retained Mr Gavin Simonds KC to bring a successful motion for an injunction against their misguided opponents.

Few subjects were so serious that they could not be subjected to irony or ridicule if Atkin thought the argument misconceived. In *Fender v Mildmay*,[8] where at least the minority of Lords Russell and Roche considered that the solemnity of the institution of marriage itself had been called in question, Atkin discussed the proposition that a promise by a married man to marry another woman on the death of his wife was unenforceable. 'Here', he said, 'the judges appear to have thought that a promise made in such circumstances tended to cause immoral relations. They may be right; speaking for myself I really do not know whether that result would follow as a rule. I can only say that if a lady yields to a promise with such an indefinite date she is probably of a yielding disposition . . . As to the suggestion that such a promise is bad because it tends to induce the husband to murder his wife, I reject this ground altogether. Alderson B in *Egerton v Brownlow* incontinently classes such objections as ridiculous. They appear to afford another instance of the horrid suspicions to which high-minded men are sometimes prone'.[9]

Above all his compassion came from a sympathetic understanding. What he so clearly and unusually understood were the needs and hopes of working men and their families. Other judges seldom shared his perception. Lord Justice Lawrence thought it 'somewhat fantastic' to suppose that a broken sash cord could make a house unfit for habitation and that the utmost that could be said was that the room was rendered 'less comfortable'. But if the house had only a kitchen on the ground floor and a front and back bedroom above, in which

7　Ibid.
8　[1938] AC 1.
9　At 15.

a man lived with his six children, Atkin knew that one of the two bedrooms could not be ventilated, and in his view the house was unfit.[10]

So in 1924 he would not accept that a wife's adultery should forever bar her from access to or custody of her children:

> '. . . but certainly', he said, 'if access were never to be allowed to children on the part of either father or mother, if the father or mother was not always perfectly discreet and wise, there are a great many parents who never would have the opportunity of seeing their children again, and to my mind the love and affection of a mother outweigh many foolish or indiscreet acts on the part of the parent in question.'[11]

Nowhere was the quality of compassionate understanding seen to better advantage than in Lord Atkin's contributions to the debates in the Lords on the Marriage Bill during 1937. The Bill is usually credited to A. P. Herbert who had long campaigned for a more humane divorce law. Until it became law, dissolution was allowed only on the ground of adultery, and Herbert's Bill added cruelty, desertion and incurable insanity. The purpose of the measure was to recognise that divorce was a misfortune rather than a crime, and Atkin strongly supported that. However, as it came up from the Commons, the Bill contained in clause 1 an absolute bar on any petition for divorce presented within five years of the date of the marriage. The clause had been agreed to by the sponsors of the measure and Herbert himself had said: 'The idea is that during five years the notion of divorce shall not be present in the mind of anybody'.[12]

But the five-year bar was given a rough reception in the Lords, Atkin himself describing the clause as 'terrible'.[13] The Archbishop of Canterbury confessed that he had no great enthusiasm for it, thinking it 'arguable that it may be interpreted as a statutory declaration that the first five years of marriage may be regarded as an experimental period'. But he was not prepared to oppose it because it laid down 'a certain time in which the parties may settle down and adjust their personalities'.[14]

The Archbishop's trumpet had given an uncertain sound but Atkin experienced no hesitations: 'I venture to think that the supporters of this clause have not realized what the real facts of divorce cases are', he said ominously, and proceeded to give some painful examples:

> 'Take the working-class husband who commits adultery with a woman or with women. Is he to return to a wife from the arms of his mistress

---

10　*Morgan v Liverpool Corp* [1927] 2 KB 131, CA. Atkin's dissenting view was vindicated in the House of Lords in *Summers v Salford Corp* [1943] AC 283.

11　*B v B* [1924] P 176 at 191, CA. The judgment of the Court of Appeal (Pollock MR and Warrington and Atkin LJJ) was unanimous.

12　Standing Committee 'A', HC, 3 December 1936.

13　105 HL Official Report col 755, 24 June 1937: see *C v C* [1979] 2 WLR 95 at 98.

14　105 HL Official Report cols 747–8, 24 June 1937.

and sleep with her in the wedding bed? Your Lordships will remember that among the working classes there is no question of separate rooms or even of separate beds. That is an insult from which a working-class woman is entitled to be relieved, and that is a normal, ordinary divorce case.

I do not know what the supporters of this clause have in their minds when they talk of matrimonial difficulties in respect to which people ought to stop and think. What ought they to think about when that happens? What room is there for stopping and thinking? That woman is entitled to relief from the terrible position in which she has been placed; and she would have no remedy. She has a remedy now by divorce. She would have a remedy under a later clause of this Bill by getting a separation; but I thought that the one thing that the promoters of this Bill wished to do was to diminish separations, because they all know of the terrible difficulty and the sad immorality which are the result of making young people who have been married, and in whom the flames of passion have been rightly kindled, live apart in separation.

Take the case on the other side, the normal case, when a man discovers that his wife has committed adultery with another man. What is he do do? Why has he to stop and think? Think about what? Is he to have a spurious child brought into his family? I thought that for generations it had been an accepted view that the manly thing to do in those circumstances, the right thing to do, is to turn the wife out of doors. That is what a husband has done from time immemorial, and that, it seems to me, is what he has a right to do. But in these circumstances he has either to stop and think or they have to adjust their personalities together while she is perhaps bearing the child of her paramour, and he is keeping her in his house and, I suppose, sleeping with her in his bed. It seems to me to be perfectly distressing.'[15]

The clause, he said, was defended on the ground that it would prevent people from rushing into marriage. But did that show a real appreciation of human nature? Did people choose partners by considering whether and when they could divorce them? 'The real truth is that this clause in the Bill is avowedly a compromise ... It looks like saying to those who do not approve of divorce at all, "At any rate you shall have five years without divorce". It is a kind of $12\frac{1}{2}$ per cent discount offered to the opponents of the Bill. In matters of life of vital importance to the community such as this, you have got no business to compromise.'[16]

In the result, the clause did emerge as a compromise, a bar for three years for all cases other than those of exceptional hardship or exceptional depravity. But Atkin was right. If a broken marriage was in truth an unhappiness rather than a sacrilege, as public opinion was increasingly coming to accept, there could be no logical case for any suspensory period. If anyone doubted that, he had only to

15   106 HL Official Report cols 88–9, 7 July 1937.
16   105 HL Official Report cols 758–9, 24 June 1937.

consider the cases which Atkin had put before the Lords. 'Law cannot command love', Milton had written in a magnificent phrase, 'without which matrimony hath no true being, no good, no solace, nothing of God's instituting, nothing but so sordid and so low, as to be disdained of any generous person'.

During the debates on the Marriage Bill, Lord Atkin moved an amendment that each member of the Welsh clergy should have a right corresponding to that given by the Bill to the clergy of the Church of England to give or withhold consent for the use of his church for the second marriages of divorced men and women. His purpose in doing so was simply to put the Welsh clergy on an equal footing with their English brethren. But by an ironic twist this led directly to a breach between him and the Bishops of the Church in Wales.[17]

On 29 January 1938 the Welsh Bishops issued a general direction, to be read from the pulpits of all churches within the Province, that the marriage of any divorced person whose husband or wife was still living should not be solemnized in church; and that if any such person should be remarried in a civil ceremony, he or she should not be admitted to Holy Communion without leave of the Bishop. Atkin considered both these directions, which applied alike to the innocent and guilty parties in a divorce, to be illegal. A serious dispute developed between himself and the Bishops. Although he had taken an important part in framing the constitution of the disestablished Welsh Church and had ever since held important positions as a lay member of the Church, including membership of the Governing Body, he did not hesitate to press his view that the Bishops' letter was 'an unlawful intrusion upon the rights of the laity'. This view which he advanced in correspondence with Archbishop Green,[18] and published in an open letter to the press,[19] was castigated as 'Erastian' and 'irrelevant' in an editorial in *The Church Times*.[20] Nonetheless he announced his intention of moving a resolution at the meeting of the Governing Body of the Welsh Church on 28 September 1938 requesting the Bishops to reconsider

---

17 106 HL Official Report col 188, 7 July 1939. Atkin added further unconscious irony by writing to the Secretary of the Governing Board of the Church in Wales and agreeing to move the amendment: 'This is probably the only amendment I propose that the Archbishop will approve!' The amended clause, which was the form in which it was enacted, ran: 'No clergyman of the Church of England or of the Church in Wales shall be compelled to solemnize the marriage of any person whose former marriage has been dissolved on any ground and whose former husband or wife is still living or to permit the marriage of any such person to be solemnized in the Church or Chapel of which he is the Minister'.

18 See Appendix 6 for the text of the letters.

19 *Western Mail and South Wales News*, 9 June 1938.

20 *The Church Times*, 17 June 1938. In an editorial in the issue for 23 September 1938 *The Church Times* referred to the forthcoming meeting of the Governing Body and declared: 'If . . . the clergy and laity rally round their episcopate . . . they will confirm on the whole Anglican Communion the much needed lesson that the teachings of Christ cannot yield to the laws of Caesar'.

their direction. As it happened, the dispute was submerged in the hysteria of the Munich Crisis and 28 September was the very day when, in the course of giving an account to the House of Commons of the negotiations with the Dictators, Chamberlain was handed his fateful invitation to go to Munich for a final effort to preserve peace. Because it seemed to him 'essential that men and women should be able to say that the Church had put aside all controversy, that it spoke with one voice, and that it prayed for peace', Atkin withdrew his resolution and it was never put.

Lord Atkin's point of view in the dispute exactly reflected that which he had advanced in the debates on the Marriage Bill. This was that although some might find scriptural authority for a different conclusion,[21] the parties to a broken marriage did not deserve to be treated as outcasts. Moreover, and this was the basis for the charge of Erastianism, if as a result of the new Act 'the divergence between the law of the State and the rule of the Church [had] been seriously widened', as the Bishops claimed, the law must be paramount. As his own resolution would have expressed it, the episcopal letter 'casts a slur unmerited and not justified in law upon the honour and reputation of innocent people who in the exercise of their Christian liberty have contracted such marriages'.

At almost the same time as the Marriage Bill was being debated in the Lords, the appeal in *Fender v St John Mildmay*[22] was being argued before Lords Atkin, Thankerton, Russell, Wright and Roche, and a very similar issue was joined: should a strict moral code backed by religious obligation give way before social realities?

Miss Fender, a state registered nurse, had met the defendant, Sir Anthony St John Mildmay, at a nursing home where she was working and he was a patient. He told her that he was unhappy with his wife and asked her to marry him if he could obtain a divorce. She agreed and became his mistress. Lady Mildmay then petitioned for divorce on the ground of her husband's adultery with Miss Fender and a decree nisi was pronounced. Immediately afterwards Sir Anthony promised to marry Miss Fender so soon as the decree was made absolute. That occurred but Sir Anthony then let Miss Fender know that he did not intend to honour his promise and in fact married someone else. The issue in the case was whether the promise of marriage was enforceable. The promise itself had been made between decree nisi and decree absolute, the waiting period imposed in divorce proceedings in order to ensure that full disclosure had been made to the Court, and that there had been no collusion between the parties to the marriage. Was a promise to marry made at that time against public policy because until decree absolute 'the marriage bond remains unimpaired and unloosened' and the law will not enforce

---

21   Eg Matthew 5 at 32: referred to in the Bishops' letter of 29 January 1938.
22   [1938] AC 1.

promises of marriage made by people who are already married; or was such a promise harmless in the eyes of the law 'for the simple reason that after decree nisi the bottom has dropped out of marriage'?

For Lord Russell, with whom Lord Roche agreed, the solemnity of marriage was in question, and that institution had long been on a slippery slope. 'What was once a holy estate enduring for the joint lives of the spouses is steadily assuming the characteristics of a contract for a tenancy at will.' The view which he had formed 'would only compel a person already married to await with decency until he or she is no longer a married man or woman before becoming the subject of a fresh betrothal'.[23]

Lord Atkin, who presided and whose judgment was the leading one for the majority, began with some general observations about public policy, the doctrine which judges invoke in order to make unenforceable those obligations of which they disapprove. From time to time, he said, 'judges of the highest reputation have uttered warning notes as to the danger of permitting judicial tribunals to roam unchecked in the field': the doctrine should not depend on 'the idiosyncratic inferences of a few judicial minds . . . In popular language, following the wise aphorism of Sir George Jessell . . . the contract should be given the benefit of the doubt'.[24]

He conceded however that the doctrine did exist so as to make unenforceable not only a promise to do a harmful thing, but also promises which had harmful tendencies. He conceded too, that a promise to marry during wedlock did violate the obligations of married life. 'If the normal ideal and the legal obligation are expressed in the promise to love and cherish it may well be doubted whether they can exist unimpaired in the presence of a betrothal to another.'

But what had that reasoning to do with the actual circumstances after decree nisi?

> '. . . let us consider how far the normal obligations and conditions of marriage continue in ordinary circumstances after decree nisi. They have disappeared: there is no consortium and the parties are living apart: they owe no duties each to the other to perform any kind of matrimonial obligation: the custody of the children has been provided for by the court: the maintenance of the wife, if petitioner, is similarly provided for: the petitioning spouse has said: "I have done with you". In these circumstances what possible effect can a promise to marry a third person have by way of interference with matrimonial obligations?'[25]

---

23   At 35.
24   At 12. The 'wise aphorism' was: 'if there is one thing which more than another public policy requires it is that men of full age and competent understanding shall have the utmost liberty of contracting, and that their contracts when entered into freely and voluntarily shall be held sacred and shall be enforced by Courts of justice': per Jessel MR in *Printing & Numerical Registering Co v Sampson* LR 19 Eq 462 at 465.
25   At 16.

The majority, led by Atkin, preferred that promises freely given should be enforced; they also preferred substance to form. It was true that the marriage subsisted between decree nisi and decree absolute. It followed that sexual intercourse with a third party at that time would be adulterous. But it was fanciful to suppose that real harm would flow from such considerations. In the words of Lord Justice Greer who had dissented in the Court of Appeal, nothing but a shell of the marriage was left.

Then Lord Atkin made a historical digression at the end of his speech.[26] He seemed to detect 'a resurgence of ecclesiastical principles', as he put it. The ecclesiastical courts had used to consider separation agreements between husband and wife unlawful, because they implied a renunciation of duty from which the authority of civil society and religion alike had insisted that the parties could not release themselves. The Reformation brought with it the superiority of the common law over ecclesiastical law, but it was not until 1848 that 'the final emancipation of law and equity from ecclesiastical domination' was established when Lord Westbury declared that voluntary separation was not contrary to the policy of the law. Now if separation agreements were not tainted and illegal, how could it be sensible to refuse to enforce the promise made to Miss Fender, seeing that the decree nisi had the same practical effect as a separation agreement and the promise created an obligation which the law welcomed?

The digression was significant. Lord Russell had drawn attention to the sacramental character of marriage before the Reformation, and had said that although it had ceased to rank as a sacrament when England abandoned the old faith, its solemnity was hardly impaired. In Atkin's view, the shadow of priestly authority which had once outlawed separation agreements needed to be dispelled. He would not for a moment have disputed with Russell the solemn character of marriage, but in accord with the current of public opinion which was then carrying Herbert's Bill through Parliament, that consideration would have to yield to human needs and real circumstances. At the root of his view lay the quality of compassion.

That quality was perhaps even more evident in a series of other cases concerned with the wretchedness of the human condition, stretching throughout Atkin's judicial career. *Everett v Griffiths*[27] was such a case: the plaintiff sued the Chairman of a Board of Guardians and a doctor for having certified him to be insane on grounds which were totally inadequate, and as a consequence of which he was unjustly detained in the asylum at Colney Hatch. Everett did much to dispel any suggestion that he might have been insane by arguing his own case with conspicuous ability. In the Court of Appeal, Atkin

26   At 18.
27   [1920] 3 KB 163, CA.

dissented from Lords Justices Bankes and Scrutton, holding that both defendants owed a duty of care to Everett.

> 'Grievous as is the wrong of unjust imprisonment of an alleged criminal, I apprehend that its colours pale beside the catastrophe of unjust imprisonment on an unfounded finding of insanity. Modern organisation has no doubt done much to remove the horrors that were associated with Bedlam in the days when the victims were subject to public exhibition. Probably even now the insane ward or reception ward is not without its revolting incidents. But it is the effect on the mind sane, even if feeble, that knows itself wrongly adjudged unsound that produces the most poignant suffering.'[28]

Here was one of the cases in which he was working towards a general duty of care[29] and he ended his judgment by asserting that 'it is just as it is convenient that the law should impose a duty to take reasonable care that such persons, if sane, should not suffer the unspeakable torment of having their sanity condemned and their liberty restricted; and I am glad to record my opinion, ineffectual though it may be, that for such an injury the English law provides a remedy'.[30]

Fifteen years later Atkin delivered the only speech in the House of Lords in another case affecting a boy in miserable circumstances.[31] Wilfred Hall was born in 1916 in Leicestershire, the illegitimate son of Lucy Hall. Within a month of his birth he moved to live with a foster mother in the city of Leicester and remained there until 1927. In that year he went to live with and was adopted by a Mr and Mrs Wall, also of Leicester. Then in 1931 he entered the Gordon Boys' Home at Woking, and in the following year at the age of sixteen he became chargeable under the Poor Laws to the County of Surrey. The Surrey Justices immediately ordered his removal to Coventry where his mother Lucy Hall was then living.

The Poor Laws as they then stood, and which continued a tradition stretching back to the reign of Elizabeth, laid down the duties of the family and the local authorities for the relief of the poor. The county and borough councils were to 'set to work' in workhouses all those who had neither means to maintain themselves nor trade to get their living; and to provide relief for those who were 'lame, impotent, old, blind and such other persons as are poor and not able to work'.[32]

---

28 At 211.
29 Other examples include *Hambrook v Stokes* [1925] 1 KB 141, CA and *Oliver v Saddler* [1929] AC 584.
30 At 223. Although Atkin's dissenting judgment was not upheld when the case reached the House of Lords, Lord Haldane described it as 'a powerful piece of reasoning displaying anxiety to guard against a possible miscarriage of justice': [1921] 1 AC 631 at 652.
31 *Coventry Corpn v Surrey CC* [1935] AC 199.
32 Poor Law Act 1930, s 15.

The contest between Coventry Corporation and the Surrey County Council, each of whom was concerned to throw on to another authority the obligation of relief of the unfortunate boy, was whether the boy's place of settlement was Coventry, his mother's place of settlement, (as was argued by Surrey) or Leicester, the residence of his adopted parents (as was contended by Coventry).

The case turned on the interaction of the Poor Law and the Adoption law. 'Settlement', as Atkin explained, was a kind of Poor Law domicil, or an indication of permanent home. By the Poor Law Act of 1930 an illegitimate child took the settlement of his mother; but because of the Adoption Act of 1926 the boy was, it was said, in the same position as if he had been born in wedlock and had been living with legitimate parents. That being so, he could not have been removed from Leicester under the Poor Laws while he was living there with his adoptive parents, and his place of settlement had become Leicester.

The Court of Appeal had decided that the boy was chargeable to Coventry. The House of Lords unanimously reversed this decision, and Atkin's own speech was coloured with scorn. Referring to the forerunner of the Poor Law Act of 1930, he said:

> 'It is well known that it was passed to remedy one of the scandals of the old Poor Law, the breaking up of families by distributing parents and children to different settlements. The effect of the decision under appeal is to disregard the formation of the strong family ties created by adoption and to revive for an adopted family the former scandals that attached to breaking up a natural family. The only Lord Justice who thought it necessary to refer to this consequence of the decision referred to it as "inconvenient". He might have permitted himself the stronger term formerly applied in this House, "tragic".'[33]

Thomas v Jones[34] was another such case, decided in 1921 when Atkin was in the Court of Appeal, and in which a bachelor farmer was charged with being the father of an illegitimate child. He took in the mother, his housekeeper, when she was in labour, sent for a doctor and then allowed her to remain in his house for five weeks after the birth. 'What else could an innocent person have done?' Atkin asked. 'There was nobody else either to light a fire, or to make tea, or to give her brandy . . .' Then he pointed out the importance of real corroborative evidence in paternity suits and gave a penetrating reason. There were cases, he said, 'where charges are so easily brought and with such difficulty refuted, and where there is a strong

---

33   At 204. The reference was to Slesser LJ: [1934] 1 KB 211 at 224, CA.
34   [1921] 1 KB 22, CA.

temptation either to conceal the identity of the real father or to impose liability upon the person who is best able to bear it'.[35]

It was natural that Atkin's outlook would make him liberal in cases between employer and workman, and where, as in so many instances, the issue was compensation for death, injury or illness suffered by the workmen, he was distinctly a 'plaintiff's judge'. But he was not alone. A majority of his contemporaries in the Lords were similarly disposed,Lords Macmillan, Wright, Thankerton and Porter, and those judges with Atkin were responsible for a remarkable series of decisions in the 30s, shifting the emphasis in favour of workmen claimants.

Because claims at common law against employers were still rooted in Victorian thinking, particularly notions of moral fault and the voluntary assumption of risk; and because it was in any case often difficult to establish exactly how an accident took place, the Workmen's Compensation Acts were enacted to enable workmen to be compensated without proof of fault. But these Acts occasioned difficulties of their own. They bred a host of technical points, many of which had to be fought to the House of Lords. In one case, sixty earlier decisions were cited and argued about.[36] The House itself did much valuable work in cutting through technicality, but it could not make the Acts easily workable, or even adequate. Compensation was based only on loss of earning capacity, which might fall short of an injured man's real needs.

For these reasons, common law actions for damages against employers continued to be brought before the courts, but again the workmen faced formidable obstacles. One was the defence of 'contributory negligence'. If the employer could demonstrate that the workman himself had been careless and had contributed to the accident, then whether or not the employer was also partly to blame, the workman's claim would fail altogether. The social consequences of exposing injured workmen and their dependants to litigious hazards of this type were serious; and the social purpose behind the decisions in the more important workmen's cases in the 30s was not hard to discern.

Caswell v Powell Duffryn Associated Collieries[37] was a characteristic example. Caswell was a young man of twenty-two whose work

---

35 At 44. In supporting the use of blood tests as corroborative evidence in bastardy cases he said: 'To my mind they are the most difficult cases of fact that come before the Court' (III HL Official Report col 705, 8 February 1939). In the same debate he also gave it as his view that 'it is almost impossible that you could find a more satisfactory tribunal' for these cases than a Bench of magistrates because of their 'thorough knowledge of the manners and customs of the people from whom these complaints come' (col 706).

36 *Noble v Southern Rly* [1940] AC 583. At 597 Atkin said: 'The County Court Judge had twenty cases cited to him, we had sixty; I suppose with a due sense of proportion the Court of Appeal had forty'.

37 [1940] AC 152.

underground in a pit was to clean rollers through which passed a belt carrying coal from the face to the point where it could be conveyed by trams to the pit bottom. The circumstances leading to Caswell's death were never satisfactorily established, but in his speech Atkin described in words of affecting simplicity how his body was found:

> 'They went to the machine, and there they found the dead body of the unfortunate Caswell; his right hand was outstretched, caught between the belt and the roller and his head was drawn up against the roller; his neck was broken. The body was drawn up so that his feet were two feet from the ground, and beneath his feet and lying in water beneath his feet was one of the iron scrapers . . .'

At the trial at Cardiff Assizes before Mr Justice Humphreys and in the Court of Appeal, the employers had argued, and argued successfully, that the machinery had been properly fenced, and that although it could not be proved affirmatively, the most likely cause of death was that Caswell himself had removed and failed to replace the protective plate, so causing the accident. The argument was put again by Sir William Jowitt in the Lords. But this time it did not succeed. The only possible act of negligence on Caswell's part was that he did not replace the plate. In their careful reconstruction of events and by means of inference, Lord Atkin and Lord Wright concluded that it was perfectly possible for the machinery to be restarted while Caswell was at work, there being no system of signalling between the cleaner and his fellow-workman who started and stopped the mechanism by a lever some distance off. If that had happened it would have been perilous for Caswell to attempt to replace the plate; for it would have been necessary to lift it to within inches of the moving parts. No contributory negligence was therefore proved by the employers.

Having disposed of the defence Atkin took the occasion to say something general. 'I find it impossible', he said, 'to divorce any theory of contributory negligence from the concept of causation . . . And whether you ask whose negligence was responsible for the injury, or from whose negligence did the injury result, or adopt any other phrase you please, you must in the ultimate analysis be asking who "caused" the injury; and you must not be deterred because the word "cause" has in philosophy given rise to embarrassments which in this connection should not affect the judge.'[38] Then pointedly: 'It may be said finally that if contributory negligence is not regarded from the point of view of causation it is difficult to see how damage comes to be divided under the Admiralty rule which is adopted in ordinary cases of injury in other systems of jurisprudence, and which persons of authority think should be adopted in ours'.

38   At 165.

Atkin ended his speech by approving as sensible and practical a saying of Mr Justice Lawrence that 'it is not for every risky thing which a workman in a factory may do in his familiarity with the machinery that a plaintiff ought to be held guilty of contributory negligence'. It was the duty of the judges to understand what it was actually like to work in a factory or mine.

> 'But having come to that conclusion', he said finally, 'I am of opinion that the care to be expected of the plaintiff in the circumstances will vary with the circumstances; and that a different degree of care may well be expected from a workman in a factory or a mine from that which might be taken by an ordinary man not exposed continually to the noise, strain, and manifold risks of factory or mine.'[39]

Another difficulty lying in the way of common law actions by workmen was the archaic doctrine of common employment which continued to plague claimants until it was abolished by statute in 1948.[40] The history of the doctrine was reviewed by Lord Atkin in *Radcliffe v Ribble Motor Services*.[41] 'At the present time', he said speaking in 1939, 'this doctrine is looked at askance by judges and text book writers. "There are none to praise, and very few to love".' It had originated with a case of 1836[42] in which a butcher's boy was injured when travelling in an overloaded van belonging to the butcher. Lord Abinger who heard the case was alarmed that if he allowed the claim a master would be liable for the carelessness of all his 'inferior agents', his coach-maker, his harness-maker, or his coachman. 'The master, for example, would be liable to the servant for negligence of the chambermaid for putting him into a damp bed; for that of the upholsterer, for sending in a crazy bedstead, whereby he was made to fall down while asleep and injure himself.' It was the old familiar argument of the judicial conservative that to uphold the claim would be to open Pandora's box.

By 1858, Atkin remarked, Chief Baron Pollock had been so intoxicated by the doctrine as to say, 'I believe there was never a more useful decision, or one of greater practical or social importance in the whole history of the law'.[43] Such superlatives are always suspect, and the open reference to the social importance of the rule could not go unnoticed. Its roots lay in the view that an employee must be supposed to have contracted with his employer for his wages on the basis that he would accept the risk of injury caused by the carelessness of a fellow-employee.

The problem in *Radcliffe's Case* was the scope of the rule. A motor coach driver was knocked down by another coach owned by

---

39 At 166. Lord Wright took the same point at 176.
40 By the Law Reform (Personal Injuries) Act 1948, s 1.
41 [1939] AC 215.
42 *Priestley v Fowler* [1837] 3 M & W 1.
43 *Vose v Lancashire and Yorkshire Rly Co* [1858] 27 LJ Ex 249.

the same company. At the time of the accident the driver who was fatally injured had for some unexplained reason stopped his coach on the way home from a trip and was standing in the street beside it. Lords Atkin, Macmillan and Wright were unanimous in their view that the doctrine did not apply. 'But in regard to driving in the streets of Liverpool', said Atkin, 'the one [driver] was no more interested in the skill of the other than in that of the drivers of the myriads of other vehicles in whose vicinity he might happen to drive. In other words, for the purposes of this doctrine, the risk of injury in the streets by a vehicle driven by a fellow servant is not one of "the natural risks and perils incident to the performance of his service".'

It may be that it was the advocacy of Sir Stafford Cripps who appeared for the driver's widow which induced the House of Lords to reverse the Court of Appeal's decision in *Radcliffe's Case*; but, reading the case now, the limitation which the House then put on the doctrine seems entirely fair and logical. That could hardly be said of the remarkable decision a year earlier in *Wilsons & Clyde Coal Company v English*[44] in which by reasoning deserving the name of casuistry, Lords Atkin, Thankerton, Macmillan, Wright and Maugham went far to emasculate the doctrine.

English was crushed and injured by machinery as he was walking along an underground road in a coal mine at the end of the day shift. He claimed that his employers should necessarily as part of a safe system of work have ensured that the haulage machinery be stopped during the period when the shifts changed. The employers had appointed an agent and a mine manager for each of their collieries, whose duties including the carrying out of the safety regulations under the Coal Mines legislation. That legislation precluded an owner from taking part in the technical management of a mine if he had appointed a manager for that purpose; and the employers maintained that, having delegated their duties as they were bound to do, any carelessness of the agent or manager was not their carelessness and by reason of the doctrine of common employment, they were not liable.

The House held unanimously that, in performing the owner's duty to provide a safe system, an agent is not engaged in common employment with a workman. Lord Atkin who presided merely agreed with the other four Law Lords. Lord Wright described the doctrine as 'illogical', 'certainly one not to be extended', and having 'little regard to reality or to modern ideas of economics or industrial conditions'. Lord Macmillan pointed out that the doctrine was in conflict with the principle of vicarious responsibility by which an employer is responsible for the negligence of his servant acting within the scope of his employment. How were the two to be reconciled?

44 [1938] AC 57.

For Lord Macmillan the 'conclusive answer' was that 'the agent engaged in discharging the owner's duty of providing a safe system of working in the mine is not engaged in a common employment with the ordinary workman in the mine. He is not collaborating with them; he is performing the duty of the owner, not the duty of an employee'.[45] Lord Wright's formulation was: 'When it is said that the workman takes the risk of his fellow-workman's negligence, it must be added that he does not take the risk of his master's negligence'.[46] He conceded that 'it may often be difficult to draw the line in any particular case'; and in that concession was revealed the weakness of the argument. Is a foreman, charge hand or safety man in common employment with 'an ordinary workman'? Is his negligence the negligence of the master? Is he collaborating with the workman or performing the duty of an owner? In truth in a complex modern industrial concern every employee, exalted or humble, must carry out the purposes and duties of the employer, and there was no room for a doctrine of common employment at all, if it were not to whittle away the responsibility of an employer to provide his employees with conditions of reasonable safety.

That the judges who gave these decisions would have liked to abolish outright the doctrine of common employment is clear enough. But they did not feel themselves able to do so. 'It is too well established to be overthrown by judicial decision' Atkin said in *Radcliffe's Case*. They therefore resorted to techniques of erosion, combined with broad hints to the legislature. The hints eventually produced results. Contributory negligence was put on a rational footing in 1945, the doctrine of common employment was abolished in 1948;[47] and many of the shortcomings of the Workmen's Compensation Acts were remedied by the National Insurance Acts passed shortly after the end of the Second World War. The judiciary, and especially the outstandingly liberal Lords of Appeal led by Atkin, are entitled to much of the credit for these changes. Just as in 1858 Chief Baron Pollock saw a social importance in employees accepting the risk of carelessness by their fellows, Lords Atkin, Macmillan and Wright had a social purpose in wearing away at the doctrine eighty years later. It no longer made sense in modern industrial conditions where there was an overriding need for employers to see that work was carried on without unreasonable danger to the safety of their workmen. It was not tolerable that men should risk death or maiming without being fairly compensated. Social justice, it has been said by a distinguished judge,[48] is for the lawmaker and not the judge, and no doubt it is true that if judges concern themselves with abstract

45   At 76.
46   At 82.
47   Law Reform (Contributory Negligence) Act 1945; Law Reform (Personal Injuries) Act 1948.
48   Lord Devlin 'Judges and Lawmakers' 39 MLR 1 at 7.

social issues, they may abdicate their responsibility to administer the law fairly in individual cases. But it would be quite unrealistic to think that cases like *English* and *Radcliffe* were decided without regard to their social context, or that there was not a broader purpose behind those decisions. It was Chief Justice Holmes who said:

> 'I think that the judges themselves have failed adequately to recognise their duty of weighing considerations of social advantage. The duty is inevitable, and the result of the often proclaimed judicial aversion to deal with such considerations is simply to leave the very ground and foundation of judgments inarticulate, and often unconscious, as I have said.'[49]

No one could fairly convict Lord Atkin of that charge.

There was no milk-and-water sentimentality about Lord Atkin's humanity. For him, wrongdoing once identified ought to be punished, and punished severely. That is why he said so plainly in the Marriage Bill debates that a man should be entitled to put his adulterous wife out of doors. When it came to sentencing he was a criminal judge of some severity,[50] and he held particularly firm views about juvenile criminals. The right punishment for malicious children who brutally illtreated other children or animals was, 'something short and sharp, the punishment which children of that kind would be or ought to be given in their own homes'.[51] And in a letter to *The Times* in 1943 he criticised the newspapers for softness towards young offenders, saying incidentally that the proper place for social workers was not on the Magistrates' Bench but in helping juvenile criminals to make a fresh start.

> 'But may I with respect comment', he wrote, 'on the sentence in your leading article of August 23 in which you say the main preoccupation of the juvenile courts should be to refit the back-slider to take a natural and creditable place in society, which of course means the society of his contemporaries? I would say that of course it means something different — i.e. the ordered society of which he is a member consisting of young and old, rich and poor, employers and employed, and which includes small shopkeepers and householders who are entitled to protection from the loss and damage to property caused by thieves and housebreakers even though their age be 14 to 16.'[52]

In his attitude to German war crimes Atkin was quite uncompromising.[53] When the Allied governments set up a War

---

49   'The Path of the Law' 10 Harvard LR 466 at 77 Vol II.
50   See eg *Clay, Grant, Vale* (1918) 13 CAR 193: sentences imposed by Atkin of four and three years penal servitude for larceny and receiving reduced in CCA and described as 'very severe'.
51   84 HL Official Report col 726, 9 June 1932.
52   *The Times,* 31 August 1943.
53   There is little doubt that had Atkin lived on, he would have added strength to the cause of those who favoured trials for war crimes. It was a difficult subject and there was much hesitation and doubt in Britain about whether it was just or wise to try the German war criminals.

Crimes Commission in the Autumn of 1943 he was invited to serve as representative of the Australian Government. Simon attempted to dissuade him on the ground of 'the character of the proposed Commission and from a feeling that Australia is bringing in a 91-ton gun to what may be a minor task',[54] but Atkin was not deflected. In fact, Bruce,[55] the Australian High Commissioner was 'particularly anxious that steps should be taken to ensure that Lord Atkin is treated as a full member of the Australian Delegation and not seated in a subordinate position.'[56] He attended the first twelve meetings of the Commission on behalf of Australia between October 1943 and March 1944, until his final illness made it impossible for him to continue, and he was a member also of the sub-committee on enforcement.

The work of the Commission was to investigate and record evidence of war crimes, and to report to and advise the Allied governments on the procedure for trying the crimes and the preparation of evidence. Atkin held strong views on the whole of this vexed subject, having written to his son Bill in 1940 that the Blitz 'only hardens people's resolve to see that there shall be no more rope for the Huns except on the drop'. During the period of the early work of the Commission, Lord Cecil suggested at a meeting of the League of Nations Union that the tribunal should include one international judge to guarantee that 'nothing grossly unfair would be done',[57] and that a British judge should be included. The suggestion provoked a sharp reaction because it was feared that offence would be given to the continental countries which had suffered under the German occupation; and Lord Vansittart wrote to *The Times* to say that the Allies might well join the Germans in thinking that the British had a 'governess mind'.[58] A few days later on 22 December 1943 Professor Goodhart contributed a longer and more considered letter. The correspondence between Lord Cecil and Lord Vansittart had, he thought, served the useful purpose of bringing this subject to a head. To his mind the punishable acts were of two classes, those which fell outside the established criminal law of the individual states, and those which constituted ordinary crimes. Those in the first class, he said, were acts of policy and not covered by any existing

54 Viscount Simon to Lord Atkin, 30 September 1943.
55 Stanley Melbourne Bruce, first Viscount Bruce of Melbourne; b 1883 at Melbourne, Australia; ed Melbourne Grammar School and Trinity Hall, Cambridge; called to the Bar, Middle Temple 1906; Hon Bencher Lincoln's Inn 1932; Member for Flinders 1918–29, 1931–33; represented Commonwealth at League of Nations Assembly 1921–38; Australian representative Council of League 1933–6; President of Council 1936; Prime Minister of Australia and Minister for External Affairs 1923–29; High Commissioner for Australia in London 1933–45; representative of Commonwealth Government in UK War Cabinet and Pacific War Council 1942–45; rowed in winning Cambridge Eight 1904; d 1967.
56 Communication from Dominions Office to Foreign Office, 19 October 1943.
57 Report in *The Times*, 11 December 1943.
58 *The Times*, 14 December 1943.

body of law. They should be punished by 'a political Act of State', and he cited the imprisonment of Napoleon on St Helena as a correct precedent. 'It has been argued', he wrote, 'that a judicial trial is necessary so as to convince the Germans of their guilt, but when in history has a trial of this nature ever succeeded in convincing anyone?' As for the second category, they were 'acts in violation of existing State law', and could be tried under the criminal law of the place where the acts were committed; and he thought that there was 'much to be said for the view' that the British and Americans should be concerned only with crimes against their own nationals, or the giving of assistance in collecting evidence and making arrests.

Atkin disagreed root and branch with the Professor's view, which he thought a deal too legalistic — an interesting reaction from someone who had held judicial office for thirty years. He saw that there would be technical difficulties in trying any war crimes under an ordinary penal code; but more important by far, the outraged conscience of humanity demanded that those who had perpetrated unprecedented barbarities should be brought to justice, and not merely punished. He set out these views in a letter to *The Times*, published on 30 December and expressed with such conviction and passion that it deserves to be read in full.

TO THE EDITOR OF THE TIMES

Sir, — I venture to think that the division of war criminals in Professor Goodhart's letter published on December 22 is possibly fallacious. He refers to those who commit acts "in violation of existing State law." The reasoning appears to be that an invading force is subject to all the laws of the invaded State, but that those laws recognize war as a justification for some acts, those that are not so justified by the laws of the invaded State remaining criminal. I would not venture a decided opinion upon this statement of the law; but I doubt whether it could be maintained.

Invading armies come not under the law of the invaded country, but against it. They owe it no allegiance and they receive no corresponding protection, tests which have been stated by legal authorities to have weight in such matters. Are they subject to all the laws — police laws, for instance, or to the laws as to civil obligations? Could a member of the invading forces be sued for trespass or conversion of goods or use and occupation of land in a tribunal of the invaded country either if functioning during the invasion or after the peace? I hesitate to affirm that either British or American soldiers can be made liable criminally or civilly by existing Fascist courts in Italy in respect of such acts as those courts may deem not justified by war.

But even if the proposition stated could be supported, it is a matter for the grave consideration of the allied Powers whether war criminals should be tried in accordance with it. It involves that the punishment of these crimes depends upon the separate provisions of the penal laws of each invaded State. Procedure, evidence, and appeal introduce varying conditions as to delay and possibly conviction; while in some countries, as I understand, capital punishment has been abolished. Moreover, if there is to be a fixed venue, there may be real difficulties in administering justice, for the crime may have taken place in one country while the witnesses may be, and often will be, in another, and there will be no power of compelling attendance. The accused may have a genuine plea of alibi or mistaken identity dependent on the production of witnesses abroad. It must be possible in proper cases to change the venue. Another very important factor in the trial of these crimes is the plea of superior orders. The effect to be given to it may vary in the existing laws of the countries in question. It seems probable that it must be treated uniformly by a rule laid down by the allied Powers.

A further difficulty in the way of trying war criminals in accordance with the existing laws of the country in which the crimes are committed is that it provides no remedy for crimes committed in the country of the enemy, and possibly lawful by the law of that country. We hear of terrible iniquities practised in Germany, Bulgaria, and elsewhere; the crimes against Jews in the various enemy countries would pass unpunished. The offences I mention do not appear to be those mentioned by the Professor in his first category, which seems to be confined to those whose policy has brought on this war. If I may express a personal opinion, it is that the trial and punishment of these war criminals should remain under the control of the allied Powers. There is a danger lest we approach the subject in too legalistic mood. The crimes of which some of the barbarian enemy have been guilty transcend all domestic laws. They are offences against the conscience of civilized humanity. What is desired is not revenge, but a vindication of civilization to be achieved by imposing retribution on the criminals so as to ensure so far as possible that in no war in the future shall like horrors be perpetrated. I hold that the allied Powers should name the black crimes for which they demand punishment — the wholesale murder of men, women,and children, whether hostages or not; the deportation of whole races of people; the carrying off into brothels of captive women. The matter to be determined is whether particular persons accused are guilty of those crimes.

This should be determined by tribunals, courts — call them what you will — consisting of just persons who, on the material before them, will say whether they are honestly satisfied that those persons are guilty or not. I would have no technical rules of procedure or evidence, and the extreme penalty should be death, to be mitigaged as the tribunal might decide. By all means try them if possible, as the Powers seem to have decided in Moscow, in the country of the crime; but the tribunals will have to be what the allies decide, which does not exclude making national tribunals international *ad hoc*.

Contrary to the Professor's view, I think that there is very little to be.said for his suggestion that the British and Americans should concern themselves only with the trials of those charged with having committed crimes against their own nationals. The conscience of the whole civilized world has been aroused by these barbarities, and surely we are all concerned in seeing that the criminals should be brought to justice. I do not believe that even a small minority of British or American people would wish to stand aside at the trial of German, Japanese, or other barbarians for crimes against, for instance, the Jews in Europe. They would not if they could; but they could not if they would.

Yours, &c.,

ATKIN

December 26

It was wholly consistent with Lord Atkin's uncompromising attitude to the Nazi war criminals that he should be sympathetic and welcoming to the victims of oppression when they sought refuge here. On 1 May 1940, shortly before the fall of France, he spoke in Gray's Inn at a reception for refugee lawyers organised by the British Council. Among those who were present was Dr Ernst Wolff who, before Hitler came to power, had been President of the Berlin Bar and of the General Council of the German Bar, and who was later to become President of the Supreme Court in the British Zone of Germany. After the reception he wrote to Lord Atkin, saying, 'your Lordship's kind words of sympathy for our situation went to our hearts. It is the same spirit of piracy under which we had to suffer that your country is now fighting and it is in the interest of the real Germany as well as in the interests of the other countries that the Nazi Germany is destroyed so that law can again prevail and the society of self-governing nations for which a German, Kant, pleaded in his treatise on Perpetual Peace 200 years ago can be established'.

Lord Atkin's humane and compassionate spirit was the most constant feature of his work for more than thirty years on the English Bench. It would be an exaggeration to assert that it informed all his judgments because in some fields of the law there was no room for it to find place. Yet still it is the quality for which he should be first remembered. The law could not diffuse itself into every phase of human conduct. Promises made between husband and wife, as he said in a famous passage, could not be visited with legal sanctions because, 'the consideration which obtains for them is that natural love and affection which counts for so little in these cold Courts', and for those promises 'each house is a domain into which the King's writ does not seek to run, and to which his officers do not seek to be admitted'.[59] But where the writ did run, justice was to be administered with humanity. This led Atkin only on the rarest occasions to an exaggerated reaction because he was 'a progressive within the law'.[60]

59   *Balfour v Balfour* [1919] 2 KB 571 at 579.
60   The phrase is Lord Denning's who kindly contributed a personal recollection. An example of Lord Atkin's very rare hyperbole is *Nokes v Doncaster Amalgamated Collieries* [1940] AC 1014.

His often declared purpose to do justice with compassion provides one of the many interesting contrasts between his own approach and that of Sir Thomas Scrutton, his pupil master and fellow judge in the Court of Appeal for more than ten years. For Atkin in *Everett's Case*, as has already been noticed, it was just as it was convenient that the law should impose a duty to take reasonable care that paupers or people of weak mind, if sane, should not 'suffer the unspeakable torment of having their sanity condemned and their liberty restricted'. Lord Justice Scrutton's contrary view was that it was necessary 'not only to protect the individual who will suffer if wrongly imprisoned, but also the community who will suffer if real lunatics are not imprisoned, because the officers appointed to certify are afraid of the cost and annoyance of actions alleging improper certification, even if those actions fail'.[61] Atkin thought that the strength of Everett's evidence was his demeanour and the conspicuous ability with which he arged his case in person. Scrutton took the view that few lunatics think they are properly incarcerated and 'most of them enjoy an action in which the individual has always a better chance of getting the sympathy of the jury than the officers of the State who are performing the unpleasant duty of incarcerating him'. As for Everett's legal acumen: 'Great cleverness', he said using a word more often than not having pejorative overtones, 'frequently goes with great mental instability. "Great wits are sure to madness near allied, And thin partitions do their bounds divide" '.[62]

Scrutton's reputation is for robustness and his decision in *Everett's Case* certainly had that quality; but it lacked something of compassion.

It is sometimes asked whether a judge's character shows through his judgments but like so many attempts at generalisation about the judge's business the enquiry is likely to prove barren. There need however be no reservation in saying that compassion was the cardinal quality in Atkin's make up. It lay upon the surface of so many of his judgments. In any case, those who knew him put it in the forefront of their assessments. He sat with the magistrates at Towyn and Machynlleth whenever he could and was known there for his sympathetic understanding.

This view is borne out by many stories of his work with the magistrates: all attest to his being both kindly and modest. When he was in Aberdovey it was well known that he would always spare time to advise informally on some problem afflicting one of the local people, and a favourite time for these interviews was before lunch on Sundays. The meal was often held up on this account. And on his appointment to the High Court Bench in 1913 he received an address from 'the Inhabitants of Aberdovey and the Surrounding

---

61 *Everett v Griffiths* [1920] 3 KB 163 at 197.
62 At 198.

Country' which referred to 'the reputation for conscientious justice and integrity combined with a considerable and genial courtesy . . .'

The assessments of Lord Atkin's own family are similar. He was an unassuming yet warm host, invariably modest. He never lost touch with the influences of his childhood and early youth; when in rural Merioneth he had that freedom to roam and make friendships where he would which is denied to a child of the cities. I do not think that he absorbed when young the principles of Welsh liberalism, if such there be, so much as the habit of being in the company of all sorts and conditions of children. That and the powerfully beneficent influence of his grandmother seem more likely to have impressed his character with its simplicity and understanding.

As his daughter, Mrs Robson, points out, he was a man of undemanding, and occasionally low, tastes, choosing to travel by bus and for entertainment the music halls. Edgar Wallace was his favourite author but it would have been a mistake to suppose that he read only low-brow books, as his children discovered when they took him to task about his reading habits. Nothing gave him more pleasure than the success of his daughter, Nancy, on the West End stage at the age of eighteen; although it was unusual, to employ a neutral word, for a High Court judge's daughter of the 20s to go on the stage.

Lord Atkin's compassion was grounded in these things. They gave him understanding which is the precondition of compassion. They also freed him from all trace of self-importance. There was a perfect aptness about the text which his family chose for his memorial in Aberdovey church:

> 'Finally be ye all of one mind, having compassion one of another, love as brethren, be pitiful, be courteous.'[63]

63   1 Peter 3 at 8.

Donoghue v Stevenson

Some few days before judgment was given in the House of Lords in
Donoghue v Stevenson Lord Wright wrote to Lord Atkin to say:

> Dear Atkin,
>
> I have been reading with admiration your magnificent and
> convincing judgment in the snail case — also Macmillan's which is
> very good. I am glad this fundamental rule of law will now be
> finally established.
>
> It seems as if (alas!) I were fated to differ from old Scrutton in the
> first two cases from his Court I have had to deal with!
>
> I hope you will have a pleasant vacation.
>
> > Yrs.
> > Wright
>
> I find Buckmaster on snails very disappointing. I have not seen
> Tomlin's efforts on the same subject.[1]

The summary was unkind to Lord Buckmaster but not overstated
as regards Lords Atkin and Macmillan.

The greatest civil case between the Wars was thrown up by humble
circumstances which are best recited by the original Scots pleading:

> 'At or about 8.50 p.m. on or about 26th August 1928, the pursuer was
> in the shop occupied by Francis Minchella and known as Wellmeadow
> Café, at Wellmeadow Place, Paisley, with a friend. The said friend
> ordered for the pursuer ice-cream, and ginger-beer suitable to be used

---

1 Lord Wright to Lord Atkin, 12 May 1932. Lord Wright had been appointed a Lord of
Appeal direct from the High Court Bench only a month before the letter was written, on
11 April 1932. Both Atkin and Wright had been pupils of Scrutton and both overtook
him, Scrutton never being promoted beyond the Court of Appeal. Of the two appeals
from Scrutton's court which Wright mentions, one was certainly the celebrated decision
in *Hillas v Arcos* [1932] All ER 494 which was heard on 3, 4 and 5 May. It is difficult to
be sure which was the other. In *King Line v Westralian Farmers* (1932) 48 TLR 598, the
appeal was heard on 10 and 12 May by a Board including Wright and the Court of
Appeal were again reversed, but Scrutton had dissented. The next occasion when Wright
participated in the reversal of a decision of Scrutton was in *Sociedad Anonima
Commercial de Exportacion e Importacion v National Steamship Co* (1932) 49 TLR 50,
but the decision was not given until 11 November. Possibly Wright already knew in May
what the decision was to be but it is unlikely.

with the ice-cream as an iced drink. Her friend, acting as aforesaid, was supplied by the said Mr. Minchella with a bottle of ginger-beer manufactured by the defender for sale to members of the public. The said bottle was made of dark opaque glass, and the pursuer and her friend had no reason to suspect that the said bottle contained anything else than the aerated-water. The said Mr. Minchella poured some of the said ginger-beer from the bottle into a tumbler containing the ice-cream. The pursuer then drank some of the contents of the tumbler. Her friend then lifted the said ginger-beer bottle and was pouring out the remainder of the contents into the said tumbler when a snail, which had been, unknown to the pursuer, her friend, or the said Mr. Minchella, in the bottle, and was in a state of decomposition, floated out of the said bottle. In consequence of the nauseating sight of the snail and in said circumstances, and of the noxious condition of the said snail-tainted ginger-beer consumed by her, the pursuer sustained the shock and illness hereinafter condescended on. The said Mr. Minchella also sold to the pursuer's friend a pear and ice.'

These at any rate were the facts which were alleged, for the action was never tried or the facts proved. The manufacturer of the ginger-beer, who was sued,[2] objected that the claims were irrelevant and the case went to the House of Lords on the preliminary question of whether such a claim could ever be well-founded: assuming that the facts alleged by the plaintiff were proved, in law could she make the defendant manufacturer liable?

Ten years after the decision Lord Justice MacKinnon in his Holdsworth lecture for 1942 declared that there never had been a snail in the bottle. 'To be quite candid', he said, 'I detest that snail. I think that my friend, Lord President Normand, explained to you that the problem in that case arose on a plea of relevancy — the Scots equivalent of a demurrer. I think that he did not reveal to you that, when the law had been settled by the House of Lords, the case went back to Edinburgh to be tried on the facts. And at that trial it was found that there never was a snail in the bottle at all! That intruding gasteropod was as much a legal fiction as the Casual Ejector.'

When Atkin and Macmillan read that passage, they both doubted MacKinnon's assertion, and Macmillan wrote to Lord Normand, who as Solicitor-General for Scotland, had argued the appeal for the manufacturer. Normand replied that the account was not accurate. 'The case never went to trial', he wrote. 'I speak from recollection, but I think it can be trusted, and what I remember is that the defender died soon after the H.L. decided the point of relevancy. The pursuer

---

2   The action was originally begun against the manufacturer alone, but later Minchella, the café owner, was added as a defender. Later still, Mrs Donoghue 'after some wavering of opinion' (as the Respondent's printed Case had it) dropped her claim against Minchella. The case commented: 'The averments of the Appellant, as they now are, retain, however, traces of the metamorphoses through which the action has passed'.

did not move to have the defender's executor cited as a party and there were no further proceedings. So much for the sake of history.' He went on:

> 'Privately I may say that I would all along have preferred a proof before answer. But I was instructed to fight the relevancy point at the risk of an appeal to the H.L. and did what I could. I personally thought that the H.L. would decide as they did in fact decide, but that we had a very strong case on the facts. If the case had gone to proof I think it would have been fought and possibly won on the issue whether there was a snail in the bottle, and I may have told MacKinnon this. It may interest you to know that Condie Sandeman, with whom I discussed the case, at an early stage, was confident that the H.L. would decide just as they did decide. You may tell Lord Atkin all this and if you are writing to him please remember me to him. But what I thought or advised or what Condie thought should probably not get loose among the public!'[3]

There is no reason to doubt Lord Normand's tactical judgment that the manufacturer would have done better to fight the case on the facts. But if that had happened — and the decision lay with Normand's own client — the foundation of the modern law of negligence might never have been laid as it was; for a decision on the facts in favour of the manufacturer, as for instance that there never had been a snail in the bottle, would have made unnecessary a statement of principle about legal negligence. On such chances of litigation hangs the development of the law.

Macmillan reported to Atkin and sent him a copy of Normand's letter. 'You may take it as quite certain', Macmillan wrote, 'that the case never went to trial. Whether there was or was not a snail in the bottle must remain one of history's unsolved problems! I am happy to hear that you are practising "l'art d'etre grand pere" in the peaceful seclusion of Aberdovey and I hope you are benefiting greatly by the rest.'

In 1932 the law on civil liability for carelessness was in a chaotic state, a fair example of what Tennyson meant when he wrote of

> 'That codeless myriad of precedent,
> That wilderness of single instances,
> Through which a few by wit or fortune led,
> May beat a pathway out to wealth and fame.'[4]

As Lord Macmillan acknowledged after summarising the earlier cases, 'the current of authority has by no means always set in the same direction'. In effect there was no single tort of negligence, but instead a number of separate torts each with its own rules; and the

---

3 Condie Sandeman: Dean of the Faculty of Advocates; b 1866; called to Scottish Bar 1889; KC 1909; Sheriff of Perth; recreations fishing and golf; d 1934.
4 'Aylmer's Field'.

conservatives among the judiciary treated the categories as closed. The owner of something inherently dangerous, a gun or a horse, was bound to be careful how he used it or let it be used by others, and he could be made liable for injury caused by his carelessness. Or the owner of premises that were dangerous had to take care that those who were permitted or invited to come on to the premises were not injured. Or liability could be founded on contract, so that a seller might be liable to his buyer for want of reasonable care about the thing being sold. But there was no general duty on a man to take care that his acts or omissions should not injure those whom he ought to have in mind. In some earlier cases statements of general principle had been attempted, but they had never been accepted as authoritative.

So as the law stood, a baker who allowed arsenic to be mixed with a batch of his bread might have been guilty of a crime, but it was at best doubtful whether someone who was poisoned through buying the bread from a shop which in turn had bought it from the baker could obtain redress from the criminally careless baker.[5] *Donoghue v Stevenson* was a comparable case.

It had originally been decided by the Lord Ordinary that Mrs Donoghue (who sued in the traditional Scots style as 'Mrs May M'Alister or Donoghue', the former being her maiden name[6]) had a good cause of action, but his decision was reversed by a majority of two to one in the Second Division of the Court of Session.[7] The Board who heard the appeal in the House of Lords in December 1931 consisted of two Scots, Lords Thankerton and Macmillan, two Chancery lawyers, Lords Buckmaster[8] and Tomlin, and Lord Atkin; and Counsel on both sides were all Scots lawyers with the exception of a single English junior, Mr T. Elder Jones, retained by the respondent manufacturer. In the event however no distinction between Scots and English law was made and the case was argued on both sides on the footing that the two systems of law were identical on the subject.

5   Lord Macmillan gives the illustration of the poisoned bread in his own speech in *Donoghue v Stevenson* [1932] AC 562 at 620.
6   The case was sometimes wrongly cited as '*M'Alister v Stevenson*' until Lord Macmillan contributed an explanatory note in the *Law Quarterly Review* (The Citation of Scottish Cases' 49 LQR 1) in which he said: 'Some confusion is apt to arise in the citation of Scottish decisions in consequence of the practice in Scotland of naming a married woman in legal documents and proceedings by her maiden name as well as by her married surname with the (infelicitous) disjunctive "or" interposed'. The correct designation of the case was he said '*Donoghue v Stevenson*'.
7   The Respondent's printed Case described the Lord Ordinary's decision as having been given in 'an elaborate Opinion which seems to show — if this may be said without disrespect — a disinclination on his Lordship's part to acquiesce in the law as it had been declared, rather than any real misapprehension regarding it'.
8   Lord Buckmaster's practice at the Bar became predominantly Chancery: see Heuston *Lives of the Lord Chancellors 1885–1940* p 254. He was appointed from the Bar to become Lord Chancellor and never sat as a judge of first instance or in the Court of Appeal.

It has sometimes been said that Lord Atkin brought the two Scots round to his view, thereby isolating the conservative faction of Lords Buckmaster and Tomlin.[9] Such an assertion could never be proved, although it is undoubted that Atkin was both determined and persuasive behind the scenes between the hearing and the judgment. It is also possibly significant that judgment was reserved for an unusually long period, from 11 December 1931 until 26 May 1932. But when one reads the speeches of Lords Thankerton and Macmillan, both of which contained original thought and Macmillan's at least deserving comparison with that of Atkin, it seems hardly likely that they did not make their own minds up on the basis of what they had heard in court. Indeed, one of the strengths of the majority opinion is that it consisted of three powerful statements, while Lord Buckmaster's dissent was supported by only a slight contribution from Lord Tomlin.

The rival speeches of Buckmaster and Atkin represent in classic form the voices of conservatism and advance, and each was a powerful piece of legal reasoning. Lord Buckmaster began with a familiar warning.

'The law applicable is the common law', he said, 'and though its principles are capable of application to meet conditions not contemplated when the law was laid down, these principles cannot be changed nor can additions be made to them because any particular meritorious case seems outside their ambit.'

Hard cases make bad law; and Buckmaster thought that the majority had invaded the area of impermissible judicial law making. His thinking was rooted in English contract law by which a stranger to a contract had no rights under it. A manufacturer's contract with someone to use care and skill about the manufacture of an article could not give anyone else any rights under the contract. That was a salutary rule to which there were only two exceptions: one was if the article were dangerous in itself (as bottled ginger-beer was not); and the other was if it had some defect which was actually known to the manufacturer (and no such knowledge could be imputed to Stevenson). So Mrs Donoghue's case could not be fitted into the established scheme of things, and she had had to contend for a wider principle; namely that every manufacturer owes a duty to anyone using the article to see that it has been carefully made. For Lord Buckmaster, that was 'simply to misapply to tort doctrine applicable to sale and purchase'. The consequences of such a misconception were serious indeed for trade and commerce, and the potential for

---

9   See Lord Denning *The Discipline of the Law* p 230.

mischief almost limitless, once the line of safety were crossed. 'If one step, why not fifty?'[10]

Lord Buckmaster sought to make his propositions good by a detailed analysis of the earlier cases, and as has been said, he brought to this task a tone of 'almost passionate sarcasm'.[11] The view which he favoured had not been questioned until the case of *George v Skivington* in 1869,[12] in which a successful claim was made by a lady who had suffered from the use of a noxious shampoo bought for her by her husband from the person who had made it up. The correctness of the decision was subsequently doubted and Lord Buckmaster said that he did not propose to follow its later fortunes: 'few cases can have lived so dangerously and lived so long'. Then an important attempt was made in 1893 by Sir William Brett, Master of the Rolls, to extract a general principle from the cases, but his judgment in *Heaven v Pender*[13] was dismissed by Buckmaster as a 'tabula in naufragio for many litigants struggling in the seas of adverse authority'. In his opinion it was better that both decisions 'should be buried so securely that their perturbed spirits shall no longer vex the law'.

To set against these two heretical statements there were many affirmations of orthodoxy which Buckmaster approvingly cited. He could not bring himself to accept the wide and novel contention of Mrs Donoghue. If it were right it would cover even the careless construction of a house; but it was well established that if because of carelessness a ceiling fell and caused injury, an action against the builder could not succeed in England, 'although' as he said, 'I believe such a right did exist according to the laws of Babylon'.

Lord Atkin's approach was wholly different, and the direction of approach was all-important. 'Where as in cases like the present, so much depends upon the avenue of approach to the question', Lord Macmillan said, 'it is very easy to take the wrong turning.'[14] For Atkin the law so far had not achieved any unifying statement of principle, only redress for a random assortment of injuries. 'It is remarkable', he observed, 'how difficult it is to find in the English authorities statements of general application defining the relations between parties that give rise to the duty'; but that was because the

---

10   Lord Buckmaster's quotation was from *Winterbottom v Wright* 10 M & W 109 at 115, per Alderson B. Generally, Buckmaster adopted the reasoning of the Respondent's printed Case, which was that a manufacturer's basic responsibility was contractual and owed to the person who bought the article from him; exceptions to this rule were narrowly defined; and that it would be quite wrong to impose a duty to persons 'of whom the traders know nothing, and who receive the goods under circumstances of which the traders are entirely ignorant, and after adventures which they cannot ascertain'. In contrast Atkin's speech owed little to the Appellant's printed Case.
11   Heuston *Lives of the Lord Chancellors* p 309.
12   LR 5 Ex 1.
13   11 QBD 503.
14   At 611.

courts concerned themselves with the individual circumstances of each dispute, and it was sufficient to say in each case whether the duty existed or no. 'And yet the duty which is common to all the cases where liability is established must logically be based upon some element common to the cases where it is found to exist.' The principle or 'general conception', as he called it, lay below the surface and all that was visible through the cases were illustrations of its application.

Both Atkin and Buckmaster knew that the appeal raised a question which could have revolutionary consquences for the law of civil liability for carelessness, and Atkin began his speech by remarking that he did not think that a more important problem had ever occupied the House in its judicial capacity. It provided a test for the legal system and would demonstrate whether that system was congruent with or remote from the everyday needs of society. He had himself tried this out with his family over the lunch table at Aberdovey after the hearing and before judgment, and his eldest grandson, Toby Low, now Lord Aldington, who was there as a boy has described the incident.

> 'During the summer holidays of 1931 I was staying at Craig-y-don with other members of the family. In those days the family went to Matins at the Aberdovey Church every Sunday morning and there was a large family lunch with Aunts and cousins presided over by my Grandfather, who took much pride in his carving of the joint. He often used the carving time and the carving weapons to conduct a discussion. I remember on several occasions that the post-church discussion about the snail and the ginger beer bottle case — who is my neighbour? — was an easily understandable theme immediately after church. I was then at Winchester aged 17 — an enthusiastic classical student and ignorant of the law, but fascinated by the arguments, and proud of having a Grandfather who was so concerned with human relationships and responsibilities. Later on, when I came to read Law myself at Oxford, I remember rehearsing these discussions with my Tutor.'

Atkin had become convinced that there was some thread linking the cases in which a duty to be careful had been established, and in a series of his own judgments he had been moving towards the formulation of a general principle.[15] In October 1931 he gave a lecture on 'Law as an Educational Subject' which revealed the direction of his thinking:

> '. . . as far as the law is concerned, it is perpetually laying before the student standards of conduct which it is desirable to have maintained in the social state. It is quite true that law and morality do not cover identical fields. No doubt morality extends beyond the more limited range in which you can lay down the definite prohibitions of law; but,

15   Eg *Everett v Griffiths* [1920] 3 KB 163 at 210; *Hambrook v Stokes* [1925] 1 KB 141 at 156; *Oliver v Saddler* [1929] AC 584 at 596.

apart from that, the British law has always necessarily ingrained in it moral teaching in this sense: that it lays down standards of honesty and plain dealing between man and man. The idea of law is that the obligations of a man are to keep his word. If he swears to his neighbour, he is not to disappoint him. In other words, he is to keep his contracts. He is not to injure his neighbour by word. That is to say, he is not to libel or slander him. He is not to commit perjury in respect of him, and he is not to defraud him into acting to his detriment by telling him lies. He is not to injure his neighbour by acts of negligence; and that certainly covers a very large field of the law. I doubt whether the whole of the law of tort could not be comprised in the golden maxim to do unto your neighbour as you would that he should do unto you.'[16]

He had thus come to see the field of civil wrongs and legal liability for carelessness as depending on moral obligation. It was this moral basis of responsibility, related to but narrower than Christian morality, which made so memorable his great statement.

'At present I content myself with pointing out that in English law there must be, and is, some general conception of relations giving rise to a duty of care, of which the particular cases found in the books are but instances. The liability for negligence, whether you style it such or treat it as in other systems as a species of 'culpa' is no doubt based upon a general public sentiment of moral wrongdoing for which the offender must pay. But acts or omissions which any moral code would censure cannot in a practical world be treated so as to give a right to every person injured by them to demand relief. In this way rules of law arise which limit the range of complainants and the extent of their remedy. The rule that you are to love your neighbour becomes in law, you must not injure your neighbour; and the lawyer's question, Who is my neighbour? receives a restricted reply. You must take reasonable care to avoid acts or omissions which you can reasonably forsee would be likely to injure your neighbour. Who, then, in law is my neighbour? The answer seems to be — persons who are so closely and directly affected by my act that I ought reasonably to have them in contemplation as being so affected when I am directing my mind to the acts or omissions which are called in question.'[17]

Lord Atkin went on immediately to say that the same doctrine seemed to him to have been laid down by Sir William Brett in *Heaven v Pender*, at least when qualified later by the same judge. Although the two cases were separated by fifty years, a comparison shows how much common ground was traversed.

In the earlier one the plaintiff was employed by a ship's painter and was injured when a rope broke causing staging which had been

16 (1932) Journal of the Society of Public Teachers of Law 30.
17 At 580 of the Report. It is of interest that against the Parable of the Good Samaritan (Luke 10,29) the Phillips Modern English Version of the New Testament (1960) has a head-note: 'Jesus shows the relevance of the Law to actual living'; whereas the Authorised Version of 1611 has: 'Christ teaches the lawyer how to attain eternal life'.

supplied by the dock owner to collapse: the claim against the dock owner succeeded.

Like Atkin, Brett thought that the cases illustrated some underlying principle. 'It follows, as it seems to me', he said, 'that there must be some larger proposition which involves and covers both sets of circumstances. The logic of inductive reasoning requires that where two major propositions lead to exactly similar minor premises there must be a more remote and larger premise which embraces both of the major propositions.' And he stated the 'proposition', which corresponded to Atkin's 'general conception', in these words: '. . . whenever one person is by circumstances placed in such a position with regard to another that everyone of ordinary sense who did think would at once recognise that if he did not use ordinary care and skill in his own conduct with regard to those circumstances he would cause danger of injury to the person or property of the other, a duty arises to use the ordinary care and skill to avoid such danger'. Brett, too, had introduced his proposition by an appeal to morality: 'And everyone ought by the universally recognised rules of right and wrong, to think so much with regard to the safety of others who may be jeopardised by his conduct.'[18]

Having stated his proposition, Brett applied it to the facts of his case, and went on to say that it would apply also to the supply of an article to be used immediately by someone before there was any opportunity for discovering a defect caused by 'a neglect of ordinary care or skill as to its condition'.

The similarity between the thinking of Brett and Atkin is very striking. Brett even added gratuitously that his principle would apply in circumstances which exactly fitted *Donoghue v Stevenson*. Yet all the judges in that case, including Atkin himself, were at one in saying that Brett had stated his proposition too broadly.[19] It had had to be 'qualified' and 'explained', they said (two favourite judicial expressions for smoothing out the roughnesses left by the doctrine of precedent), in the later case of *Le Lievre v Gould*.[20] Sir William Brett, by then Lord Esher, was a party to that decision, but it was concerned with the very different problem of whether a surveyor who had carelessly issued inaccurate certificates was liable to mortgagees who had not employed him but who had relied on his certificates. It was to be another seventy years after *Le Lievre's Case*, and thirty after *Donoghue v Stevenson*, before it was fully accepted that the law of negligence applied to words as well as to deeds.[21]

---

18   11 QBD 503 at 508.
19   Lord Buckmaster at 573 and 576; Lord Atkin at 580; Lord Macmillan at 614. In 1922, Atkin had described Brett's propositions as 'somewhat wide' (*Hodge v Anglo-American Oil Co* 12 Ll L Rep 183 at 191) and had carefully limited his observations on liability for negligence to articles which were dangerous in themselves.
20   [1893] 1 QB 491.
21   *Hedley Byrne v Heller* [1964] AC 465.

Lord Esher understandably thought that *Heaven v Pender* had no bearing on the surveyor's case, and said that *Heaven's Case* 'established that, under certain circumstances one man may owe a duty to another, even though there is no contract between them. If one man is near to another, or is near to the property of another a duty lies upon him not to do that which may cause a personal injury to that other, or may injure his property'. This he prophetically called the idea of 'contiguity or neighbourhood', and added: 'That is the effect of the decision in *Heaven v Pender*, but it has no application to the present case'.[22]

It is clear enough, as Atkin himself said, that Lord Esher was not referring only to physical proximity when he spoke of 'contiguity or neighbourhood', but was speaking metaphorically of nearness; and it also seems clear that he was not qualifying in any way what he had earlier said in *Heaven v Pender*. If the law laid down by the majority in *Donoghue v Stevenson* had really been stated by Sir William Brett fifty years earlier, why had it not become accepted wisdom?

The first and most obvious reason is that Brett was unable to carry with him his fellow judges in the Court of Appeal. Both declined to concur with him 'in laying down unnecessarily the larger principle which he entertains'.[23] But more important by far was the gulf which separated the judgments of Atkin and Brett in quality and style.[24] Atkin had a rare facility with precedents, to which he brought a profound understanding of the old procedures and formalised pleadings which so constricted the conclusions open to the judges. He took eleven pages of his speech to deal with the cases which had been cited against the view he favoured. In all but one of those cases he explained with complete convincingness that nothing stood in the way of the application of his general conception; and in that single exception he conceded, as he always did when intellectual honesty required it, that it would not yield to explanation, and that the decision (by two judges of first instance) must be criticised for seeking 'to confine the law to rigid and exclusive categories'.[25] The

---

22   [1893] 1 QB 491 at 497.
23   11 QBD 503 at 516. The use of the word 'unnecessarily' was significant.
24   'The precision of a neat draftsman has never been counted among Lord Esher's accomplishments': Sir Frederick Pollock 'The Snail in the Bottle and Thereafter' (1933) 49 LQR 22 at 25. The same writer's opinion was that Esher's attempt to give a comprehensive definition 'may now be regarded as based on a conception sound in principle, even if the expression cannot be accepted as satisfying in form'.
25   At 594.
     The exceptional case was *Blacker v Lake & Elliot* 106 LT 533, a decision of Hamilton and Lush LJJ. Atkin's superior understanding of the significance of the old forms of pleading is illustrated by a comparison of his treatment of *Winterbottom v Wright* (at 588 of the Report) with that of Buckmaster (at 568) and of Brett in *Heaven v Pender* (11 QBD at 513). Only Atkin appreciated that no negligence apart from breach of contract had been pleaded, and that the decision was accordingly not an obstacle to Mrs Donoghue's claim.

analysis of the state of the law and the revelation of its shortcomings carried great force.

Dr Johnson once remarked that 'authority from personal respect has much weight with most people, and often more than reasoning' and the same could be said of the force of style. The majority took a momentous step in *Donoghue v Stevenson*; but the manner of doing it was as important as what was done. By taking as his text the parable of the Good Samaritan and showing in arresting language how it could be applied to legal thinking, Lord Atkin gave to English jurisprudence its most quoted metaphor. If that passage is compared with the ponderous prose of Sir William Brett it becomes easier to understand why Atkin succeeded where Brett had failed.

Some misunderstanding has derived from the way in which Lord Atkin cast his judgment. He stated his 'general conception of relations giving rise to a duty of care', and from that he drew out a proposition about manufacturers' liability which was the true decision in the case. This proposition was that 'a manufacturer of products, which he sells in such a form as to show that he intends them to reach the ultimate consumer in the form in which they left him with no reasonable possibility of intermediate examination, and with the knowledge that the absence of reasonable care in the preparation or putting up of the products will result in an injury to the consumer's life or property, owes a duty to the consumer to take that reasonable care'. That proposition of law has stood and has never since been doubted.

But the general conception was not a statement which was intended afterwards to be directly applied. It was a leading mark from which other specific propositions could and have since been derived. It would have been, as Lord Devlin said, a misuse of the conception for judges to attempt to decide cases by saying whether or no there was a sufficient degree of proximity between plaintiff and defendant — English law does not develop in that way.[26] And Atkin himself warned against the risk of vague and misleading generalisations. Because in the field of civil wrongs the administration of justice depends on judges applying general principles which they themselves have formulated, 'it is of particular importance to guard against the danger of stating propositions of law in wider terms than is necessary, lest essential factors be omitted in the wider survey and the inherent adaptability of English law be unduly restricted. For this reason it is very necessary in considering reported cases in the law of torts that the actual decision alone should carry authority, proper weight, of course, being given to the dicta of the judges'.[27]

The conception of the neighbour opened up the possibility of further classes of case being brought within the law of negligence so

---

26 In *Hedley Byrne v Heller* [1964] AC 465 at 524. See also *Dorset Yacht v Home Office* [1970] AC 1004 at 1060, per Lord Diplock.
27 At 584.

that it could be truly said, 'The categories of negligence are never closed'.[28]

In fact Lord Atkin and his fellow judges of the majority determined to do precisely what Lord Buckmaster feared, to mark out new ground so that legal liability for carelessness could be extended. The new principle might have been observable from the cases but it had never before been stated, except unavailingly by Sir William Brett. Lord Macmillan said that 'The grounds of action may be as various and manifold as human errancy': that was to make possible the taking of the fifty steps which the conservatives thought impermissible.

Lord Macmillan's special contribution to the debate was to liberate the law of negligence from the shackles of the old rule that no stranger to a contract can take a benefit under it. In his view the confusing state of the old cases was to be explained by the fact that 'two rival principles of the law find a meeting place where each has contended for supremacy'.[29] One was that only a party to a contract can complain of its breach, and the other that negligence gives a right of action to someone injured by it. There was no reason why the two rights should not exist side by side. If an injured claimant could not establish a contractual right then that of itself should not preclude an action for negligence. It was in that sense that Macmillan emphasised the importance of the avenue of approach to a case.

The decision worked a legal revolution. According to the style of the modern appellate judgment, the majority did not content themselves with a conclusion wide enough only to decide the dispute. They surveyed the entire field and found the state of the law wanting. In order that the debris of the old cases should not stand in the way of development which was consonant with both common sense and social needs, a framework had to be worked out within which the law of negligence could grow, unconstrained by illogical or nice distinctions. To achieve this the reactionaries had first to be beaten out of their entrenchments. When seven years later Lord Atkin was presented for an honorary doctorate at Liverpool University, his eulogium described him as 'what is very rare in England, a legal scientist, a judge who is not content merely to settle present disputes, but seeks always to expand and develop those underlying principles which are to be applied to other disputes'; and went on to contrast him with those judges 'who lack his imaginative courage'.

---

28   At 619, per Lord Macmillan.
29   At 609.
   Lord Macmillan's approach to the problem in *Wilsons and Clyde Coal v English* [1938] was similar conceptually, where he said (at 74): 'In this appeal your Lordships have to consider and accommodate the spheres of operation in the law of master and servant of two competing doctrines, the doctrine of vicarious liability and the doctrine of common employment'.

'They are content to be guided and seek for authority as an easy substitute for independent action. They take refuge in precedent as in a protective shell; like the mollusc, they attain safety at the price of flexibility and mobility, and practitioners and students alike search their judgments in vain for those general ideas which are the life of the law.'

Courage of that order was necessary, and judgment too, for however obvious the good sense of the decision now seems, it was less evident then than the dangers of the limitless field which had been opened up.

Yet the revolution was not destructive. That was why Atkin particularly, but his fellow judges of the majority also, took such pains in analysing and explaining the old cases. They were not tempted to smash the clay and start again. The growth was organic and was later described by Lord Devlin in these words:

'What *Donoghue v Stevenson* did may be described either as the widening of an old category or as the creation of a new and similar one. The general conception can be used to produce other categories in the same way. An existing category grows as instances of its application multiply until the time comes when the cell divides.'[30]

It is a feature of English law that most of its best modern jurisprudence is to be found in the great opinions and judgments in the Law Reports and not in academic writings. The most thoughtful attempts to analyse the methods and effects of the decision of the majority in *Donoghue v Stevenson* are to be found in two later decisions of the House of Lords in the same field which were themselves milestones, *Hedley Byrne* in 1963[31] and the *Dorset Yacht* Case in 1970.[32] Here it was said for the first time with authoritative clarity that Lord Atkin's 'general conception' of neighbourhood is not a universal rule of law to be applied literally as if it were a statute, but is a guide to the circumstances in which a duty of care may be held to exist. The most lasting value of the case will be to show 'how the law can be developed to solve particular problems'.

In the *Dorset Yacht* Case, Lord Diplock asserted that all three decisions had extended the English law of civil wrongs so as to impose liability where it had not been imposed before[33] — although, he observed, the judges hesitate to acknowledge the process of law-making, and 'little conscious thought has been given to analysing its methodology'. Then, in a remarkable passage, he undertook his own analysis.[34]

The first stage, he said, is for the court to consider how far the older cases have gone. The search through the cases involves the

---

30   *Hedley Byrne* at 525.
31   [1964] AC 465.
32   [1970] AC 1004.
33   At 1058.
34   At 1058–1060. It is difficult to discern what was the purpose of the analysis.

analyst having some general idea of what he is looking for, that is the types of conduct and relationship which ought to give rise to a duty. This is an inductive process because it sets out to identify the characteristics which are common to those older cases, and leads to a proposition which can be stated as:

> 'In all the decisions that have been analysed a duty of care has been held to exist wherever the conduct and relationship possessed each of the characteristics A, B, C, D etc., and has not so far been found to exist when any of the characteristics were absent.'

The process then becomes deductive and the proposition is restated as: 'In all cases where the conduct and relationship possess each of the characteristics A, B, C, D etc., a duty of care arises'.

But because a milestone decision involves a new departure, a policy decision by the court becomes necessary in order to decide whether a duty of care ought to exist if any of the relevant characteristics were absent; and that policy decision will be influenced 'by the same general conception of what ought to give rise to a duty of care as was used in approaching the analysis'.

Lord Diplock pointed out that the proposition used at the deductive stage is not a true universal because of the sheer volume of reported cases. So that proposition ought to be qualified to exclude cases in which the conduct or relationship had characteristics 'obviously absent' in the case for decision, and would then run:

> 'In all cases where the conduct and relationship possess each of the characteristics A, B, C, and D, etc., *but do not possess any of the characteristics Z, Y or X etc. which were present in the cases eliminated from the analysis*, a duty of care arises.'

This, said Lord Diplock, is an important qualification and one which Lord Atkin himself introduced when warning of the danger of 'stating propositions of law in wider terms than is necessary, lest essential factors be omitted in the wider survey and the inherent adaptability of English law be unduly restricted'. It is for this reason that Lord Atkin's 'general conception' should not be treated as a universal rule of law. The parable of the Good Samaritan, observed Lord Diplock, itself illustrates conduct, by the priest and the Levite who passed by on the other side, which had as its probable consequence injury to the health of the thieves' victim, yet for which they would not have been liable in English law.

The passage deserves to be read in full. It is a rare, perhaps unique, essay by a judge in analysing the underlying mental processes by which an important judicial conclusion is reached. And it was made with *Donoghue v Stevenson* directly in view. Yet it does less than justice to the qualities which Lords Atkin, Thankerton and Macmillan brought to the decision: courage, judgment, simplicity of expression, and above all vision. Even on the mechanistic level at which Lord

Diplock's propositions were stated, the essential step — that of the 'policy decision' to extend legal responsibility into a new area, is hardly discussed. Lord Diplock saw that step as deriving from the cumulative experience of the judges. Weight must certainly be given to the earlier cases which led up to *Donoghue v Stevenson* and which were so painstakingly analysed by Lord Atkin; but those decisions did not speak in unison and in the case itself five judges were in favour of admitting Mrs Donoghue's claim and four against; one would look far for a more dramatic difference of outlook than in the speeches in the House of Lords itself.

Very recently Lord Wilberforce has reminded the legal profession that 'at the margin, the boundaries of a man's responsibility for acts of negligence have to be fixed as a matter of policy'; and he went on to explain that the way in which Lord Atkin stated the neighbour principle requires 'that foreseeability must be accompanied and limited by the law's judgment as to persons who ought, according to standards of value or justice, to have been in contemplation'.[35] To found liability for negligence within the framework of Lord Atkin's general conception, it is not enough that the defendant ought to have foreseen that damage would result from his carelessnesss — otherwise the Levite would be liable in English law. The judges must also be satisfied that the plaintiff is within the class of those who ought to be compensated. It may be objected that this is not a helpful guide, or even begs the vital question. But the history of Atkin's neighbour principle since it was first formulated supplies the answer to the objection. It has provided a practical guide relied on more regularly and more frequently than any other judicial statement of this century.

Considering that Lord Atkin thought and said that no more important problem had occupied the Law Lords, their decision on *Donoghue v Stevenson* received only a modest welcome in the professional journals of the day. Sir Frederick Pollock contributed a short article to the *Law Quarterly Review* entitled 'The Snail in the Bottle, and Thereafter'[36] in which he praised 'the Scots Lords of Appeal for overriding the scruples of English colleagues who could not emancipate themselves from the pressure of a supposed current of authority in English Courts'. Professor Winfield wrote: 'it cannot be doubted that the decision meets the needs of the community',[37] and the opinion of the *Solicitors' Journal* was that it would 'govern millions of small transactions every day in the whole of the United ingdom'.[38] But no writer appreciated the significance of the general conception of foreseeability which Atkin had propounded. Where it was discussed it was generally misunderstood. Within a few weeks

35 *McLoughlin v O'Brian* [1982] 2 WLR 982 at 988.
36 49 LQR 22.
37 51 LQR 249 at 254.
38 76 Sol Jo 387. The writer noted in passing that the decision had not attracted much public notice.

of the House of Lords' decision, the Court of Appeal presided over by Lord Justice Scrutton had to decide a case in which it was argued that *Donoghue v Stevenson* had changed the law.[39] The jib of a crane had fallen and killed a skilled erector who had noticed that some cogwheels did not fit well, but had not appreciated the extent of the danger and had started to work the crane. His widow's claim against the manufacturer had been withdrawn from the jury by Mr Justice McCardie, and the Court of Appeal refused to disturb the decision. Scrutton adopted a minatory tone. 'English judges' he said, 'have been slow in stating principles going beyond the facts they are considering. They find themselves in a difficulty if they state too wide propositions and find that they do not suit the actual facts.' In his view Lord Atkin had stated his general proposition too widely, and the real ground of the decision was no more than the definition of 'a manufacturer's liability to the ultimate consumer when there is no reasonable possibility of intermediate examination of the product'.

Fears about the implications of Atkin's general conception continued to trouble some. As late as 1941, the writer of a note in the *Law Quarterly Review* seized on a phrase of Atkin's in a recent case that 'Every person, whether discharging a public duty or not, is under a common law obligation to some persons *in some circumstances* to conduct himself with reasonable care so as not to injure those who are likely to be affected by his want of care', and supposed that in so saying Atkin had repented and accepted that 'the criterion of "neighbourly duty", was not a universal one'. The qualification would, the writer thought, 'bring tranquillity to many minds that, for the past nine years, have been sorely harrassed in the attempt to reconcile the decision in that case with the normal trend of the development of our law'.[40]

The reception which was accorded to the decision in the Commonwealth showed more understanding than at home. A full and thoughtful article in the *Canadian Bar Review*, although written from Oxford, said that 'Lord Atkin's judgment is at once stamped as perhaps the most impressive and certainly the most authoritative effort ever made to generalise the English law of negligence', and described the neighbour principle as 'a guide to judges where before there was none'.[41]

And Mr Justice Evatt, with whom Atkin seems to have corresponded regularly, wrote from the High Court of Australia in March 1933:

39 *Farr v Butters Bros* [1932] 2 KB 606.
40 P. A. Landon, 57 LQR 179 at 183.
    In *Grant v Australian Knitting Mills* [1936] AC 85 it was contended by the manufacturer defendant, for whom Wilfrid Greene KC appeared 'that if the decision in Donoghue's Case were extended even a hair's breadth, no line could be drawn, and a manufacturer's liability would be extended indefinitely' (at 107, per Lord Wright).
41 F. C. Underhay, 10 Can Bar Rev 615.

'. . . The Snail Case has been the subject of the keenest interest and debate at the Bar and in the Sydney and Melbourne Law Schools: on all sides there is profound satisfaction that, in substance, your judgment and the opinion of Justice Cardozo of the U.S.A. coincide, and that the common law is again shown to be capable of meeting modern conditions of industrialisation, and of striking through forms of legal separateness to reality. There is an article in the Canadian Bar Review which expresses the Australian view as well as that of Canada . . .'.[42]

The revolution brought about by *Donoghue v Stevenson* was so quiet that it passed completely unnoticed by the general public who were so closely affected by it; and its true nature was perhaps not fully understood even by the profession until Lord Devlin's speech in 1963 in the *Hedley Byrne* Case. The general conception of neighbourly duty was not a proposition which had been stated too widely. It was a statement which called the law of negligence into existence as a separate civil wrong, and enabled that branch of the law to develop on common sense lines so as to become the most important and far-reaching of all civil wrongs. In the fifty years which have passed since the decision it has renewed itself again and again, and has demonstrated its usefulness in all manner of circumstances.[43] There is no sign that its power of adaptability is waning, nor is there any reason why it should. This power is due more than anything else to the moral spirit which animated Lord Atkin's speech, an object lesson, as Lord Wright said, of liberal thought in the handling of principles which has influenced the common law in all its branches.[44]

Atkin and his colleagues found a tangled mass of old decisions but no decision of the House directly in point. The step which they took to bring order to the chaos was one which was impelled by the ordinary needs of British society and the assumptions which it made about right and wrong. They were doing something which every legal system requires of its law makers, parliamentary or judicial, that of constantly relating the law to the tacitly accepted moral principles of their own society.

In retrospect the decision now seems so clearly right and just that it makes one marvel at the state of the law before 1932; but the increasing certainty which time brings that an important decision is right is the highest tribute that can be accorded to the judgment of those who made it.

42   The reference to the decision of Cardozo J is to *Macpherson v Buick Motor Co* 217 NY 382 — see 598 of the Report of *Donoghue v Stevenson*. The article in the *Canadian Bar Review* seems to be that referred to in note 41 above.
43   See eg *Awad v Pillai* reported in *The Times* for 5 June 1981 under the heading 'Extending the "neighbour principle" '; and '*The Irene's Success*' [1982] 1 All ER 218.
44   Lord Wright 'In Memoriam Lord Atkin of Aberdovey' 60 LQR 332.

Commercial Law

Commercial law was Lord Atkin's métier. He made his reputation at the Bar in the field, and he had done his pupillage with Thomas Scrutton, with whom he sat for nine years in the strongest common law Court of Appeal of this century. It is not easy to define the qualities which made up Atkin's greatness as a commercial lawyer, but foremost was a determination that the intellectual problems presented by mercantile cases should never be degraded into puzzles to be solved by mere cleverness. The law for Atkin had always to be useful and realistic, the servant of the commercial community and not its arbiter.

For this reason the bargains made by traders must stand, and it was not the business of the judges either to attempt to improve on them or to incur the reproach of having destroyed them because they lacked something of clarity. 'Nothing is more dangerous', he said in *Bell v Lever Brothers*, 'than to allow oneself liberty to construct for the parties contracts which they have not in terms made by importing implications which would appear to make the contract more business like or more just.'[1] As so often, he summed it up in popular language by saying that the contract should be given the benefit of the doubt.[2]

It was possible to go further and conceive of commercial law (or at least that part which was not codified by Parliament) as being no more than judicial confirmation of the general usages of traders. This was the view of Sir Alexander Cockburn, a judge whom Atkin revered throughout his professional life, and whose concern Atkin shared that commercial law and commercial practice should not be allowed to drift apart.

> 'It is true that the law merchant is sometimes spoken of as a fixed body of law, forming part of the common law, and as it were coeval with it. But as a matter of legal history, this view is altogether incorrect. The law merchant thus spoken of with reference to bills of exchange

1 [1932] AC 161 at 226.
2 *Fender v St John-Mildmay* [1938] AC 1 at 12.

and other negotiable securities, though forming part of the general body of the *lex mercatoria*, is of comparatively recent origin. It is neither more nor less than the usages of merchants and traders in the different departments of trade, ratified by the decisions of Courts of law, which, upon such usages being proved before them, have adopted them as settled law with a view to the interests of trade and the public convenience . . . Usage, adopted by the Courts having been thus the origin of the whole of the so-called law merchant as to negotiable securities, what is there to prevent our acting upon the principle acted upon by our predecessors, and followed in the precedents they have left to us? Why is it to be said that a new usage which has sprung up under altered circumstances, is to be less admissible than the usages of past times? Why is the door to be now shut to the admission and adoption of usage in a matter altogether of cognate character, as though the law had been finally stereo-typed and settled by some positive and peremptory enactment?'[3]

Those passages are from a judgment of Lord Cockburn which Atkin described as one of the charters of the liberty of the common law,[4] and he accepted entirely Cockburn's views. Very early in his own judicial career he had made it clear that if usages changed, the law should change with them. 'The object of the Courts in construing commercial contracts', he said, 'is to try and give effect to the intention of both the contracting parties and not to impose upon businessmen terms which they never contemplated. If old forms are now used to express different meanings from those read into them in earlier days the Courts should be prompt to recognize the altered use if they are satisfied that there is in fact a change.'[5]

But the language of the business document is not so easy to interpret: it is often cryptic leaving much unsaid, and what is written can be formless or illogical. Moreover, the commercial community clings tenaciously to established forms, which become changed and botched according to the exigencies of the transactions in which they are used. Atkin occasionally, and Scrutton more frequently and more trenchantly, showed irritation about the way commercial men framed their agreements. Atkin once said that half the disputes which came before the courts were caused by the 'extraordinary inability' of businessmen to express themselves in a way which was incapable of being mistaken,[6] but his worst strictures were reserved for policies

---

3 *Goodwin v Robarts* (1875) 10 Ex 337 at 346, 352. Benjamin QC had argued that temporary scrip issued in England by Rothschilds as agents for the Russian Government, was not negotiable, and no usage could make it so.
4 *Rex v International Trustee* [1937] AC 500 at 531.
5 *Groom v Barber* [1915] 1 KB 316 at 325.
6 Public lecture on 'The Place of Law in University Education' given at the London School of Economics on 5 October 1923.

of marine insurance, things of shreds and patches which he described as past praying for.[7]

But the contribution of both great judges in the field which was their own lay especially in giving effect to, rather than in holding up to ridicule, what traders had agreed upon. For this Sir Thomas Scrutton brought to bear his formidable irony. In *Rose and Frank v Crompton* Mr Justice Bailhache had decided that a clause in a contract stating that it was not 'a formal or legal agreement and shall not be subject to legal jurisdiction . . .' should be rejected because it was repugnant to the rest of the document. Scrutton dismissed that: '. . . before this heroic method is adopted of finding out what the parties mean by assuming that they did not mean part of what they said, it must be clearly impossible to harmonize the whole of the language they have used'.[8]

Similarly dismissive, Atkin castigated as 'a logical absurdity which I do not find it necessary to admit into our law' the proposition that goods were 'entrusted' to a jeweller's customer who fraudulently gained possession of two valuable necklets by pretending that she wanted to show them to her husband and another person. 'She stole them', he said, 'just as completely as though she had secretly taken them off the counter and hidden them in her bag.'[9]

In order to make commercial agreements effective it is always necessary to pay regard to commercial reality and commercial probabilities. Lord Atkin had an acute perception of these, a quality well illustrated by his dissenting judgment in the Court of Appeal in 1921 in *Howard Houlder v Union Marine Insurance*.[10] A cargo of molasses to be carried from the West Indies to Canada was insured with London underwriters by American cargo owners for an agreed value of £26,025 which was then equivalent to US $108,000. The policy contained a clause reading: 'Claims, if any, to pay at the rate of 4.15 dols. to the £1 sterling'. A total loss occurred and the underwriters paid out £26,025. In the meantime the dollar had appreciated against sterling and the assured claimed an additional £3,000 odd to enable him to recover $108,000.

Of nine judges who heard the case, Atkin was the only one who would have decided in favour of the assured. In the Court of Appeal, Lords Justices Bankes and Warrington, and later all five Law Lords

---

7   *Trade Indemnity v Workington Harbour and Dock Board* [1937] AC 1 at 17.
    Marine policies seem always to have been singled out for opprobrium: cf *Burges v Wickham* (1863) 3 B & S 669 at 685-6, per Cockburn CJ; and more recently *The Salem* [1981] 2 Lloyd's Rep 316 at 323 per Mustill J.
8   *Rose and Frank v Crompton* [1923] 2 KB 261 at 287.
9   *Lake v Simmons* [1926] 2 KB 51 at 70, 71. Atkin's view did not find favour with his brethren, Bankes and Warrington LJJ, but his dissent was upheld in the House of Lords on other grounds ([1927] AC 487). The woman had been convicted of larceny by the time the action, which was brought on a Lloyd's policy, was tried by McCardie J.
10   (1921) 6 Ll L Rep 551.

took the view that the policy was a contract made and to be performed in England. It was a sterling policy and the clause could not have the drastic effect of converting it into a dollar policy. As Lord Sumner had it, 'The effect of the transaction would be to add to a contract of indemnity against marine risk already completed, an additional contract of indemnity against a totally different kind of risk which arises out of the fluctuations of exchange'.[11]

Atkin approached the meaning of the document differently. This he thought was a case where the parties would have contracted so as to protect the assured. He had a cargo worth $108,000, admittedly to be insured in sterling, but on terms that would protect his dollar property. If he was considering the risk of a total loss, he would be saying to the underwriters:

> 'We want to be sure that if we do lose the whole cargo we recover its whole value, that is 108,000 dols., and we therefore ask that you pay us the sum insured at the same rate at which we fixed the sum insured, in other words at 4.15 dols. In this way we shall recover no more and no less than 108,000 dols.: you will pay us for every $100 insured either 415 dols. or such a sum in sterling as will produce to us where we carry on business 415 dols.'

This, he thought, was exactly what the assured might ask and the underwriters assent to. But Atkin's view, so convincing commercially, did not prevail and the opposite conclusion has not since been challenged in England. Indeed, Lord Dunedin said of the case that, mercifully, it was so peculiar that it could not possibly be an authority for any other. Nonetheless, a similar point arose two years later in the United States and the Fourth Circuit Court of Appeals declined to follow the House of Lords' decision in *Houlder's Case* although expressly invited to do so. The court pointed out what had been at the root of Atkin's thinking, that since the First War, sterling no longer remained the most stable measure of value that could be found. 'American ships and cargo owners', said the court, 'were no longer content with a promise to pay pounds. They wanted to know, if a loss happened, how many dollars pounds would mean to them, for there were many indications that dollars would be worth more and pounds less than for more than a century had been the case.'[12]

Atkin's commercial points were often made by a simple decisive illustration. When discussing whether an exemption clause in a towage contract should be held effective in circumstances where the tugs had supplied only six hours' efficient towage out of an intended fifteen, and the tow was lost as a consequence, he asked:

> 'If the tugs on the orders of the defendant had cast off the tow in a storm on a lee shore for the purpose of engaging in a more profitable

11 (1922) 10 Ll L Rep 627 at 628.
12 *Marine Ins Co v McLanahan* (1923) 290 F 685. I am indebted for this reference to Dr F. A. Mann *The Legal Aspect of Money* (4th edn) p 206.

salvage operation, and the two were in consequence damaged, could it be suggested that the intention of the contract was that the defendant should be protected?'[13]

Or when charterers agreed to load steel at a specified freight rate, and a cargo was loaded which was partly general goods commanding a higher rate, the Court of Appeal decided that the shipowners were entitled to more than nominal damages. Atkin made the point this way:

> 'If I order from the wine merchant twelve bottles of whiskey at so much a bottle and he sends me ten bottles of whiskey and two of brandy, and I accept them, I must pay a reasonable price for the brandy. That is the position here.'[14]

It is not surprising to discover that Atkin had a determination to clear away the accumulated debris of the past whenever it stood in the way of a just and realistic result. This was the necessary preliminary before a modern law of negligence could develop; and it was as essential in commercial matters.

In the *Fibrosa* Case towards the end of his career, he with Lords Russell, Macmillan and Wright, overturned the old rule established in the cases that followed the postponed coronation of King Edward VII, that if a contract is frustrated, money which has already been paid cannot be reclaimed. In so doing Atkin reached a conclusion 'that I venture to think would occur to most people, whether laymen or lawyers . . . that the buyer ought to get his money back, having had nothing for it . . .'[15]

But in the work of removing anomalies, nothing bears comparison with the decision of the House of Lords in *United Australia v Barclays Bank*.[16] In that case, a cheque drawn in favour of the plaintiffs had been wrongfully endorsed in favour of a company called M.F.G. Trust, the initials of which were those of the wife of an undischarged bankrupt financier, described by Atkin as a 'lady of fortune'. Later the books of the United Australia Company were discovered to record a loan in favour of M.F.G. but there was no minute authorising any loan. Proceedings were started against M.F.G. for the return of money lent and for money had and received, but M.F.G. went into liquidation before the action could be tried. The plaintiffs proved in the liquidation but nothing was done about their proof. They then began proceedings against Barclays Bank for carelessly collecting the cheque and crediting the proceeds to M.F.G. The Bank's main defence was that because the plaintiffs had sued M.F.G. for the return of money lent, they had 'adopted' the transaction of loan,

13   *The Cap Palos* [1921] P 458 at 471.
14   *Steven v Bromley* [1919] 2 KB 722 at 728.
15   [1943] AC 32 at 50.
16   [1941] AC 1.

although it was admittedly fraudulent, and treated M.F.G. as a debtor, or in the picturesque language of the old pleaders, they had 'waived the tort'.

Both Mr Justice Goddard and the Court of Appeal reluctantly upheld the defence.[17] Lord Denning, who appeared as leading counsel for the plaintiffs, has described how apprehensive he felt in opening the appeal in the Lords with a history of failure in the courts below; and how the case was 'argued for him' by Lord Atkin who encouraged and prompted him quietly with a few incisive questions. Lord Denning had had the impression that Atkin had done this as much as anything to show his hand and to bring his colleagues round.[18] In the result Viscount Simon and Lords Atkin, Thankerton, Romer and Porter unanimously allowed the appeal.

Atkin pointed out in his speech that in the ordinary case where a thief is sued for the return of stolen goods, 'the plaintiff has never the slightest intention of waiving, excusing or in any kind of way palliating the tort'.

> 'I protest', he said, with the rhetorical flourish which he occasionally used, 'that a man cannot waive a wrong unless he either has a real intention to waive it, or can fairly have imputed to him such an intention, and in the cases which we have been considering there can be no such intention either actual or imputed. These fantastic resemblances of contracts invented in order to meet requirements of the law as to forms of action which have now disappeared should not in these days be allowed to affect actual rights. When these ghosts of the past stand in the path of justice clanking their medieval chains the proper course for the judge is to pass through them undeterred.'

For those who would defend such absurdities, it was necessary, as Burke had once said, to beat them out of the entrenchments of Gothic rubbish under which they hoped to remain impregnable. But the arid science of pleading exercised a baleful charm. Lord Campbell had permitted himself the reflection that 'in the exquisite logic of special pleading rightly understood, there is much to gratify an acute and vigorous understanding';[19] and Lord Romer recalled that one of the old common lawyers had been moved to break into verse on the subject.[20]

To Lord Atkin's mind, the crystallised refinements of equity also contributed much to the obstruction of progress and tended to prevent a business-like solution.

17 [1939] 2 KB 53.
18 Personal communication from Lord Denning.
19 *Life of Lord Ellenborough* quoted by Lord Simon [1941] AC 1 at 22.
20 Lord Romer referred to 'The Circuiteers: An Eclogue' by Sir F. Pollock, the elder, sometime the Queen's Remembrancer, printed in 1 LQR 232. The poem is an imaginary dialogue by the banks of Windermere at sunset between Addison, a special pleader, and Sir Gregory Lewin, a criminal lawyer, in which they 'rest beside this prattling burn, And sing of our respective trades in turn.' Addison sings: Thoughts much too deep for tears subdue the Court, When I 'assumpsit' bring, and god-like waive a tort.'

In the Spring of 1936 Lord Atkin wrote to his old friend Professor Gutteridge about the House of Lords decision in *Russian and English Bank v Baring Bros*[21] and expressed his antagonism to Chancery niceties in plain terms:

> 'We had an interesting case some time ago winding up a dissolved Russian Bank: business against Chancery. It shocked the purists that anything dissolved should be allowed to sue: on the other hand if the statute says you are to wind it up, unless you deem it to exist it has no assets, no creditors, no debtors: and what winding up means heaven only knows. As in one of the other cases the question arose because one of the big financial houses holds about £100,000 belonging to the defendant bank: and has the greatest reluctance (from the highest possible motives of course) to hand it over.'

Business against Chancery was a recurrent theme of Atkin's time in the Lords and is well illustrated by the *Russian and English Bank Case*. Another example was *Southern Foundries v Shirlaw*[22] where Lords Atkin, Wright and Porter decided over the dissent of Lords Maugham and Romer that it was an implied term of a managing director's service agreement that the employing company should not remove him from the Board during the currency of the agreement, surely the better commercial view. The danger which the intrusion of equity carried into mercantile questions was that in straining after fairness in hard cases, it would create complicted exceptions to the simple certainties which should be the concern of the law merchant. This was the central point of *Re Wait*,[23] an important decision on the sale of goods.

Wait had bought a quantity of wheat on cif terms and sub-sold part on a similar basis. The sub-buyers paid in advance of delivery to them of any document of title, Wait paid in their cheque, pledged the bill of lading and went bankrupt. His trustee in bankruptcy redeemed the pledge and claimed to retain all the wheat, leaving the sub-buyers to an unsecured claim in damages. The Court of Appeal held by a majority (Lord Hanworth and Lord Justice Atkin, Lord Justice Sargant dissenting) that the trustee's claim must be upheld.

Sargant represented the Chancery viewpoint. To his mind, the agreement for sub-sale was an equitable assignment enforceable against the wheat in the trustee's hands. The view had about it a certain fairness, for the sub-buyers had after all paid for the goods. But it did not commend itself to Atkin. The wheat which had been sub-sold was neither 'specific' nor 'ascertained' goods for which a decree of specific performance could be ordered under the Sale of

21   [1936] AC 405.
22   [1940] AC 701. For recent examples of 'business against Chancery', see *British Eagle v Air France* [1975] 2 All ER 390 (the opposing speeches of Lords Morris and Cross); and *Sudbrook Estate Ltd v Eggleton* [1982] 3 All ER 1.
23   [1927] 1 Ch 606.

Goods Act; the parcel of wheat to be sub-sold was less than the whole of what Wait had bought, and had never been identified or appropriated.

That was a strict, even harsh, view, but it was a necessary one. The Sale of Goods Act was a code and, 'It would have been futile in a code intended for commercial men to have created an elaborate structure of rules dealing with rights at law, if at the same time it was intended to leave, subsisting with the legal rights, equitable rights inconsistent with, more extensive, and coming into existence earlier than the rights so carefully set out in the various sections of the Code'.

More important still was the effect that the view to which he was opposed would have had on business transactions. Nearly all important transactions were financed by banks or financial houses:

> 'They would have to satisfy themselves on being paid off that the equitable interests were not being defeated, and their own powers of disposition if their customer made default would be enormously restricted. Presumably they would have to communicate with each sub-purchaser. [This] would throw the business into confusion, for credit would be seriously restricted.'

The appreciation of the commercial consequences of a decision was characteristic. Lord Justice Sargant could only answer the point by saying that ordinary business is not conducted dishonestly; but as to that Atkin thought the test of honesty was inadequate, either too wide or too narrow to resolve commercial disputes. There was no dispute about the existence of the principles of equity, but he concluded dismissively, 'They are well settled, and beyond doubt in their own sphere beneficial'.

It is sometimes possible to sense a personal tension in the tussle for a majority in the House of Lords between the proponents of business and of Chancery. Certainly Atkin felt it himself, for he wrote to his son, Bill, in 1935: 'I am sitting this term in the House of Lords: after the next case I shall only have two Chancery colleagues, Tomlin and Russell, and hope to bring them into line'; and in 1938 to W. R. Wallace, Chief Clerk to the Judicial Committee, of Lord Romer's promotion to Lord of Appeal: 'This is a good new appointment though I mislike a preponderance of Chancery men. Let us hope that brotherly love will not continue!'[24] In fact, Atkin was seldom in the minority, and then only in the cases in which his dissent was solitary and memorable as in *Liversidge* or the *East Suffolk Rivers Case*.[25] The more usual division was an alliance of the Scots and common lawyers on one side, and the Chancery men on the other, as in *Donoghue v Stevenson*.

24   Atkin to Wallace, 5 January 1938.
25   [1941] AC 74.

Atkin's most formidable adversary in the House was Lord Russell: each was capable of expressing himself in the forceful language of the advocate. In the *Portuguese Banknote* Case,[26] Atkin said of a consequence of one of the arguments and quoting a phrase of Russell's: 'I should have thought this result, in the language of one of your Lordships, manifestly impossible; but rules of law have to be tested in these days, and must survive the application of first principles'; and he asserted that the case could not be decided in favour of Waterlows 'without reversing a number of authorities which have governed our commercial law, as I understand it, from earliest times'. Lord Russell, who was in favour of determining the appeal in favour of Waterlows, replied:

> 'One of your Lordships in his speech has, in effect, accused those of us who differ from him in this case, of upsetting a number of authorities governing our commercial law. Personally, I am unconscious of any such assault upon authority. I am only conscious of deciding that the Bank have not proved that they have suffered the enormous damages which they claim to recover from Messrs. Waterlow. I confess, however, that I derive some consolation from the knowledge that, in this alleged act of violence I am abetted by one whose pre-eminence as a commercial lawyer is both well established and long established.'

Lord Russell referred to Lord Justice Scrutton and he was right to point out that the division of opinion in the case was not on traditional lines. Mr Justice Wright, Lords Justices Greer and Slesser and Lords Sankey, Atkin and Macmillan ultimately prevailed over Lord Justice Scrutton and Lords Warrington and Russell. Mr Gavin Simonds, who led Norman Birkett, James Wylie and Bensley Wells for the appellants, Waterlows, evidently delivered a reply so forcible that it came close to carrying the House, for no less than three of the Law Lords mentioned his argument in terms of praise.[27]

This historic case, which supports those who think that Law Reports can be read for pleasure, was concerned with the nature of money itself. The Central Bank of Portugal which had the exclusive right to issue bank notes as legal tender in Portugal, ordered a quantity of notes bearing on their face a portrait of Vasco de Gama, to be printed by Waterlows. The paper currency of Portugal was at that time inconvertible, that is to say it was not backed by gold and the only obligation which the Bank incurred when it issued a note was, on demand, to give another note in exchange for it. Nor was there any likelihood that the currency would become convertible. A quantity of the notes were duly delivered to the Bank, but, by reason of an audacious fraud practised on Waterlows, they were induced to deliver a further quantity to an international gang led by one Marang

---

26   *Banco de Portugal v Waterlow* [1932] AC 452.
27   Lord Warrington (at 485), Lord Russell (at 499), Lord Macmillan (at 508).

and including the Portuguese Minister at the Hague, which surreptitiously put a large number into circulation in Portugal. In order to protect its currency, the Bank felt bound to withdraw the whole Vasco de Gama issue, good and spurious, and it was accepted that this was a reasonable and indeed inevitable step for the Bank to take. It therefore invited all holders of notes of this type to surrender them in exchange for notes of a new issue but the same denomination. The Bank sued Waterlows for breach of contract, the issue between the parties being, what was the Bank's recoverable loss?

As Lord Macmillan put it, 'Your Lordships were presented with a choice between two extremes. No possible middle course was suggested. Which is right?' The Bank had given good and valid notes in exchange for worthless forgeries. What loss did this occasion? On one hand it was said for Waterlows that all that the Bank had lost was the cost of paper and printing. On the other side it was submitted that the Bank had lost the full face value of the good notes which it had been compelled to issue for the bad. For the resolution of this question it was necessary to enquire into the nature of inconvertible paper currency.

Lord Russell asked what sum would compensate the Bank for having undertaken, on the issue of a good new note, the obligation of exchanging it one demand for another. No evidence of loss had been tendered beyond the cost of paper and printing.

Lord Macmillan, in an elegant and lucid speech, took the opposing view. The argument that by issuing the new notes the Bank had lost only the value of some stationery, was in his opinion fallacious. 'It overlooks the cardinal fact that a note when issued by the Bank of Portugal becomes by the mere fact of its issue legal tender for the sum which it bears on its face. The issued note represents so much purchasing power in terms of commodities. It can be used by the holder of it to purchase at current prices any commodity in the market, including gold and securities. It can equally be used by the Bank to purchase commodities, including gold and securities, or to discharge debts due by it. It must be accepted by the Bank in discharge of debts due to it.'

Lord Atkin's speech was a contrast in style with Macmillan's, but to the same effect. It was the hard-hitting, driving, speech of the advocate, seeking always the weaknesses in the opposing view and reducing it to absurdity. Of one contention he said that it was 'a proposition which I do not wish to qualify with an epithet'. He considered that 'the Bank by issuing its note like the trader issues its promise to pay a fixed sum, issues a bit of its credit to that amount . . .' Its damages should be measured by the liability it had incurred, and, he said, 'There is one final and conclusive proof of the fallacy of the defendant's contention to which I have not heard an answer. By issuing a note the Bank provides the holder of it with a piece of currency which he can bring to the Bank the next day and compel the Bank to receive in discharge of his overdraft or in payment under a contract to buy securities or bullion'.

From this, the majority view, it has been said, it is possible to draw the general conclusion, 'that according to its intrinsic nature money represents purchasing power'.[28]

As he disapproved of the separate paths which had been taken by the common law and equitable jurisdictions, so Lord Atkin also thought it wrong for special classes of document to have their own rules of interpretation and enforcement. Separation deeds were a prime example of such an unwelcome development and of them Atkin said:

> 'We have to deal with a separation deed, a class of document which has had a chequered career at law. Not recognized by the Ecclesiastical Courts, such contracts were enforced by the common law. Equity at first frowned. Lord Eldon doubted but enforced them ... Full effect has therefore to be given in all Courts to these contracts as to all other contracts. It seems not out of place to make this obvious reflection, for a perusal of some of the cases in the matrimonial Courts seems to suggest that at times they are still looked at askance, and enforced grudgingly. But there is no caste in contracts. Agreements for separation are formed, construed and dissolved and to be enforced on precisely the same principles as any respectable commercial agreement, of whose nature indeed they sometimes partake.'[29]

For the same reason he deplored the contortions in which judges sometimes indulged in the interpretation of wills. For him, a will was a business document, and the sole object which the courts should have in view was the accurate ascertainment of the testator's intentions. Judges should be relieved, he once said, 'from the thraldom, often I think self-imposed, of judgments in other cases believed to constrain them to give a meaning to wills which they know to be contrary to the testator's intention'.[30]

An opportunity to assimilate the rules of law and equity presented itself to the Court of Appeal in 1920 in *Banque Belge v Hambrouck*[31] where the subject was tracing. Hambrouck was a clerk in an engineering works whose owner banked with the Banque Belge. Hambrouck fraudulently obtained over £6,000 by means of cheques

---

28   Mann *The Legal Aspect of Money* (4th edn) p 28. It is interesting today to read Lord Atkin's view on the proper volume of the note issue ([1932] AC 452 at 487): 'In any civilized State it will not be permitted to issue notes to an unlimited amount; it will, if honestly conducted, in any case determine its obligations by its possible resources; but the State will require that behind the promises to pay there stand solid resources in the form of gold and liquid securities; and it will impose a positive restriction on the issue of notes beyond an amount which it considers necessary.'

29   *Hyman v Hyman* [1929] AC 601 at 625.
Similarly he saw 'no logical absurdity' in applying the doctrine of frustration to leases ([1922] 2 AC at 199–200), a view now approved by the House of Lords in *National Carriers v Panalpina* [1981] 2 WLR 45.

30   *Perrin v Morgan* [1943] AC 399 at 415.

31   [1921] 1 KB 321.

drawn on his employer's account, and having passed them through his own bank account, he paid them by means of further cheques to his mistress, Mlle Spanoghe. She paid them into a deposit account with a third bank. The Banque Belge sued to recover the money in the deposit account. The difficulty was whether the money which had admittedly been stolen by Hambrouck could be traced through Hambrouck's bank into Mlle Spanoghe's deposit account.

All three of Lords Justices Bankes, Scrutton and Atkin considered that the funds could be traced, but the interest of the decision lies in their differing approaches to the same conclusion. Bankes' view was that the common law claim succeeded because Mlle Spanoghe had never paid any money into her deposit account except the proceeds of Hambrouck's fraud: there had been no mixing of funds. Scrutton was inclined to think that the Banque Belge could not succeed at law because Hambrouck's payment of the Banque Belge's money into his own bank, 'and his drawing out other money in satisfaction, had changed its identity . . . at any rate if the money was mixed in Hambrouck's bank with other money'. But that was no matter, because the claim certainly succeeded in equity, the equitable extension of the doctrine of tracing having enabled money to be traced even though it had changed its character or been mixed.

In a long and careful judgment, Atkin considered whether the distinction which his brethren had drawn or implied between the common law and equitable remedies was really justified. He quoted at length from *Taylor v Plumer*,[32] the leading case on common law tracing decided in 1815 by Lord Ellenborough, and doubted the restricted significance it had later been given by Lord Haldane. 'But if', he said, 'in 1815 the common law halted outside the bankers' door, by 1879 equity had the courage to lift the latch, walk in and examine the books.'[33] In his view, the approach of the common law had always been to ask, had the means of ascertainment failed? That being so, the Banque Belge could make out a claim at common law as well as in equity.

The leading commentators on the subject support Lord Atkin's view as consistent with the earlier cases, and have pointed out that on that view the common law right would in practice be similar to the equitable, or even more extensive.[34] It would permit tracing into a mixed fund, thought otherwise to have been the peculiar contribution of equity, and that without the complex refinements which have been developed around the equitable doctrine. In its simplicity and generality, the question, 'Had the means of ascertainment failed?' might have assumed an importance in the field comparable with that of the neighbour principle in negligence.

32   3 M & S 562.
33   *Re Hallett's Estate* (1879) 13 Ch D 696.
34   Goff and Jones *The Law of Restitution* (2nd edn) pp 52–53.

But the opportunity was not taken and although in 1948 Lord Denning asserted that it was no longer appropriate to draw a distinction between law and equity,[35] the two systems have developed separately: or more accurately, the common law rule has remained debilitated and its equitable counterpart has grown its own complications. Atkin would have regretted both.

Lord Atkin's judgment in the *Banque Belge Case* is an illustration of another aspect of his thinking, a preoccupation with general principles. This was not merely the extraction of a principle from the earlier cases, a process which is in any event necessary for the decision of most cases, but the perception of a general underlying idea, which may sum up what has gone before but is also capable of illuminating the future.

The pre-eminent example of this quality is in Atkin's great speech in *Donoghue v Stevenson*, but there are other cases where the same tendency can be seen.

Another important instance is in his dissenting speech in *East Suffolk Rivers Catchment Board v Kent*[36] where Lord Atkin for the first time voiced the opinion that any authority discharging a public duty must take care not to injure anyone likely to be affected by a want of care, even if acting under statutory powers. This conception of a dual responsibility, statutory and under common law, has led directly to a whole new development in the field of public law, the implications of which as yet are far from being fully worked out.

Bell v Lever Brothers[37] is another example: here the elusive topic of contractual mistake arose for decision and Atkin remarked significantly that 'if this case results in establishing order into what has been a somewhat confused and difficult branch of the law it will have served a useful purpose'. The issue in the case was: can a contract stand where one party has obtained something different in quality from that which he bargained for?

Bell and Snelling were managers of a large company and had service contracts with some years to run. As a result of a merger of the company's business it became necessary to cancel their contracts and the company paid substantial compensation in order to do so. It was later discovered that the company's expenditure and expressions of regard for their employees had been misplaced. Both Bell and Snelling had been speculating covertly in cocoa, a product in which the company dealt, and had this been known, they could and would have been dismissed summarily without compensation. The company sued for recovery of the money which it had paid as compensation, but, having succeeded before Mr Justice Wright and

---

35   *Nelson v Larholt* [1948] 1 KB 339 at 343, described by Goff and Jones (op cit, p 53) as 'an expression of hope rather than a statement of reality'.
36   [1941] AC 74.
37   [1932] AC 161.

in the Court of Appeal, lost in the House of Lords by the narrow majority of three (Lords Blanesburgh, Atkin and Thankerton) to two (Lords Hailsham and Warrington).

The decision has been fought over and criticised, as much for its apparent injustice as for the confusing reasoning of four separate speeches. The House of Lords failed to settle the law in a peculiarly difficult field and only Atkin attempted a general review. His formulation of the test in a case like *Bell v Lever Brothers* was that before consent was to be nullified and the contract declared void, the mistake had to be 'as to the existence of some quality which makes the thing without the quality essentially different from the thing as it was believed to be'; and he concluded 'on the whole' that an agreement to terminate a broken contract was not so essentially different from one to end an unbroken contract that it could not satisfy his test. That conclusion has been attacked by commentators and it has been asked: if the test is not satisfied in Bell's case, how can it ever be satisfied, for while 'the contemplated subject matter of the bargain was a service contract of great value to Bell, the actual subject matter was worthless'?[38]

Such criticisms are fair but they have tended to obscure the principle which underlay Lord Atkin's reasoning, and which he made explicit at the end of his speech. 'The result is that in the present case servants unfaithful in some of their work retain large compensation which some will think they do not deserve. Nevertheless it is of greater importance that well established principles of contract should be maintained than that a particular hardship should be redressed.' If contract parties fail to protect themselves by including stipulations in their agreements, they must bear the risk that events will turn out unfavourably, for the paramount consideration is that their agreements should stand.

The long-term effect of the decision is that it has become virtually impossible to avoid a contract at common law for mistake on the ground of some misconception as to the quality of the subject-matter of the contract, a result which was doubtless intended and would have been welcomed by Atkin and his colleagues of the majority. But again equity has intervened, and will grant relief where the common law will not, although the circumstances in which it will do so are now very far from clear. In *Bell v Lever Brothers*, the House of Lords did not distinguish between law and equity; their intention, and particularly that of Lord Atkin, was to settle the law. In that respect, the decision must be accounted a failure.

A decision whose implications were not so obvious to the judiciary as some commentators would have wished was that of Lords Justices Bankes, Scrutton and Atkin in *Société des Hotels le Touquet Paris-*

---

38   See eg Cheshire & Fifoot *Law of Contract* (10th edn) p 208.

Plage v Cummings;[39] yet it must take its place among the forces which eventually carried away the unjust and anomalous English rules about the recovery of foreign currency. The *Le Touquet Case* was decided in 1921, but it was more than fifty years afterwards before the so called 'breach-date rule' was finally buried.[40] By this rule, a debt in foreign currency was, for the purposes of recovery in England converted into sterling (the only currency in which judgment could be given here) at the date when it fell due; so that if sterling were to depreciate against the foreign currency between the date of maturity and the date when payment was finally made (in modern times, more than an academic possibility) the creditor was the loser. A campaign against the rule had long been waged in academic writings and the *Le Touquet Case* had been used as a base for the attack.[41]

The Court of Appeal decided that if a debtor owing French francs was sued in this country but afterwards paid his debt to his creditor in francs, he satisfied his obligations in full. So stated, the result seems not only to accord with sense but to be self-evident. But the contrary was vigorously argued, for the franc had fallen sharply against sterling in the period between the time when the debtor ought to have paid and the date of actual payment. Moreover Mr Justice Avory awarded a sterling sum calculated at the rate of exchange current when the debt fell due.[42] His decision was reversed, Lord Justice Scrutton observing that the plaintiffs, who were owed Frs 18,035 payable in France, must be content with Frs 18,035 paid in France.

Atkin agreed with Scrutton but he added some significant observations of his own which cast a long shadow towards the final rejection of the old anomalies. It could not be right, he thought, that once a writ was issued in England, the franc debt became a sterling debt at the rate of exchange ruling at the date of maturity. 'If such were the effect of the transaction, it would follow that the defendant on January 1, 1915 [the day after the date of maturity] incurred obligations to pay to the plaintiffs sums in the manifold currencies of the many countries of the world where she might eventually be sued.' Then, at the very end of his judgment he posed the question which was not to be settled for another fifty years, and gave more than a hint of what his provisional view was.

> 'For the purposes of this action I have not thought it necessary to decide at what date the exchange should be calculated had the plaintiffs succeeded. . . . But no case that I know of has yet decided what the position is when a foreign creditor, to whom a debt is due in his

---

39   [1922] 1 KB 451.
40   By the House of Lords in *Miliangos v George Frank Textiles Ltd* [1976] AC 443.
41   See eg Dicey's *Conflict of Laws* (7th edn) pp 916–7; Kahn-Freund 'Foreign Currency Obligations and the Devaluation of Sterling' 68 LQR 163;
Mann *Legal Aspect of Money* (2nd edn) p 320.
42   [1921] 3 KB 459.

country in the currency of his country, comes to sue his debtor in the Courts of this country for the foreign debt. Much may be said for the proposition that the debtor's obligation is to pay, say, francs, and so continues until the debt is merged in the judgment which should give him the English equivalent at that date of those francs. It is a problem which seems to require very full consideration, and which I personally should desire to reserve.'[43]

Lord Atkin's contribution to the development of commercial law included many statements of principle which have stood unchallenged ever since. Two examples must suffice. In *Ariadne Steamship Co v James McKelvie & Co*[44] he explained comprehensively the circumstances in which an agent who signs a contract as such may be personally liable, in two pages of terse prose to which no summary or extract can do justice. A year earlier, the Court of Appeal in *Joachimson v Swiss Bank Corpn*[45] had decided that it was necessary for a customer to demand repayment of a credit balance on current account before suing. In the course of his judgment, Atkin described the attributes of the contract between banker and customer:

'The question seems to turn upon the terms of the contract made between banker and customer in the ordinary course of business when a current account is opened by the bank. It is said on the one hand that it is a simple contract of loan; it is admitted that there is added, or superadded, an obligation to the bank to honour the customer's drafts to any amount not exceeding the credit balance at any material time; but it is contended that this added obligation does not affect the main contract. The bank has borrowed the money and is under the ordinary obligation of a borrower to repay. The lender can sue for his debts whenever he pleases. I am unable to accept this contention. I think that there is only one contract made between the bank and its customer. The terms of that contract involve obligations on both sides and require careful statement. They appear upon consideration to include the following provisions. The bank undertakes to receive money, and to collect bills for its customer's account. The proceeds so received are not to be held in trust for the customer, but the bank borrows the proceeds and undertakes to repay them. The promise to repay is to repay at the branch of the bank where the account is kept, and during banking hours. It includes a promise to repay any part of the amount due against the written order of the customer addressed to the bank at the branch, and as such written orders may be outstanding in the ordinary course of business for two or three days, it is a term of the contract that the bank will not cease to do business with the customer except on reasonable notice. The customer on his part undertakes to exercise reasonable care in executing his written orders so as not to mislead the bank or to facilitate forgery.'[46]

43   [1922] 1 KB 451 at 465.
44   [1922] 1 KB 518 at 535–6.
45   [1921] 3 KB 110.
46   At 126–7.

One textbook writer has described the judgment as one of the most important ever delivered on the subject of banking law, and the quoted passage as a text on which a considerable part of his book is a sermon.[47] The description of the banking contract has indeed never been improved upon nor doubted. The decision in the case, at first blush perhaps surprising, was amply justified by all the members of the court (Lords Justices Bankes, Warrington and Atkin) as necessary in a commercial sense on the ground that '. . . the parties must have intended that the money handed to the banker is only payable after a demand. The nature of the contract negatives the duty of the debtor to find out his creditor and pay him his debt. If such a duty existed and were performed, the creditor might be ruined by reason of outstanding cheques being dishonoured'.

Atkin always insisted on high moral standards in commercial dealings and dealt severely with a lack of probity wherever it appeared. It was an integral part of his outlook that human relationships should be regulated by a strict code and that wrongdoing should be sharply treated. In this respect he was able to import into his work in the commercial field his own personal standards. So, in a case where a bankrupt who was unaware that a receiving order had been made against him had been lent money, his trustee in bankruptcy was ordered by the Court of Appeal to refund the money to the lender. The court was pressed with the argument that the administration of bankruptcy would be made difficult if judges decided according to what they considered high-minded, and without regard to the law. But Atkin and his brethren were of the view that if it would be dishonourable for the debtor to use the money to pay his creditors, it would be equally dishonourable for an officer of the court, knowing the facts, to do the same.

> 'I think these difficulties are exaggerated', he said, 'but while one may agree that opinions as to rules of honesty differ, the difficulty of recognizing honesty when she appears, affords [an] inadequate reason for discarding her altogether. The advantages of maintaining a high standard of commercial morality in my judgment far outweigh the suggested inconveniences of administration. If I may repeat the words of Lord Esher the proposition strikes me as a good, a righteous and a wholesome one, and I eagerly desire to adopt it.'[48]

The court (Lords Justices Warrington, Duke and Atkin) were unanimous, but it is in Atkin's judgment that the moral considerations are most conspicuous. So too were they in a decision with important implications for stock exchange dealings, decided in the Privy Council in 1937 on appeal from the Supreme Court of Canada,

---

47 Chorley *Law of Banking* (6th edn) p 26.
48 *Re Thellusson* [1919] 2 KB 735 at 764. See also *Rhodes v Macalister* 29 Com Cas 19.

Solloway v McLaughlin,[49] and in which Lord Atkin delivered the opinion of the Board. Brokers instructed to buy for a client on margin and to carry the purchase for him, simultaneously sold shares in the same company, and used the client's shares to complete the sale. They also sold shares which the client had lodged with them as margin. When later the client closed his transaction, the brokers went into the market, which had by then fallen substantially, bought the necessary number of shares and delivered them to the client. The brokers raised the familiar argument that the client had lost nothing as a result of their, the brokers', dealings, for he had got the shares he had instructed the brokers to buy. Moreover, it was objected, if judgment were to be given for the client for the full amount he had been charged for the shares purchased, and for the price which the brokers had obtained for the margin shares, the client giving credit only for the value of the shares delivered to him, the client would be put in a better position than if he had not been defrauded at all.

Atkin gave these arguments short shrift:

> 'All that this amounts to', he said, 'is to recognize that fraudulent brokers have often sounder judgment than their clients as to the future course of markets. If the shares had been converted and not returned, there can be no question that the client would have been entitled to receive the proceeds of the conversion though he himself had planned to hold and thought he had succeeded in holding the shares until a time when the value was nothing. Fortunately for the commercial community the law has many effective forms of relief against dishonest agents, and no injustice is done if the principal benefit, as he occasionally may, by the superior astuteness of an unjust steward in carrying out a fraud.'[50]

Although Lord Atkin's 'constructive intuition' enabled him in his greatest judgments to point the way the law could develop and grow, he was at bottom a judge who felt the force of tradition more than the need to innovate. There were certain fundamentals which must withstand the pressure of change. It was for this reason that he told Lord Simon that the majority of the House in *Liversidge v Anderson* had missed the opportunity 'of upholding old traditions of justice', and his dissenting speech in that case was concerned first and last with consistency of meaning. He was conservative also, and especially

49   [1938] AC 247.
50   At 259.
  On the occasion of the award to Atkin of an honorary Doctorate of Civil Law at Oxford in 1931, the address ran:
  'Frustra huius oculis Autolycus ad omnem fraudem igeniosus tenebras offuderit; frustra ad homines in commerciis circumscribendos clam cum aliis coierit, consenserit, coniurarit.'
  [In vain would the crafty Autolycus himself, skilled as he was in every kind of fraud, have tried to pull the wool over his eyes; quite vain would have been all his secret alliances, plots and conspiracies with others designed to cheat men in their business dealings.]

so, in the view he took that the judiciary should not arrogate to itself functions which were properly those of the executive. He would have agreed with Madison that power is of an encroaching nature, and such encroachments by the judges were to be avoided. 'A conflict is not to be contemplated between the Courts and the Executive', he said in a remarkable decision in which, with obvious reluctance, he accepted a statement from the Home Secretary that a spot in the middle of the Bristol Channel was outside territorial waters.[51] And on another occasion, when dealing with racial discrimination: 'Questions of policy, or in other words, how the legal powers shall be exercised, are not matters for the legal tribunal but have to be determined by the appropriate constitutional authority'.[52] Equally conservative was his formulation of the absolute doctrine of sovereign immunity in 'The Cristina',[53] put forward in two propositions:

> 'The first is that the courts of a country will not implead a foreign sovereign, that is, they will not by their process make him against his will a party to legal proceedings whether the proceedings involve process against his person or seek to recover from him specific property or damages.
>   The second is that they will not by their process, whether the sovereign is a party to the proceedings or not, seize or detain property which is his or of which he is in possession or control.'

In that case the House decided that the owners of a ship registered in Bilbao and which had been requisitioned by decree of the Spanish Republican Government could not obtain the assistance of the English courts to recover possession of her in Cardiff, because such assistance would necessarily involve impleading a foreign sovereign. Atkin's statement represents the pure theory of sovereign immunity, later described by Lord Wilberforce as a 'classic formulation',[54] although later also substantially qualified.

Less than a year after the decision in 'The Cristina' the Spanish Civil War threw up another dispute which tested in a more acute form the views of the judiciary on sovereign immunity.[55] Lord Atkin again presided in the House of Lords and the Republican Government was again represented by Mr G. St. C. Pilcher KC, Mr Owen Bateson and Mr John Foster. The 'Arantzazu Mendi' was registered in Bilbao and in 1937 was requisitioned by the Republican Government while on the high seas, after that port had been captured by Franco's Nationalist forces. In March 1938, while the ship was in London, General Franco issued a decree requisitioning her and

---

51   *The Fagerness* [1927] P 311.
52   *Commissioner for Local Government Lands and Settlement v Kaderbhai* [1931] AC 652 at 654. An East African case, in which the Commissioner, being empowered to sell plots of land by auction, had imposed the condition that only Europeans should bid.
53   [1938] AC 485.
54   In *I Congreso del Partido* [1981] 3 WLR 328 at 335.
55   *SS Arantzazu Mendi v Government of the Republic of Spain* [1939] AC 256.

other vessels, and in the following month the owners and the master made national declarations that they held the vessel at the disposal of the Nationalist Government. On the same day the Republican Government issued a writ claiming possession, which the Nationalist Government sought to set aside on the ground that it impleaded a foreign sovereign. Mr Justice Bucknill and the Court of Appeal ordered the writ to be set aside. The House of Lords unanimously affirmed the decision.

In doing so, Lords Atkin, Thankerton, Russell, Macmillan and Wright were faced with a direct conflict between the two sides in the civil war. Each claimed possession of the ship and each claimed sovereignty. However, the only issue in the case was whether the Nationalists were entitled to immunity and that depended on whether they constituted a sovereign authority. According to the usual practice, the court asked for guidance from the Foreign Secretary. This was given in a letter dated 28 May 1938 which read as follows:

'Sir, With reference to your letter of May 25, regarding the case of the Arantzazu Mendi, I am directed by Viscount Halifax to return the following answer to the question asked in para. 5:–

(1) His Majesty's Government recognises Spain as a foreign sovereign state.

(2) His Majesty's Government recognises the government of the Spanish Republic now having its seat in Barcelona as the de jure government of Spain.

(3) No government other than that referred to in the preceding subparagraph is recognised by His Majesty's Government as the de jure government of Spain or any part thereof.

(4) The Nationalist Government of Spain is a government in conflict with the government of the Spanish Republic established at Barcelona. It claims to be the government of Spain and is seeking to overthrow the government of the Spanish Republic and to establish its authority over the whole of Spain.

(5) His Majesty's Government recognises the Nationalist Government as a government which at present exercises de facto administrative control over the larger portion of Spain.

(6) His Majesty's Government recognises that the Nationalist Government now exercises effective administrative control over all the Basque provinces of Spain.

(7) His Majesty's Government has not accorded any other recognition to the Nationalist Government.

(8) The Nationalist Government is not a government subordinate to any other government in Spain.

(9) The question whether the Nationalist Government is to be regarded as that of a foreign sovereign state appears to be a question of law to be answered in the light of the preceding statements and having regard to the particular issue with respect to which the question is raised.'

It was argued for the Republican side that the effect of the Foreign Office letter was merely to accord to the Nationalists recognition as insurgents, and that it was contrary to the principles of international law to concede sovereign status to a body which confessedly had not attained its full aim. In any case, it was said, sovereignty pertains to a state and not a government.

In his speech Atkin remarked that it did not seem necessary to discuss the case at much length: the only question was 'whether the Nationalist Government of Spain represent a foreign sovereign State in the sense that entitled them to immunity from being impleaded in these Courts . . .' The judge had taken the course of making enquiries of the Foreign Office; 'not only is this the correct procedure', he said, 'but . . . it is the only procedure by which the Court can inform itself of the material fact whether the party sought to be impleaded, or whose property is sought to be affected, is a foreign sovereign State . . . The reason is, I think, obvious. Our State cannot speak with two voices on such a matter, the judiciary saying one thing, the executive another. Our Sovereign has to decide whom he will recognize as a fellow sovereign in the family of States; and the relations of the foreign State with ours in the matter of State immunities must flow from that decision alone'.

Observing that the Nationalist decree affecting merchant shipping in the Basque Provinces emanated from the territory specifically mentioned in the sixth paragraph of the Foreign Office letter, and that there was no difference 'for the present purposes' between recognition of a state de facto and de jure, he concluded that the Nationalist Government had made out its claim to sovereign immunity.

It was a much-criticised decision. That de facto recognition can carry as a consequence a right to immunity from suit by the government recognised de jure has been described as a 'non sequitur', and offensive to principles of international law.[56] It has also been pointed out that at the time when the House of Lords gave their decision (23 February 1939) the political and strategic situation in Spain would have made any other result unreal, so near to victory then were Franco's forces. The Foreign Office was doubtless embarrassed by the questions addressed to it, and in the final paragraph of its answer sought to transfer responsibility for the decision back to the courts. But neither considerations of logic nor the sensitivities of the political situation deflected Atkin and his colleagues from what they conceived to be of overriding importance, an absolute refusal to become embroiled in the business of the executive.

56   See eg H. Lauterpacht 'Recognition of Insurgents as a "de facto" Government' 3 MLR 1; Mann *Studies in International Law* p 408. HM Government does not now accord recognition to governments, but only to states: — Statement by Lord Carrington in the House of Lords on 28 April 1980: 408 HL Official Report col 1121.

'The non-belligerent State', Atkin said, 'which recognizes two Governments, one de jure and one de facto, will not allow them to transfer their quarrels to the area of the jurisdiction of its municipal courts.'[57]

Lord Atkin's adherence to the separation of powers was formed in an age before the incursions of the state had reached into every corner of daily life. Some of the consequences of his strict view are not so apt today: would he for example have taken the same absolute view of sovereign immunity forty years after '*The Cristina*'? But such a question implies no criticism of his conservative stance in its own time. In any case no one could doubt the rightness of his determination to curb the ambitions of the executive. *Liversidge v Anderson* may have been a case about the proper construction of subordinate legislation, but its moral was that judges were not to be more executive-minded than the executive. His vigilance in this matter came from a sense of the history of the seventeenth century, and he seems always to have had in mind the lessons which that troubled age held for the judges. In *A-G v Wiltshire United Dairies*,[58] decided in 1921, both he and Lord Justice Scrutton quoted the Bill of Rights in holding ultra vires the imposition by the Food Controller of a charge of twopence per gallon as a condition of the grant of licences to purchase milk. The vagueness of the alleged purpose to which the money was to be applied, he said, 'illustrates the wisdom of Parliament in retaining, in its own hands, the control of the expenditure of public money'.

The return to old fundamentals was characteristic. Another such fundamental was that a single well-defined system of commercial law should prevail throughout the English jurisdiction. The common law Court of Appeal of which Atkin was a member for almost nine years held strongly to this view. If it were not so, the way would be open for the over-mighty subject to make his own rules. But how was this to be reconciled with arbitration procedures? Here the parties choose their own tribunal and must be taken by so doing to accept its decisions whether good, bad, or indifferent. For this reason most systems of law do not allow for any review of arbitral decisions by the courts except in cases of manifest injustice or irregularity. But this had never been the point of view of English law, under which the courts have traditionally had a jurisdiction to supervise the proceedings of arbitrators and to review questions of law decided by arbitrators, virtually upon demand by either party to the dispute.

That traditional English view was affirmed decisively by Lords Justices Bankes, Scrutton and Atkin in the case of *Czarnikow v Roth*,[59] which settled for sixty years and until the legislature

---

57   At 265.
58   (1921) 37 TLR 884.
59   [1922] 2 KB 478.

intervened,the issue of whether parties could validly agree that questions of law were to be finally settled by arbitrators, and were not to be reviewed by an English court. Each member of the court, 'whose combined authority in matters of commercial law is probably unequalled', as the 1978 Report on Arbitration by the Commercial Court Committee described them,[60] disposed of the question with a magisterial negative. So important did the Committee of 1978 consider the judgments that lengthy extracts from each were appended to their Report.

Lord Justice Bankes said:

> 'The importance of maintaining in its integrity the rule of law in reference to public policy is in my opinion a matter of considerable importance at the present time [1922]. Powerful trade organizations are encouraging, if not compelling, their members and persons who enter into contracts with their members to agree, as far as they can lawfully do so, to abstain from submitting their disputes to the decision of a Court of law ... to release real and effective control over commercial arbitrations is to allow the arbitrator, or the Arbitration Tribunal, to be a law unto himself, or themselves, to give him or them a free hand to decide according to law or not according to law as he or they think fit, in other words to be outside the law. At present no individual or association is, so far as I am aware, outside the law except a trade union ... Unlimited power does not conduce to reasonableness of view or conduct ...'

Lord Justice Scrutton:

> 'Arbitrators, unless expressly otherwise authorized, have to apply the laws of England. When they are persons untrained in law, and especially when as in this case they allow persons trained in law to address them on legal points, there is every probability of their going wrong, and for that reason Parliament has provided in the Arbitration Act that, not only may they ask the Courts for guidance and the solution of their legal problems in special cases stated at their own instance, but that the Courts may require them, even if unwilling, to state cases for the opinion of the Court on the application of a party to the arbitration if the Courts think it proper. This is done in order that the Courts may insure the proper administration of the law by inferior tribunals. In my view to allow English citizens to agree to exclude this safeguard for the administration of the law is contrary to public policy. There must be no Alsatia in England where the King's writ does not run. ... I am ready to go very far in ignoring technicalities and irregularities on the part of arbitrators, unless there is some real substance of error behind them, but I think commercial men will be making a great mistake if they ignore the importance of

60   Cmnd 7284.
 That Atkin and his colleagues were fully alive to the possibility of abuse of the special case procedure, through which the court's supervisory jurisdiction was mainly exercised, appears from *Aronson v Mologa* (1928) 138 LT 470.

administering settled principles of law in commercial disputes, and trust to the judgment of business men, however experienced in business, based only on the facts of each particular case, and with no knowledge of or guidance in the principles of law which must control the facts and which arbitrators must administer . . .'

Lord Justice Atkin:

'I think that it is still a principle of English law that an agreement to oust the jurisdiction of the Courts is invalid. . . . The jurisdiction that is ousted in this case is not the common law jurisdiction of the Courts to give a remedy for breaches of contract, but the special statutory jurisdiction of the Court to intervene to compel arbitrators to submit a point of law for determination by the Courts. This appears to me to be a provision of paramount importance in the interests of the public. If it did not exist arbitration clauses making an award a condition precedent would leave lay arbitrators at liberty to adopt any principles of law they pleased. In the case of powerful associations such as the present, able to impose their own arbitration clauses upon their members, and, by their uniform contract, conditions upon all non-members contracting with members, the result might be that in time codes of law would come to be administered in various trades differing substantially from the English mercantile law. The policy of the law has given to the High Court large powers over inferior Courts for the very purpose of maintaining a uniform standard of justice and one uniform system of law. Analogous powers have been possessed by the Court over arbitrators, and have been extended by the provisions of s. 19. If an agreement to oust the common law jurisdiction of the Court is invalid every reason appears to me to exist for holding that an agreement to oust the Court of this statutory jurisdiction is invalid . . .'

It must have been an awesome court. Lord Denning appeared before it ('one of the strongest Courts of Appeal') as a junior. 'Often there was a difference between Scrutton and Atkin, each trying to win over Bankes. Scrutton with robust common sense, Atkin with a fine rapier mind. The Court spoke just enough. They also listened well — especially to youngsters — Atkin did not interrupt much — but when he did, it was with devastating effect.' Scrutton's heavy irony was legendary, and he was fond of observing that he supposed no one would pay any attention to what he said. In one of the series of scuttling cases which followed the collapse of the marine freight market after the First World War, he said:

'The underwriters allege, whether correctly or not I do not know, that just about this time, when insured values were much above the market values of shipping, an extraordinary multitude of disasters fell upon Greek ships, including this one, by which mines attacked them in places where fortunately no loss of life occurred to the crew and where incidentally the loss of the ship was a gain to her owner.'[61]

---

61   *Graham v Motor Union Insurance* [1922] 1 KB 563 at 579.

But Atkin, who admired Scrutton greatly and was a close personal friend, perceived that that rugged figure also had a passion for justice. For it was also Scrutton who said:

> 'It is indeed one test of belief in principles if you apply them to cases with which you have no sympathy at all. You really believe in freedom of speech, if you are willing to allow it to men whose opinions seem to you wrong and even dangerous.'[62]

As a young man, Atkin had walked the courts in search of a pupil master, and no one impressed him so much as an advocate as Thomas Scrutton. He therefore sought him out and persuaded him to take him as a pupil. Many years later, the pupil paid his master a notable compliment in a speech at Gray's Inn.

> 'I had the great advantage', Atkin said, 'of having as a colleague on the Bench when I was appointed, my old Tutor, Mr. Justice Scrutton, one of the greatest lawyers whom the last century produced and a Judge who was devoted to the cause of justice.'

Possibly an even greater compliment was paid to both judges by Sir Arthur Greer who wrote to Atkin:

> 'On one occasion I said to the late Mr. Justice Bailhache that the qualities required for a perfect Judge consisted of ability to grasp all the details of a case and at the same time not to lose sight of the general principles of the law. His answer was: "No such person exists." I disagree with his view, as I have known two instances of these qualifications for judicial office — one was Ld. J. Scrutton, the other a pupil of his to whom this letter is addressed.'

The contrasting prose styles of Scrutton and Atkin are so marked that many passages from the judgments of each could be identified without attribution. It is tempting to suggest that the whole judicial style of each could be characterised metaphorically as hammer and rapier, but that would do justice to neither. For Atkin was as strong a judge as Scrutton. And he too could command a destructive irony, as when he described underwriters as 'very often depicted by Counsel in these Courts as being persons whose knowledge of any particular business is blank, and so guileless that they would lose money if they only did business with a society for missionaries'.[63] Each judge's style owed much to his earlier experience as an advocate, and in the best judgments of that remarkable court, the reader has the sensation of being swept along to an irresistible conclusion.

Atkin and Scrutton constantly disagreed; while there seem to be only two reported occasions when Lord Justice Bankes dissented,[64]

---

62   *R v Secretary of State for Home Affairs, ex p O'Brien* [1923] 2 KB 361 at 382.
63   *Niger Company v Guardian Assurance* 6 Ll L Rep 239 at 249.
64   In *Roberts v Poplar Assessment Committee* [1922] 1 KB 25; and *R v Roberts* [1924] 2 KB 695.

either Atkin or Scrutton dissented as often as the court was unanimous. 'They fought for the body of Bankes' as Lord Denning put it.[65] In the study of decision making by the English judiciary, more attention might be paid to the struggle for mastery behind the scenes in the appellate courts. It is clear that Atkin was outstandingly difficult to dislodge from a view, once formed, and he said himself that he found it easier to determine a case than to hear it.[66] There is little reason to think that Sir Thomas Scrutton was any more persuadable.

It comes as something of a surprise to discover that Atkin did not much enjoy his time in the Court of Appeal. There he was able to devote a great part of his work to the resolution of commercial questions in a court of three whose combined experience in that field was incomparable. Yet in June 1927 he wrote to his son Bill to say:

'I am beginning to feel rather tired of the Court of Appeal where I shall have been nine years next Spring and have been junior Common Law Lord Justice all the time: quite unprecedented. If I were offered a Law Lordship in the next year I should probably take it. If not I propose to resign, and see whether I cannot raise an equal or perhaps larger income by joining some bank and/or insurance company. I think my commercial law might be useful. However all this is rather in the air.'

This was not just a passing mood, for his daughter, Mrs Robson, has recalled that he hardly ever told his family about his daily work in the Court of Appeal, saying only in answer to the evening question: 'Nothing: very dull'. But within a year of his letter to his son, he was promoted to the House of Lords over his two more senior colleagues. Although he had more commercial cases to decide in the Court of Appeal than at any other period of his judicial career, he evidently chafed at being junior member for so long. Perhaps also he felt that he was neither master in his own court, as he had been as a judge of first instance, nor in the supreme appellate tribunal where the law was capable of real development. But whether that speculation is right or wrong, the legacy which he left with Lords Justices Bankes and Scrutton is a permanent one. It is unlikely that commercial law will again be stamped simultaneously with the authority of three such judges.

65   Personal communication from Lord Denning.
66   Speech at Gray's Inn House Dinner to celebrate the completion by Lord Atkin of 25 years of judicial office, 15 December 1938.

Privy Council

Lord Atkin's own opinion of the Judicial Committee of the Privy Council was that it was the greatest and most important of all English tribunals. Its jurisdiction involved, as he said, 'knowledge of some four or five or more, completely different kinds of jurisprudence, dating from the unknown past', and he saw it as 'the only agency for securing any measure of uniformity in legal development over the whole of this vast empire'.[1] He did not add, as he might have done, that the course of history had imposed on the Judicial Committee the wholly unforeseen jurisdiction of a constitutional court in parallel with its original jurisdiction of redressing individual wrongs by appeal proceedings from courts overseas.[2]

The judicial work of the Privy Council grew out of the royal prerogative to hear appeals from all the King's courts, wherever they might be. Any subject who considered that justice had not been done in his cause could petition the King for redress, and these petitions were heard in Council. Under the authority of Acts of Parliament or Orders in Council, provision was made in the colonies and plantations for appeals from the local courts to the King. In addition the Crown preserved a prerogative power to grant special leave to appeal to the Privy Council from the courts of the colonies without regard to any limitation which might be imposed by local ordinance. In 1833 the jurisdiction was put on a statutory footing and the Judicial Committee was formed to deal with appeals from the East Indies and the plantations and other dominions of His Majesty abroad.[3]

The emphasis which Lord Atkin laid on the development of uniform legal principles throughout the Empire was consonant with the original purposes of the jurisdiction. Consistency and certainty were as important as the need to redress grievance throughout the

---

1 Atkin 'Appeal in English Law' (1927) 3 Cambridge Law Journal 1 at 7.
2 The constitutional role was unforeseen. Although during the eighteenth century the Privy Council had to consider the validity of legislation made in the American Plantations, the sort of issue which arose for decision by the Judicial Committee on the Federal Consitutions of Australia and Canada could not have been predicted.
3 Judicial Committee Act 1833 (3 & 4 William IV, c 41).

Empire. In the time in which he sat in the Judicial Committee, Atkin heard cases of wide diversity and many of them illustrate well the aim which pervaded so much of his work of securing an even growth of legal principle expressed in simple language and capable of application in a variety of circumstances. Characteristically, the language is often memorable as well as simple.

In 1931, he wrote the advice of the Board in a case about the deportation of a deposed Nigerian Chief.[4] The Chief applied for a writ of habeas corpus claiming, variously, that he was not a native Chief, that if he were, he had not been deposed, and that since there was no native custom requiring him to leave the area, the Governor had not been entitled to order his removal. The advice of the Board was that because the Governor's powers were purely executive, it was for the courts to decide the legality of his actions. Lord Atkin continued in language that was significant for the future.

'In accordance with British jurisprudence no member of the executive can interfere with the liberty or property of a British subject except on the condition that he can support the legality of his action before a court of justice. And it is a tradition of British justice that judges should not shrink from deciding such issues in face of the executive.'

The Supreme Court of Nigeria had dismissed the application for habeas corpus, but the Board's advice was that the case must be remitted for a full investigation. In passing, Atkin made some remarks about native custom. It had been suggested at the hearing that the original custom of killing a deposed Chief, being barbarous, had been commuted to a custom to banish. The Board accepted that the more barbarous customs of earlier days could 'under the influence of civilization become milder without losing their essential character of custom'. But it was nonetheless necessary to show that the milder form *had* become customary. '. . . the court cannot itself transform a barbarous custom into a milder one. If it still stands in its barbarous character it must be rejected as repugnant to "natural justice, equity and good conscience".'

Five years later came the celebrated decision in *Ambard v A-G for Trinidad and Tobago*[5] in which Atkin's language rose to rhetorical heights only rarely to be found in the Law Reports. The editor of the *Port of Spain Gazette* had been found guilty of contempt of court for an editorial article drawing attention to disparities in sentencing in the island courts. The article is set out in full in the advice of the Board, entitled 'The Human Element' and the views are expressed

---

4   *Eshugbayi Eleko v Government of Nigeria* [1931] AC 662.
5   [1936] AC 322. Cf *Debi Prasad Sharma v The King-Emperor* 70 LRIA 216, where Atkin said, in a case in which an Indian judge has been criticised in a newspaper: 'If the facts were as alleged they admitted of criticism. No doubt it is galling for any judicial personage to be criticised as having done something outside his judicial proceedings which was ill-advised. But judicial personages can afford not to be too sensitive'.

in language of careful and respectful moderation. Yet the editor was convicted and fined £25, or in default, ordered to be imprisoned for one month. The Judicial Committee could find nothing to justify the finding of the local court that the article had been written with the direct object of bringing the administration of the criminal law in the colony by the judges into disrepute and disregard.

> 'But whether the authority and position of an individual judge, or the due administration of justice, is concerned no wrong is committed by any member of the public who exercises the ordinary right of criticizing, in good faith, in private or public, the public act done in the seat of justice. The path of criticism is a public way: the wrong headed are permitted to err therein: provided that members of the public abstain from imputing improper motives to those taking part in the administration of justice, and are genuinely exercising a right of criticism, and not acting in malice or attempting to impair the administration of justice, they are immune. Justice is not a cloistered virtue: she must be allowed to suffer the scrutiny and respectful, even though outspoken, comments of ordinary men.'

As well as caring deeply for the due process of law, Atkin enjoyed the odd corners into which the work of the Privy Council led. On 20 May 1942 he wrote to his daughter, Margaret:

> 'We have just finished work today at the Privy Council by acquitting 4 Kaffirs from Swaziland who have been for 2 years in prison under sentence of death. But we thought that there was a vital irregularity in the proceedings. Won't they be surprised! I have always thought it was the most impressive part of our jurisdiction that the law can stretch its arm so far to rescue the poorest and meanest subjects . . .'

He referred to an appeal from the High Court of Swaziland convicting the appellants of murder and sentencing them to death.[6] The case for the prosecution was that they had agreed together to kill one Nkalane in order to use parts of his body to make 'medicine' and increase their crop yield. It was alleged that after the killing a 'medicine man' had been summoned to provide 'medicine' to purify the assassins. The appellants denied all the allegations, and disputed the supposed customs of medicine for crops and for purification. The trial took place before a judge of the High Court assisted by two British administrative officers and a native assessor. The main question in the appeal was whether, in order to comply with the relevant Swaziland Proclamation, the opinions of the administrative officers and assessor had to be given in open court, or whether, as here, they could be given privately to the judge in his room.

Having decided that the proceedings did not comply with the Proclamation, Lord Atkin, speaking for the Board, went on to consider whether the defect was so serious as to vitiate the trial.

6 *Mahlikilili Dhlamini v The King* [1942] AC 583.

'In this country the omission would be a fatal flaw entitling a convicted criminal to have the conviction set aside . . . There may, no doubt, be cases where the guilt of the accused is so apparent that in spite of the disregard of this essential need for publicity this Board would not consider it right to grant leave to appeal, but the present is not such a case, as a particular native custom formed an important consideration on which it was essential that the proclaimed necessity for publicity should be observed.'

A case which illustrates as well as any the extraordinary diversity of the business of the Judicial Committee in Atkin's time is *Chung Chi Cheung v The King.*[7] A cabin boy on board a Chinese Maritime Customs cruiser had shot and killed the Master of the vessel while she lay within the territorial waters of Hong Kong. Both the boy and the captain were British subjects. After the shooting, the chief officer ordered the vessel into the port of Hong Kong where the boy was arrested and charged with murder. The Chinese authorities applied for his extradition but failed because he was a British subject. Members of the crew of the vessel gave evidence at the trial and the boy was eventually convicted. By his appeal to the Privy Council he contended that the local British court in Hong Kong did not have jurisdiction.

The Judicial Committee affirmed the decision of the Hong Kong court, holding that a public armed ship in foreign territorial waters is not to be treated as a floating part of the flag-state. In writing the opinion of the Board, Lord Atkin discussed the two rival theories. The first, which he described as 'the floating island theory', is that 'a public ship of a nation for all purposes either is, or is to be treated as, part of the territory of the nation to which she belongs'. On that view no country in whose territorial waters a public ship comes can confer jurisdiction on its courts by reason of any act done on the ship, or by reason of the presence or residence of any person on board. The ship is part of a foreign country. The alternative view, which the Board accepted, is that a public ship is not part of the territory of her own nation: 'The domestic Courts, in accordance with principles of international law, will accord to the ship and its crew and its contents certain immunities, some of which are well settled, though others are in dispute'.

The conclusion of the Board was that, the attempt at extradition having failed, the Chinese authorities acquiesced in the exercise by the British court of jurisdiction in the case. This they did by permitting members of their service to give evidence in aid of the prosecution, and by leaving 'the material instruments of conviction, the revolver, bullets, etc.', without demur in the hands of the Hong Kong police.

7   [1939] AC 160.

'Here is no question', said Lord Atkin,' of saying you may treat an offence committed on my territory as committed on yours. Such a statement by a foreign sovereign would count for nothing in our jurisprudence. But a sovereign may say, you have waived your jurisdiction in certain cases, but I prefer in this case that you should exercise it. The original jurisdiction in such a case flows afresh.'

Lord Atkin's advice in this case is remarkable for its erudition. Because the subject matter was international law, the relevant rule neither need nor could be proved in the same way as a rule of foreign law. The range of enquiry is necessarily wider; and here there is a far-ranging discussion of legal writings. Atkin placed most reliance on the decision of Chief Justice Marshall in *Schooner Exchange v M'Faddan*,[8] a judgment which he said 'has illumined the jurisprudence of the world'. But he also made reference with evident enjoyment to the debate which took place in 1875 on the treatment of fugitive slaves, and which was started by a letter to *The Times* from the Whewell Professor of International Law. The dogmatic assertion of the 'floating island theory' by the Professor, Sir William Harcourt, was treated to 'a merciless dissection' by Mr Rothery, the Registrar in Admiralty, who was a member of the Royal Commission appointed to look into the whole issue.

In the course of his judgment Atkin said:

'It must be always remembered that, so far, at any rate, as the Courts of this country are concerned, international law has no validity save in so far as its principles are accepted and adopted by our own domestic law. There is no external power that imposes its rules upon our own code of substantive law or procedure. The Courts acknowledge the existence of a body of rules which nations accept amongst themselves. On any judicial issue they seek to ascertain what the relevant rule is, and having found it, they will treat it as incorporated into the domestic law, so far as it is not inconsistent with rules enacted by statutes or finally declared by their tribunals.'

That statement does not seem to justify the fears it has provoked among academic writers.[9] A fair reading of it proposes no more than that established principles of international law are readily incorporated into our domestic law unless they are repugnant to it; they are not recognised by English courts unless they are so adopted. The decision in *Chung Chi Cheung's* Case itself shows how amenable to adoption those principles are.[10]

---

8   7 Cranch 116.
9   For example, Lauterpacht *International Law: Collected Papers* (Vol 2) 'The Law of Peace' p 560.
10   Atkin expressed the same view in very similar terms in the Court of Appeal in *Commercial and Estates Co of Egypt v The Board of Trade* [1925] 1 KB 271 at 295. Bankes LJ, less cautiously, asked: 'Is the right thus described . . . a branch of international law which constitutes part of the law of the land?' (at 283).

These few examples of the jurisdiction of the Privy Council in Atkin's time confirm his own appreciation of the diversity of the work of the tribunal and its unifying force in the field of private law. But the Judicial Committee had quite other work to do. The movement of history had made it the expounder of the constitutions of the great self-governing dominions. The period of Atkin's tenure coincided with the decline in both the jurisdiction and the authority of the Privy Council, a tendency which he himself much regretted.

The Imperial Conference of 1926 followed a constitutional crisis in Canada, and the Canadian Prime Minister, Mackenzie King, was determined that the independence of the dominions should be precisely defined. He was supported by the other dominions and the new Irish Free State. The result was Balfour's definition of Dominion Status and the supersession of the compulsory sovereignty of the Empire by the voluntary association of the Commonwealth; but it was another five years before Balfour's 'last and most successful jugglery with high-sounding words'[11] gave way to language which could be interpreted by a court. The Report of the 1926 Conference had stated that 'it was no part of the policy of His Majesty's Government in Great Britain that questions affecting judicial appeals should be determined otherwise than in accordance with the wishes of the part of the Empire primarily affected'.[12] The Statute of Westminster of 1931 enabled each self-governing member of the Commonwealth to enact laws having effect outside its own territory. And, subject to certain safeguards to protect the Australian and Canadian Constitutions, it ended for the self-governing Commonwealth countries the restrictions imposed on them by the Colonial Laws Validity Act of 1865 by which local legislation which was repugnant to an Imperial Act was declared void. In practice this meant that it was open to the Dominions to end the appeal from its own courts to the Privy Council; and what led more than anything else to this option being taken was a sense of dissatisfaction with the constitutional work of the Judicial Committee.

It was in any case likely that in the flood tide of nationalism, emergent nations would wish their own courts to decide their own constitutional issues. But that apart, the constitutional work of the Privy Council in the fifty years before, and then during, Atkin's time cannot fairly be accounted a success. Many reasons may be assigned for this. The individual judges, who were mostly Lords of Appeal were not adapted by training to decide constitutional questions. In a period before long-distance travel had become commonplace they were remote from the rapidly changing needs of the countries concerned. The narrowly focussed detachment, rightly prized as indispensable for the despatch of private judicial business, is not

11 A. J. P. Taylor *English History 1914–1945* (OUP) p 253.
12 Report of the 1926 Imperial Conference, cmd 2768, p 19.

invariably advantageous for a constitutional court. The questions to be resolved were often of a frankly political character, and for that a tribunal needs as well as impartiality a political vision to give direction to its work. This point has often been made of the United States Supreme Court, the greatest of all constitutional tribunals:

> 'In its most enduring and memorable work, the Court has been careful not to read the provisions of the Constitution like a last will and testament, lest indeed they become one. Instead the Justices have been guided by the basic canon of Marshall, calculated to turn the mind away from canons: "This provision is made in a constitution, intended to endure for ages to come, and consequently, to be adapted to the various crises of human affairs".'[13]

The most serious constitutional crisis with which Lord Atkin had to deal came in 1936 when he presided in the Privy Council in a series of appeals from Canada in which the validity of much of Mr Bennett's 'New Deal' legislation was called in question. The Dominion Government, faced with a world-wide economic recession, had followed the lead of the United States and introduced an elaborate programme whose main elements were the improvement of working conditions, an attack on restrictive practices and regulation of product marketing. As was inevitable much of the legislation was 'interventionist' and interfered with free bargaining. It also affected trade within the individual Provinces, and it was the Provincial Governments who challenged its validity.

Shortly before the hearings, Atkin wrote to Sir Claud Schuster, the Lord Chancellor's Permanent Secretary, saying that he did not think that the proposed composition of the Board would command sufficient authority. It is not now clear who was originally intended to sit, but Atkin's point was that the Board should be composed entirely of Law Lords, and should not be partly staffed by judges of first instance or Lords Justices who happened to be Privy Councillors. He was conscious of a growing feeling in Australia and Canada that appeals from the courts of those countries should be heard only by judges of the highest tribunal. The Lord Chancellor, Hailsham, replied saying that he had invited Sankey, an ex-Lord Chancellor, to preside but that he was unable to accept. He pointed out that he himself had presided in every Dominion appeal until his health had prevented his continuing: 'In these circumstances', he wrote, 'I had chosen what I thought was as strong a Board as it is possible to compose, in yourself, Macmillan and Roche and Wright, who had kindly consented to come up from the Court of Appeal and Sidney Rowlatt, whose merits I regard as second to none'.

---

13   P. A. Freund 'The Supreme Court of the United States' (1951) 29 Canadian Bar Review 1080 at 1086 quoting Marshall CJ in *McCullough v Maryland* (1819) 4 Wheat 316 at 415.

He explained that Lord Thankerton had expressed a wish to sit and that he was to exchange for Lord Roche, and he concluded firmly:

> 'But I cannot agree to regard the Judicial Committee as composed of two grades of Judges, one, the Law Lords, and the other, the ex-Judges and Lords Justices who give us help from time to time. To do this would be to render it practically impossible to obtain the help of retired Judges and Lords Justices and it would render the authority of any Board which was constituted with them for Indian or Colonial Appeals very questionable.'[14]

Atkin replied in a conciliatory way and the Board was finally constituted of himself, Lords Thankerton, Macmillan, and Wright,and Sir Sidney Rowlatt. During the hearings Hailsham wrote again, saying:

> 'I am glad to tell you that I have recently heard indirectly that no less than four of the Canadian Counsel ... have severally expressed the greatest possible satisfaction at the constitution of the Board, so that obviously you are all impressing, as I felt sure you would do ... I expect the decisions, when given, will carry conviction, which, after all, is the best test of the strength of the tribunal.'[15]

The Federal Constitution of Canada is contained in the British North America Act of 1967, and the distribution of legislative powers between the central Dominion Parliament in Ottawa, and the separate provincial Parliaments, is there laid down. Subjects are classified, some being reserved to the Dominion and others assigned to the Provinces.[16] The provincial subjects include, notably, 'Property and Civil Rights in the Province' and 'Generally all Matters of a merely local or private Nature in the Province'. The Dominion has a general power to make laws 'for the Peace, Order and Good Government of Canada in relation to all Matters not coming within the Classes of Subjects by this Act assigned exclusively to the Legislature of the Provinces'; and the classes of subjects reserved specifically to the Dominion are 'for greater Certainty, but not so as to restrict the Generality of the foregoing Terms'.

The structure is therefore that the general law-making power is confided to the central Parliament, and is cut into only by those subjects expressly assigned to the Provinces. The contrast with the United States Constitution, which only delegates powers to Washington, leaving the residual legislative power with the states, was not accidental. The 1867 Act followed closely upon the end of the American Civil War, and the Canadian Founding Fathers determined not to follow the United States pattern and give too great a power to the Provinces.

14 Hailsham to Atkin, 3 November 1936. See appendix 3 for full text.
15 Hailsham to Atkin, 17 November 1936.
16 The British North America Act 1867, ss 91 and 92.

'Here we have adopted a different system', asserted Sir John A. Macdonald in the Confederation Debates. 'We have strengthened the general government. We have given the legislature all the great subjects of legislation. We have conferred on them, not only specifically and in detail all the powers which are incident to sovereignty, but we have expressly declared that all subjects of general interest not directly and exclusively conferred upon the local governments and local legislatures shall be conferred upon the general government and legislature. We have thus avoided that great source of weakness which has been the cause of the disruption of the United States.'[17]

One of the 'great subjects of legislation' assigned to the Dominion was the vital power of regulating trade and commerce, through whose counterpart the United States Congress has gone so far to govern the country.[18] But by one of the ironies of history the United States has emerged with a far stronger central government than Canada; and the more narrowly drawn commerce power in the United States Constitution has proved by far the greater instrument for binding the states together. By contrast, the Canadian commerce power has been described in the Supreme Court as 'the old forlorn hope, so many times tried, unsuccessfully, upon this court and the court above'.[19]

A further power of great importance assigned to the Dominion Parliament and Government by the British North America Act was the power to perform obligations of Canada or any of its Provinces towards foreign countries arising under 'Treaties made between the Empire and such Foreign Countries'.[20] This power of performing treaty obligations was to assume significance in the series of Canadian appeals in which Lord Atkin presided; but in considering it, it has to be remembered that the draftsman in 1867 did not conceive that Canada could have any foreign obligations which did not arise under treaties of the British Empire; for Canada then had no independent status which would enable it to make its own treaties.

17   Canadian Confederation Debates, p 33. Sir John Alexander Macdonald: b 1815 in Glasgow; came to Canada 1820; ed Royal Grammar School, Kingston, Upper Canada; 1844 elected to represent Kingston in Legislative Assembly for which he sat almost continuously until his death; 1857 Prime Minister Upper Canada; chief architect of Confederation of Canada, took foremost part in Quebec Conference 1864 and London Conference 1866; first Prime Minister of Dominion of Canada 1867 which office he held until his death except 1873–8: to his initiative are due inclusion in the Dominion of British Columbia and NW Territory, and building of Canadian Pacific Railway; KCB 1867; Privy Councillor 1879; d 1891.

18   Speaking at the 50th Anniversary of the founding of the American Bar Association Mr Justice Stone said: 'Great as is the practical wisdom exhibited in all the provisions of the Constitution, and important as were the character and influence of those who secured its adoption, it will, I believe, be the judgment of history that the Commerce Clause and the wise interpretation of it, perhaps more than any other contributing element, have united to bind the several states into a nation' [14 ABA Journal 428 at 430 (1928)].

19   *Re The Board of Commerce Act* (1920) 60 SCR 456 at 488, per Idington J.

20   S 132.

By the time the 'New Deal' legislation of 1934/5 came to be scrutinised by the Privy Council, a bias had already been established in favour of the Provinces. With this bias the names of Lords Watson and Haldane are especially associated.[21] And since it was the Dominion Parliament which was principally responsible for interventionist legislation, a tendency against state interference in the economy was also apparent.

The low point in interpretation of the power to regulate trade and commerce was reached with the decision of the Privy Council in *The Board of Commerce Case* in 1921.[22] Viscount Haldane, speaking for the Board, appeared to characterise the power as merely auxiliary, capable of overriding provincial jurisdiction over property rights in the Provinces only as an aid to the Dominion's general power of intervention, which itself could be invoked only in 'an altogether exceptional situation'. This view, a virtual emasculation of the commerce power, was rejected as heresy by the Judicial Committee ten years later in a decision of great importance, rendered by Lord Atkin.[23] But the bias against use of the commerce power as an instrument of intervention remained, and in the Canadian decisions of 1937 it was reaffirmed in Atkin's own powerful style.

The legislation upon which the Judicial Committee was called to pronounce comprised, first, three laws providing for weekly rests, minimum wages and limitation of hours of work, all based on draft conventions of the International Labour Organisation; secondly an Employment and Social Insurance Act; thirdly, a law making criminal certain unfair trade practices; fourthly, a law regulating the marketing of natural products; fifthly, a Farmers' Creditors Agreement Act; and sixthly, the Dominion Trade and Industry Commission Act. Only the third, fifth and sixth survived scrutiny, leaving the vital labour laws to be completely invalidated. Every Dominion power invoked in aid of the legislation was found wanting.

The leading decision was given in the *Labour Conventions Case*.[24] The Dominion sought to uphold the legislation on the ground of its exclusive competency to implement obligations arising under international treaties. The Treaty of Versailles had laid down that abiding peace depended on social justice, and that that in turn

---

21 For example *A-G for Ontario v A-G for Canada* [1896] AC 348 (Lord Watson); *A-G for Canada v A-G for Alberta* [1916] 1 AC 588 (Lord Haldane). Haldane much admired Watson and his contribution to the Canadian Constitution: see Haldane 'The work for the Empire of the Judicial Committee of the Privy Council' (1922) 1 Cambridge Law Journal 143 at 150. The article makes explicit the deliberate policy of both judges to redress the balance (as they saw it) in favour of the Provinces. Lord Sankey is perhaps the judge most associated with the opposite viewpoint and the greater flexibility: see eg *Edwards v A-G for Canada* [1930] AC 124 at 136; *British Coal Corpn v The King* [1935] AC 500 at 519.
22 *Re The Board of Commerce Act, 1919* [1922] 1 AC 191.
23 *Proprietary Articles Trade Association v A-G for Canada* [1931] AC 310.
24 *A-G for Canada v A-G for Ontario* [1937] AC 326.

required the improvement of conditions of labour throughout the world. For this purpose the Treaty established a permanent organisation called the International Labour Organisation with power to prepare conventions dealing with conditions of work. The Dominion legislation in question had for its object the implementation of certain of these conventions. Accordingly, the Dominion argued, the legislation fell within section 132 of the 1867 Act on the ground that it was in performance of Canada's obligations arising under the Treaty of Versailles, a British Empire treaty.

Alternatively, it was contended that it was authorised under the Dominion's general power, since it did not touch matters exclusively assigned to the Provinces.

The Supreme Court of Canada had divided equally, three to three, the Chief Justice, Sir Lyman Duff, for upholding the legislation.[25] The Privy Council ruled that the statutes were beyond the powers of the Dominion Parliament and were accordingly unconstitutional.

The decision was of crucial importance on the issue of Canada's treaty-making powers. The Chief Justice's view was that the Dominion Parliament had power to pass laws in implementation of treaties with foreign countries made by the British Empire, whether or not those laws 'trenched' on property and civil rights in the Provinces; and the Privy Council had more than once upheld that view.[26] Moreover, on one occasion the Privy Council had upheld Dominion laws based on a convention to which Canada alone (not as part of the Empire) was a party, and which also interfered with provincial property rights.[27] From these decisions it seemed clear that the Dominion had now power to legislate to implement international agreements, be they treaties or conventions, to which Canada was party. As had been pointed out in the *Radio Case* in 1932,[28] Canada had acquired a status as a self-governing Dominion which had been unthought of in 1867, and in consequence, had power to enter into international agreements by itself and not merely as part of the Empire. The authority to pass laws in pursuance of these agreements should, it was argued, be co-ordinate with that contained in section 132 of the 1867 Act relating to British Empire treaties.

All this was rejected in Atkin's speech. The Judicial Committee held that Canada's obligations in relation to the International Labour Organisation conventions arose under the conventions themselves and not under the Treaty of Versailles from which the ILO sprang. That disposed of section 132, no Empire treaty being here relevant.

---

25   [1936] SLR 461.
26   *A-G for British Columbia v A-G for Canada* [1924] AC 203; *Re Regulation and Control of Aeronautics in Canada* [1932] AC 54.
27   *Re Regulation and Control of Radio Communication in Canada* [1932] AC 304.
28   Ibid.

In order to be valid, the legislation would therefore have to be shown to be within the classes of subject assigned to the Dominion or within its general power. Atkin's approach to this issue was that 'there is no such thing as treaty legislation as such. The distribution is based on classes of subjects; and as a treaty deals with a particular class of subjects, so will the legislative power of performing it be ascertained'. It followed from this that 'no further legislative competence is obtained by the Dominion from its accession to international status'; and then, in a memorable phrase: 'In other words, the Dominion cannot, merely by making promises to foreign countries, clothe itself with legislative authority inconsistent with the constitution which gave it birth'.[29]

As for the Dominion's general power to legislate 'for the Peace, Order and good Government of Canada' in fields not expressly assigned to the Provinces, the Judicial Committee's view was that this should be confined to exceptional cases overriding the normal distribution of powers and involving 'some extraordinary peril to the national life of Canada', or the like.[30]

The Board therefore concluded that the legislation fell within the exclusive competence of the Provinces since it affected 'property and civil rights in the Provinces'. As so often in the judgments of his later years, Atkin ended with a heightened passage, in this case containing a metaphor that has become one of the most famous phrases in Canadian constitutional law:

> 'It must not be thought that the result of this decision is that Canada is incompetent to legislate in performance of treaty obligations. In totality of legislative powers, Dominion and Provincial together, she is fully equipped. But the legislative powers remain distributed, and if in the exercise of her new functions derived from her new international status Canada incurs obligations they must, so far as legislation be concerned, when they deal with Provincial classes of subjects, be dealt with by the totality of powers, in other words by co-operation between the Dominion and the Provinces. While the ship of state now sails on larger ventures and into foreign waters she still retains the watertight compartments which are an essential part of her original structure.'[31]

After the full discussion in the Privy Council's decision in the *Labour Conventions Case*, the remaining legislation could be disposed of in short order.

The Employment and Social Insurance Act provided for a scheme of mandatory unemployment insurance, the funds being provided in part by Parliament, and in part by employers and employees.[32]

29 [1937] AC 326 at 352.
30 At 353.
31 At 353–4.
32 *A-G for Canada v A-G for Ontario* [1937] AC 355. Unemployment Insurance was added to the specific subjects within Dominion competence by the British North America Act 1940.

The leading argument put forward by the Dominion was that the legislation fell within its general powers because of the special importance of the measure in times of economic depression.

The answer of the Judicial Committee, again through Lord Atkin, was that 'the present Act does not purport to deal with any special emergency ... it is an Act whose operation is intended to be permanent'. The conclusion that the Dominion's general or residual power to legislate must be confined to cases of emergency, and temporary emergency at that, could not but have grave consequences for Canada.

The Natural Products Marketing Act of 1934 established a Dominion Marketing Board whose powers were to regulate the marketing of natural products throughout Canada. The Act clearly affected trade within the individual Provinces, but also inter-provincial and export trade. The Judicial Committee held that the Act invaded the separate legislative preserve of the Provinces, and could not be saved either by the Dominion's power to regulate trade and commerce, or by its general power.[33] This last ruling was scarcely surprising in view of the decision in the *Employment and Social Insurance Case*.

The *Natural Products Case* had one peculiar feature which illustrates the anomalies to which the federal distribution of powers can sometimes give rise. Some of the Provinces supported marketing schemes such as could be established under the Act and had set up their own provincial schemes. But since the Act affected intra-provincial trade as well as intercourse between Provinces, and since the ultra vires parts could not be excised, the whole Act had to be struck down. As to the common objective of the Dominion and the Provinces, Atkin said:

'Their Lordships appreciate the importance of the desired aim. Unless and until a change is made in the respective legislative functions of Dominion and Province it may well be that satisfactory results for both can only be obtained by co-operation. But the legislation will have to be carefully framed, and will not be achieved by either party leaving its own sphere and encroaching upon that of the other.'[34]

That warning had melancholy echoes, for in 1931 a marketing Act of British Columbia had been invalidated by the Supreme Court of Canada because it interfered with inter-provincial trade.[35] The task of framing marketing legislation which passed safely between Scylla and Charybdis might prove to be beyond human skill.

The remaining three measures were upheld by the Privy Council. The first made criminal the giving of different rebates or discounts to different buyers, sales at different prices in different areas, and

33 *A-G for British Columbia v A-G for Canada* [1937] AC 377.
34 At 389.
35 *Lawson v Interior Tree Fruit and Vegetable Committee* [1931] SLR 357.

sales at artificially depressed prices in order to destroy a competitor. The Judicial Committee upheld these additions to the Canadian Criminal Code as having a genuinely criminal character.[36] The Farmers' Creditors Arrangement Act was also upheld as falling within the class, 'Bankruptcy and Insolvency', exclusively assigned to the Dominion.[37] Finally, the Dominion Trade and Industry Commission Act which established a commission to administer the Combines Act, to set commodity standards and to enquire into unfair trade practices, was also validated.[38] The Act established 'Canada Standard' as a national trademark to be owned by the Crown, and to constitute a representation that goods conformed with the relevant commodity standard. This created a civil right of a new type, but that was held to be no objection to its validity. There was no reason why 'the legislative competence of the Dominion Parliament should not extend to the creation of juristic rights in novel fields, if they can be brought fairly within the classes of subjects confided to Parliament by the Constitution'.

Canadian constitutional lawyers reacted strongly to the decisions. In most cases they thought that they had a deeply depressing significance, falsifying the Founders' intentions, weakening the cohesive force of a strong central Parliament and destroying measures which were urgent for a grave economic crisis.[39] Most serious of all were the consequences of the *Labour Conventions Case* for Canada's treaty-making and treaty-implementing powers. Atkin's view that there was no such thing as treaty legislation, and that the classification of legislation could not be altered 'merely by making promises to foreign countries' was criticised as begging the true question. This was: did not legislation implementing treaties having significance for the whole Dominion fall either within its general power to make laws for the peace, order and good government of Canada, or within the treaty-implementing powers of section 132 of the 1867 Act, liberally construed?[40]

The Provinces had put in issue the question of whether the Canadian Government had authority even to make the treaty, but

36   *A-G for British Columbia v A-G for Canada* [1937] AC 368.
37   *A-G for British Columbia v A-G for Canada* [1937] AC 391.
38   *A-G for Ontario v A-G for Canada* [1937] AC 405.
39   See references under note 40. Not unnaturally, the comment from outside Canada was more temperate, eg A. Berriedale Keith 'The Privy Council Decisions: A Comment from Great Britain' 15 Canadian Bar Review 428 (1937). Professor Keith's view was that the decisions were in accord with traditional interpretation, the Constitution might well need amendment, but 'that work should be left to the legislature'. He added that the circumstance 'that judicial interpretation is a comparatively simple way of remedying defects is not a consideration proper to be taken into account' (p 428).
40   V. C. Macdonald 'The Canadian Constitution Seventy Years After' 15 Canadian Bar Review 401 at 415 (1937); N. A. M. Mackenzie 'Canada and the Treaty-Making Power' 15 Canadian Bar Review 436 (1937); F. R. Scott 'The Privy Council and Mr. Bennett's "New Deal" Legislation' Canadian Journal of Economics and Political Science, Vol III, February 1937, 234 at 237.

the Judicial Committee had refused to be drawn. It could not therefore be said with certainty 'whether the Dominion has a right to have its representatives even go so far as to conclude negotiations with a foreign government with regard to any proposed treaty or convention until its subject matter has been properly classified'.[41] The same commentator concluded that 'Canada ceases to be a single nation in the conduct of her international relations'.[42]

Almost as serious was Lord Atkin's view in the *Employment and Social Insurance Case* that the general power to legislate which had been entrusted to the Dominion Parliament could only be exercised in a special and temporary emergency. On that Professor F. R. Scott of McGill University said 'an emergency power which the world economic crisis does not justify using is no power at all'.[43]

41   F. R. Scott 'The Consequences of the Privy Council Decisions' 15 Canadian Bar Review 485 at 486 (1937).
42   At 485.
43   At 489. In 1950 Professor F. R. Scott published the following poem (28 Canadian Bar Review 780), a sad retrospect of the 1937 decisions. The 'fresh approach' of Lord Simon to which he refers was exemplified in *A-G for Ontario v Canadian Temperence Federation* [1946] AC 193.

SOME PRIVY COUNSEL

"Emergency, emergency," I cried, "give us emergency,
This shall be the doctrine of our salvation.
Are we not surrounded by emergencies?
The rent of a house, the cost of food, pensions and health, the unemployed,
These are lasting emergencies, tragic for me."
But the only answer was "Property and Civil Rights,"
And all my peace-time troubles were counted as nothing.
"At least you have an unoccupied field," I urged,
"Or something ancillary for a man with four children?
Surely my insecurity and want affect the body politic?"
But back came the echo of property and civil rights.
I was told to wrap my sorrows in watertight compartments.
"Please, please," I entreated, "look at my problem.
I and my brothers, regardless of race, are afflicted.
Our welfare hangs on remote policies, distant decisions,
Planning of trade, guaranteed prices, high employment;
Can provincial fractions govern this complex whole?
Surely such questions are now supra-national!"
But the judges fidgeted over their digests
And blew me away with the canons of construction.
"This is intolerable," I shouted, "this is one country;
Two flourishing cultures, but joined in one nation.
I demand peace, order and good government,
This you must admit is the aim of Confederation!"
But firmly and sternly I was pushed to a corner
And covered with the wet blanket of provincial autonomy.
Stifling under the burden I raised my hands to heaven
And called out with my last expiring breath
"At least you cannot deny I have a new aspect?
I cite in my aid the new approach of Lord Simon!"
But all I could hear was the old sing-song,
This time in Latin, muttering *stare decisis*.

The inevitable conclusion of this disquiet was that Canadians would look again at the suitability of the Privy Council as their final court of appeal. It was now apparently possible for the Canadian Parliament to end that appeal. The Federal Parliament had already barred the way to the Privy Council in criminal matters, and that had been recognised as valid in 1935 in a decision to which Atkin was himself party.[44] After the Second World War, civil appeals also were to be abolished;[45] and there can be small doubt that the 1937 series of decisions gave fresh impetus in that direction. It was strongly felt that the court of ultimate appeal should be 'staffed with men fully qualified to understand the spirit which infuses the British North America Act,and the environment in which it must be made to work'.[46] Of the Privy Council: 'its members are too remote, too little trained in our law, too casually selected, and have too short a tenure'.[47]

In the longer perspective of history some Canadian constitutionalists take the view that the influence of judges like Lords Watson and Haldane has been to aggravate the country's fissiparous tendencies so far as to make the Constitution vulnerable to today's threat to its very existence. The Dominion Parliament's power to intervene in response to its understanding of national needs is from their standpoint the meaning of nationhood and a fair price to pay for federal unity. Those who share this view consider that the judges of the Judicial Committee did some mischievous work, and that those with the more conspicuous legal ability did the more conspicuous mischief.[48]

Lord Atkin's own position is not easy to define. Indeed care must be taken before ascribing a view to any individual judge in the Judicial Committee, because by the former convention, judgments were given in the form of a single 'advice' to the Crown.[49] The doubts of some may therefore be suppressed in arriving at unanimity. A startling example of this occurred in the 1937 Canadian decisions

---

44   *British Coal Corpn v The King* [1935] AC 500. It was pointed out at 520 that the Statute of Westminster (s 7) had at the request of Canada excluded the power for the Dominion and Provincial Parliaments to amend the British North America Act.
45   As regards legal proceedings commenced on or after 23 December 1949, by *An Act to amend the Supreme Court Act of Canada* (13 Geo VI SC 1949 (2nd Sess) c 37); the power to abolish appeals had been upheld in *A-G for Ontario v A-G for Canada* [1947] AC 127. The last appeals were heard about ten years later.
46   Scott (op cit), 15 Canadian Bar Review 485 at 493.
47   Ibid, at 494.
48   Private communication from Professor S. A. Scott, McGill University.
49   It had been the practice of the Privy Council, dating at least from an Order made in 1627 and providing that 'no publication is afterwards to be made, by any man, how the particular voices and opinion went', never to refer to any dissentient opinion in its report to the Crown. The practice was confirmed, so far as concerned the Judicial Committee, by the Act of 1833, but it was altered by the Judicial Committee (Dissenting Opinions) Order 1966: and any member of the Judicial Committee who dissents may now publish his dissent in open court together with his reasons. The right is seldom exercised.

themselves. Nearly twenty years afterwards, Lord Wright who was a member of the Board in all the appeals, wrote a short article of tribute to the memory of Sir Lyman Duff who had recently died, and included an outspoken criticism of the 'watertight compartment' theory expounded in Lord Atkin's judgment in the *Labour Conventions Case*, and to which he (Lord Wright) was party.[50]

On the other hand, it must generally be true that the views of the judge who writes the opinion of the Board are faithfully reflected in that opinion. That would have been especially so in Lord Atkin's case, for he had the reputation for being unyielding in his views in the private discussions which take place after the hearing among judges of appeal. When Lord Hailsham became Lord Chancellor for the second time, in 1935, he received a confidential note from Viscount Dunedin who had been retired since 1932, containing thumbnail sketches of the Lords' 'team'. Of Atkin, Dunedin said: 'Clever. And a good common lawyer. But obstinate if he has taken a view and quite unpersuadable'.[51]

Others might have said that Akin's decisiveness was an integral part of his quality of judgment, but however that may be, his reputation for being unpersuadable was probably well-founded. If only for this reason, it seems safe to treat the point of view revealed by the 1937 Canadian decisions as his own.

Atkin would have been grieved to feel that the decisions did anything to make the abolition of civil appeals to the Privy Council from Canada more likely. He felt strongly that the Statute of Westminster had been a retrograde step, and he believed as strongly in the value of a single final administration of justice as a bond of union and a focus of impartiality unaffected by local pressures. It was very much in Lord Hailsham's mind when he was writing to Atkin during the Canadian hearings that the composition of the Board could have an effect on the continuance of the right of appeal; and he began his letter by saying, 'I think you and I are agreed as to the paramount importance of retaining the appeal to the Privy Council from the Dominions of the Crown and as to the importance of constituting a Board which will inspire confidence by its decisions in all parts of the Empire'.[52] But it goes without saying that these considerations could not have had the slightest effect on the decisions themselves.

It would be less than fair to describe Atkin's views as extreme, for in the general movement towards depleting the powers of the central Dominion Government and Parliament, he did much to restrain excesses. His view of the Dominion power to legislate in the criminal field was particularly liberal. *The Proprietary Articles Case* was itself

---

50   Wright, 33 Canadian Bar Review 1123 at 1126 (1955).
51   Quoted in Heuston *Lives of the Lord Chancellors* p 481.
52   Hailsham to Atkin 17 November 1936.

under this head.[53] The Combines Investigation Act of 1927 had made it an offence, punishable by fine or imprisonment, to form or operate a 'combine' which was detrimental to the public and restrained or injured trade. In short the Act was an attack with penal sanctions on anti-competitive practices.

The main question at issue was whether the Act fell within the Dominion power to legislate on criminal matters, and it was contended by Ontario and Quebec that (quoting Lord Haldane in the *Board of Commerce Case*) it did not 'belong to the domain of criminal jurisprudence'.[54] It was argued that the Act impinged upon the provincial powers to legislate on matters relating to 'property and civil rights in the Province', and 'the administration of justice in the Province'.

Lord Atkin's judgment began with some general statements about the distribution of powers.

'Their Lordships entertain no doubt that time alone will not validate an Act which when challenged is found to be ultra vires; nor will a history of a gradual series of advances till this boundary is finally crossed avail to protect the ultimate encroachment . . .'

He then went on to trace the long history of anti-combine legislation in Canada, and pointed out the difference between the Act then being considered, and the legislation which had been invalidated in the *Board of Commerce Case*. Chief among those differences was the requirement in the later Act that the combine must operate to the detriment or against the interest of the public.

'. . . and if Parliament genuinely determines that commercial activities which can be so described are to be suppressed in the public interest, their Lordships see no reason why Parliament should not make them crimes . . . Criminal law connotes only the quality of such acts or omissions as are prohibited under appropriate penal provisions by authority of the State. The criminal quality of an act cannot be discerned by intuition; nor can it be discovered by reference to any standard but one: Is the act prohibited with penal consequences? Morality and criminality are far from co-extensive; nor is the sphere of criminality necessarily part of a more extensive field covered by morality — unless the moral code necessarily disapproves all acts prohibited by the State, in which case the argument moves in a circle.'[55]

That was a refreshingly simple definition of criminality, but necessarily so if it was to prevent subtle arguments from eating into

53 *Proprietary Articles Trade Association v A-G for Canada* [1931] AC 310.
54 At 312. The argument of Ontario and Quebec was apparently that an act did not 'belong to the domain of criminal jurisprudence' unless it was also civilly unlawful, but even Lord Haldane did not go that far. He offered incest as an example of a valid new federal crime (*Board of Commerce Case* [1922] 1 AC at 199), and so far as is known, incest is not civilly actionable.
55 At 323, 324.

the boundary of the Dominion's power to legislate on penal subjects. It remained only to add that if the legislation were authorised under one or other head of the Dominion's powers, it was 'not to the purpose to say that it affects property and civil rights in the Provinces. Most of the specific subjects in s.91 [Dominion powers] do affect property and civil rights but so far as the legislation of Parliament in pith and substance is operating within the enumerated powers there is constitutional authority to interfere with property and civil rights'.[56]

It was also argued for the Dominion that the combines legislation fell within the power to regulate trade and commerce. On this, the contention of the Provinces was that Lord Haldane's judgment in the *Board of Commerce Case* had established that the commerce power was only auxiliary; that is, it could not be invoked except in aid of another independent power entrusted to the Dominion legislature. This view, which would have reduced the vital commerce power to a cipher, was rejected by Atkin. He said only: 'No such restriction is properly to be inferred from that judgment', and he declined to say whether the Combines Act did or did not fall within the commerce power: the Board guarded itself 'from being supposed to lay down that the present legislation could not be supported on that ground'.[57]

In that oblique way judges conventionally avoid widening the ambit of their decisions beyond what is strictly necessary. But the importance of what had been done could not be disguised. The power to regulate trade was now recognised as an independent class of subject, not merely ancillary, and it would be open to the courts, if they were so minded, to give it a broad and far-reaching interpretation. Again, as in the *Dominion Trade and Industry Commission Case*,[58] Lord Atkin had avoided the extremes of the restrictive view of Dominion powers. But any hope that the commerce power would now enter into its kingdom would not have been well-founded. In his judgment in the *Natural Products Marketing Case*[59] Atkin carried the conservative tradition a step further and demonstrated how difficult it would be for the commerce power to be invoked whenever provincial property and civil rights were affected. The question would have to be faced: how could the trade of Canada be regulated without interfering with that property and those rights?

The contrast between Atkin's treatment of Dominion legislative powers in the criminal and civil fields is striking. The effective preservation of law and order throughout Canada was one

56   At 326, 327.
57   At 326.
58   *A-G for Ontario v A-G for Canada* [1937] AC 405.
59   *A-G for British Columbia v A-G for Canada* [1937] AC 377.

thing: it was quite another to extend the regulating arm of central government so that it could interfere with trade and commerce within the Provinces. Of the one, he asserted that it was 'not to the purpose to say that it affects property and civil rights in the Provinces'; of the other: 'It is therefore plain that the Act purports to affect property and civil rights in the Province, and if not brought within one of the enumerated classes of subject in s. 91 must be beyond the competence of the Dominion Legislature'. In effect the Privy Council had defined 'Trade and Commerce' to mean only international and inter-provincial trade, and Atkin would not alter that crucial definition.

Lord Atkin was a conservative in his attitude to the division of legislative competence between the Dominion and the Provinces. This was a field in which he was not disposed to innovate. Long before his time the bias of the Canadian Federation had been established by the Privy Council. The two most potent possibilities for enlarging the scope of Dominion law-making, the residual or general power to legislate for the peace, order and good government of Canada, and the power to regulate trade and commerce, had again and again been restricted by the Judicial Committee. Atkin was ready to curb the excesses of that judicial policy but he would not reverse it. Partly this was because his natural disposition was against extensions of power in a central government which could interfere with free commerce and the sanctity of bargains. But more importantly, his own view of the balance of the constitution was consistent with the historic trend of Privy Council decisions. In a revealing passage of his judgment in the *Labour Conventions Case*[60] he described the distribution of legislative powers as 'probably the most essential condition in the inter-provincial compact to which the British North America Act gives effect', and he went on to give his reasons:

> 'If the position of Lower Canada, now Quebec, alone were considered, the existence of her separate jurisprudence as to both property and civil rights might be said to depend upon loyal adherence to her constitutional right to the exclusive competence of her own Legislature in these matters. Nor is it of less importance for the other Provinces, though their law may be based on English jurisprudence, to preserve their own right to legislate for themselves in respect of local conditions which may vary by as great a distance as separates the Atlantic from the Pacific.'[61]

In 1932 Lord Atkin had to consider another constitutional case of the first importance, this time from Australia.[62] Like the Canadian *Natural Products Case* the issue was whether a system of orderly marketing enforced by public control was valid. Laws had been

60   *A-G for Canadia v A-G for Ontario* [1937] AC 326.
61   Ibid, at 351, 352
62   *James v Cowan* [1932] AC 542.

passed in Victoria and South Australia designed to compel dried fruit growers to take their fair share of the less profitable overseas market and imposing quotas on sales within Australia. Frederick Arthur James of Berri, South Australia and a litigant to whom Australians have cause to be grateful, was well known as an opponent of all government regulatory schemes and he twice successfully took governments to the Privy Council.

Under powers conferred by South Australian legislation, the Dried Fruits Board of that State determined that for 1927 the quota of fruit which could be sold within Australia was to be limited to 15 per cent of output. Having little hope that James would pay attention to this determination, the Board obtained the Minister's Order to seize and acquire compulsorily a quantity of fruit in James' packing sheds. James contended that the Order was invalid and claimed damages for trespass.

When the States of Australia came together in 1900 to form a federation, it was the common intention of all parties that the tariffs which had earlier protected each individual state would be abolished, and that there would be free trade between states with protection against the outside world. Section 92 of the Constitution accordingly stated: 'on the imposition of uniform duties of customs, trade, commerce, and intercourse among the States . . . shall be absolutely free'.

The question was: did quotas imposed by government fiat offend this provision or was it designed only to prohibit interference with inter-state trade 'as such'? The latter view for which the Government of South Australia contended, was given short shrift by Lord Atkin. The determinations, he said,

> ' . . . were intended to prevent persons in South Australia from seeking more than the fixed quota in any of the Australian States. The quota was fixed by reference to the needs of all the States; and the prohibition of the sale of the surplus was against selling to any of the States. As the determination said, "The proportion which may be marketed in the Commonwealth of Australia shall not be more than" the prescribed proportion. If this leaves inter-State commerce "absolutely free" the constitutional charter might as well be torn up.'[63]

Then it was said that interference with inter-state trade was only an incidental consequence of the powers of compulsory acquisition which the Government had. The Board disagreed: the real object of the power of acquisition was to enable the minister to place restrictions on inter-state commerce, and that being so, 'the legislation is as invalid as if the legislature itself had imposed the commercial restrictions. The Constitution is not to be mocked by substituting executive for legislative interference with freedom'.[64]

63 At 555.
64 At 558.

The further question was raised by the appeal whether section 92 of the Constitution applied to the Commonwealth as well as the individual states, that is whether Commonwealth legislation must itself avoid infringements of the absolute freedom of trade. Did the Constitution intend to prevent for all time any legislation of any government which would limit the liberty of an Australian to sell his goods wherever he wished in Australia? The point clearly did not arise directly in James' case against the South Australian Government, but it was argued on a procedural question. Issues as to the boundaries of the constitutional powers of the Commonwealth and the states could not be appealed to the Privy Council without a certificate of the High Court of Australia and none had been asked for. However, the Board did not think it necessary to decide the question because if section 92 applied to both Commonwealth and the states, 'the prohibited area is denied to both'; alternatively, if the prohibition applied to the states alone, the only question was whether the states had violated it, and the Commonwealth powers would be undisputed. Therefore 'there are no boundaries between the one and the other which come into question'. James had to bring another appeal to the Privy Council four years later to establish that the Commonwealth was bound equally with the states.

The Board in *James v Cowan* consisted of Lord Sankey, then Lord Chancellor, and Lords Blanesburgh, Hanworth, Atkin and Russell. When it became known that neither Lord Atkin nor any of his fellow judges in the earlier case except Russell was to sit in the later appeal in *James v Commonwealth of Australia*[65] there was much disquiet in Australia. Mr Justice Evatt wrote to Atkin in May 1936 sending him some press clippings, and saying, 'There is some considerable consternation in this country at your not sitting in the interstate free trade case', and a few days later he wrote again in more general terms showing that the fears which Atkin nursed as to the future of the right of appeal to the Privy Council were not groundless.

HIGH COURT OF AUSTRALIA

Judges' Chambers
Sydney 24/5/36

Dear Lord Atkin,

The prohibition of appeals from this Court (under sec. 74) was due, as you know, to the fear that our constitutional quarrels would not greatly interest British jurists. But the two great cases of 1914 (sugar) and 1932 (James v. Cowan) produced a reaction as they both cut away a great deal of dead wood from the previous decisions; and there arose something of a movement largely

inspired by W. A. Holman ex-Premier NSW, that the way to the
P.C. in constitutional cases should be made easier. The same feeling
towards the P.C. exists strongly in N. Zealand since the earth quake
(W. Compensation) decision some years ago. Consequently the
slightest appearance of indifference to great constitutional appeals
does harm and many of our Bar leaders state freely that professional
support to the continuance of appeals may depend upon, say, the
transfer to the Lords of the Privy Council jurisdiction . . .

The particular case is not of such importance as the general
practice in which I take it you will have some voice: but in the
particular case jurisdiction was assumed because of its outstanding
interest and significance and practically at the request of Judges of
this Court who made it because of the new enunciation of principle
by you. When public commentators here became concerned at
"Lord Atkin's absence" you can imagine the disappointment of
those Judges who invited specially so, the assistance of those
quorum magna pars fuisti.

I have not forgotten your kind interest on a previous occasion in
some little work of mine: and it is in the belief that such interest
continues that I have done myself the honour of addressing you
frankly on a matter so important to the future working of our
constitutional judicial system.

I am, Lord Atkin,

Yours sincerely,

H. V. Evatt[66]

In November 1936 Atkin had put pressure on Hailsham to staff
the Board for the Canadian appeals exclusively from Lords of Appeal.
Here was tangible evidence that opinion in Australia to the same
effect was running just as high as in Canada. Both countries were
acutely sensitive to anything which might be interpreted as a slight.[67]
The difficulties for Hailsham were serious, and he was as anxious as
Atkin to retain the Privy Council's appellate jurisdiction. But he
mistook the temper of the times when he wrote to Atkin in November
1936 to say

'. . . I cannot believe that the legal authorities in the Dominions are
so little aware of the merits of our Judges that they seriously think
that because a man has not been a Law Lord, he is not as well qualified
as any other member of the Judicial Committee'.[68]

In the sixteen years during which Atkin was a Lord of Appeal he
made a very substantial contribution to the work of the Judicial
Committee, much of it impressed with the strong prose style which

---

66   Evatt to Atkin, 24 May 1936.
67   Exemplified by the speculation in Canada, caused by Lord Wright's criticism in 1955
     of the *Labour Conventions Case* (see above, p 110, that that case may have been
     effectively determined by Sir Sidney Rowlatt, 'a "taxation judge", who, I am told, sat
     through the 1937 hearings in his overcoat making neither note nor comment' (B. J.
     Mackinnon, 34 Canadian Bar Review 115 at 117).
68   Hailsham to Atkin, 3 November 1936.

he made his own. In common with all his brethren the work on private law was more successful than in the field of constitutional law. Here the instinct towards the development of an embracing legal principle expressed in straightforward language, which was such a mark of his work in the fields of commercial law and civil wrongs, was less invariably apt. Yet in this field too his judgment enabled him to temper the more rigid views to which the Judicial Committee sometimes seemed prone. And when issues arose about which he felt profoundly, as in the Australian free trade cases, he was a champion without equal in his time.

Statutory Interpretation

Speaking in a debate on law reform in 1966, Lord Wilberforce said of statutory interpretation that he suspected that it was 'what is nowadays popularly called a non-subject'.[1] The suspicion was justified. There is no coherent law of statutory interpretation, and no law which can be seen to be developing. The words of the enactment seem sometimes to mean just what the judges choose them to mean. And yet the business of statutory interpretation absorbs an increasing amount of judicial time, as the output of legislation itself increases: in the 1943 volume of Appeal Cases, for instance, the last full year of Lord Atkin's career, twenty-three out of thirty-seven reported cases were concerned in one way or another with the meaning of legislation.

The question is, as Alice and Lord Atkin memorably said, whether you can make words mean so many different things. Considering that the language of a statute is intended to be peremptory, it may be surprising that it can yield to differing meanings. It has been said again and again from the Bench that the words must be given their 'plain' or 'ordinary' meanings. How then can controversy arise? The answer is that it is permissible to interpret the words so as to accord with the intention of Parliament. The Parliament whose purpose must be discovered is an impersonal, indeed an imaginary one. It is certainly not the Parliament which is made up of individual legislators who happen to compose the two chambers at the time of the passage of the Bill, for many of them may have had no interest in the measure. Nor is the intention of Parliament to be taken as the intention of the sponsors of the Bill, for they may not have been able to carry through their purpose into the final Act. In any case, the judges are not allowed to read *Hansard* in order to see what the sponsors, or any other member, may have said. This is a much criticised rule, but there is a certain amount to be said for it. The legislative processes, through which the parliamentary draftsman's work must pass, are confusing and muddled.

1 277 HL Official Report col 1294, 16 November 1966.

'A Bill', wrote Mr Frederic Harrison, 'normally goes into Parliament in the state in which it ought to come out, and comes out in the state in which it ought to go in. An ordinary statute differs from an ordinary deed much as a marriage settlement prepared by a competent lawyer differs from one which should be finally settled in a dozen fierce wrangles between the heated relatives of the happy pair. If testators when making their wills were to put in new clauses on the spur of the moment, or the respective families were to cut about the drafts of an eminent conveyancer, wills and settlements would have a strong resemblance to modern Acts of Parliament.'[2]

The freedom to search for the 'spirit of the Act' or, quaintly, the 'mischief' at which it is aimed (both synonyms for the intention of Parliament) opens the possibility of liberal interpretation, which Bentham wrote of as 'that delicate and important branch of judiciary power, the concession of which is dangerous, the denial ruinous.'[3] Given this freedom, it is a rare statutory phrase which will not yield up more than one meaning when subjected to analysis by the judges.

At one extreme stands Lord Denning who at the outset of his long career in the Court of Appeal embarked on a characteristically adventurous attempt to liberalise the interpretation of Acts of Parliament. 'We do not sit here', he said, 'to pull the language of Parliament to pieces and make nonsense of it. That is an easy thing to do and it is a thing to which lawyers are too often prone. We sit here to find out the intention of Parliament and of ministers and carry it out, and we do this better by filling in the gaps and making sense of the enactment than by opening it up to destructive analysis.'[4] For Viscount Simonds, a judge of opposite cast of mind, these heroics were 'a naked usurpation of the legislative function under the thin guise of interpretation'.[5]

As in so much, Lord Atkin's position on statutory interpretation was that of a moderate. At any rate, he avoided the language of extremes.[6] He would have agreed with Lord Watson that 'the intention of the legislature' is a very slippery phrase,[7] but he did not hesitate to state what he conceived to be the purpose of a statute. In an early case on legislation imposing a minimum wage for coal miners, he said of the Act that 'as is well known from the circumstances in which it was passed, and as can be gathered from its provisions, [it] was passed with the object of promoting industrial peace . . . and it is obvious that unless reasonable facilities are given for adapting the rates and rules to any serious change of circumstances

2   Quoted in Chalmers 'An experiment in codification' 2 LQR 133.
3   Bentham *Of Laws in General* (ed Hart, Athlone Press, 1970) p 239.
4   *Magor and St Mellons RDC v Newport Corpn* [1950] 2 All ER 1226 at 1236.
5   Ibid. [1951] 2 All ER 839 at 841.
    The word 'heroics' was Lord Denning's own: see [1950] 2 All ER 1236.
6   For a very rare exception, see *Wankie Colliery Co v IRC* [1921] 3 KB 344; below p 127.
7   *Salomon v Salomon* [1897] AC 22 at 38.

either on the part of the workmen or the employers the Act is likely to bring not peace but a sword'.[8]

Atkin was again willing to search for the underlying purpose of a Second World War statute which enabled, but did not oblige, local councils to make up the pay of their officers who were away at the war to what they would have received as local government officers. Bolton Corporation chose not to do so, and the House of Lords held that the refusal gave rise to a trade dispute which could be referred to arbitration. In his speech he said:

> 'I cannot think that the legislature did not forsee that, once the power was given . . . claims would be made and settled by the usual processes of collective bargaining with which sensible masters and workmen are now familiar . . . I think that the local authorities in this matter were not only permitted, but required, to turn their minds away from a duty to the ratepayers and direct them to a duty to the public at large . . . The intention, I should have said, obviously is to further the public welfare by encouraging the war effort, to enable local authorities, like other good employers, to secure that their servants when they undertake war service, are not worse off financially by their change of service.'[9]

But where the language of the statute was transparently plain, it was wrong to give it colour according to the temper of the times, or to strain at meaning. Atkin's dissent in *Liversidge v Anderson* was as much a plea for orthodoxy in interpretation as for the liberty of the subject. And in *Ford v Blurton*, in reaching a conclusion which was repugnant to him on the abrogation of a litigant's right to a jury in civil proceedings, he said, 'I find myself unable to formulate any restriction on the wide meaning of the word "conveniently" which would be within the realm of construction as opposed to legislation. I speak reluctantly because I cannot bring myself to believe that this far-reaching result was intended by the Legislature'.[10]

On the other hand, where there was a choice of meaning, judges should not choose one which leads to a forced or fantastic result. In *Russian and English Bank v Baring Brothers*,[11] the question was whether the Bank, dissolved under the law of the country of its incorporation, Russia, could be wound up in England so as to enable its assets here to be collected and administered. The Companies Act stated that a company which had not been registered in England

---

8   *R v Judge Amphlett* [1915] 2 KB 223 at 239.
9   *NALGO v Bolton Corpn* [1943] AC 166 at 180.
10   (1922) 38 TLR 801 at 805. A little later in the judgment he was even more explicit: '. . . though I have serious misgivings whether we are correctly interpreting the real intention of Parliament, I am unable to put any meaning upon the words other than that adopted by the other members of the Court'.
11   [1936] AC 405. Cf *Ferrier v Scottish Milk Marketing Board* [1937] AC 126 at 130 where Atkin said: 'My Lords, this Procrustean method has the almost inevitable result of stretching the meaning of words to fit the bed so constructed.'

could be wound up 'If the Company is dissolved . . .'; but, in argument, Mr Gavin Simonds had taken an objection which was satisfying to a rigorously logical mind. Only that law, he contended, which gave birth to a company could bring its life to an end. Russian law had brought the life of the Bank to an end by dissolving it, and there were no words in the English Companies Act which expressly treated foreign dissolved companies as revived. It was accordingly all a matter of implication 'that dissolved foreign corporations are to arise from the grave in full life and vigour and [become] entitled to sue to recover property' and 'that they are to be so entitled notwithstanding that they do not exist.'[12] Lord Russell confessed frankly that he found himself unequal to the task of assenting to such a view.

Lords Blanesburgh, Atkin and Macmillan were equal to the task. For Atkin, the pursuit of pure logic could end only in frustrating the purpose of the Act. 'Are we to say that the legislative enactment is completely futile: or is there another solution? My Lords, I think that we are entitled to imply, indeed I think it is a necessary implication, that the dissolved foreign company is to be wound up as though it had not been dissolved, and therefore continued in existence. This seems to me with respect the necessary result of saying that it shall be wound up in accordance with the provisions of the Act.' Here was a case where a gap had been left by Parliament, where as Atkin observed, 'one may wish that the legislature had worked out the solution itself', but where in order to avoid obstructing the evident purpose of the enactment, it was permissible to fill the gap.

In the field of Poor Law relief, Lord Atkin expressed his understanding of the purpose of the statutes in the strong language which reflected his own humane inclinations. In *Coventry Corpn v Surrey County Council*,[13] he described the Poor Removal Act of 1846, as 'passed to remedy one of the scandals of the old Poor Law, the breaking up of families by distributing parents and children to different settlements'. And in a Scots case decided a year or two later in 1936, *Duncan v Aberdeen County Council*,[14] he went further, saying:

'This is a question of construction, and for my part even if we had not in the statute itself, as I think we have, a satisfactory guide to the meaning of the words used I should have found no difficulty in accepting the construction put upon them by the appellant.'

12   Per Lord Russell, at 434.
     Lord Macmillan described the difficulties as 'more logical than real' (at 439).
     See also Atkin's letter to Professor. Gutteridge, quoted p 74
13   [1935] AC 199. See also p 37
14   [1936] 2 All ER 911.

The statute stated that, 'In affording outdoor relief to any person', the local authority was to disregard the first £1 of any disability pension which was being paid. The appellant was an ex-serviceman whose sole income for himself, his wife and five children was a disability pension of £2 per week. He applied for relief, but the local authority decided that he was not entitled to any because his pension was sufficient for his needs. The question of construction was whether the first £1 was to be disregarded, not only in deciding the amount of relief, but also in considering whether the applicant was entitled to relief at all. 'The trend of legislation is unmistakeable', said Atkin, and referring to the provision for relief:

> 'They are obviously remedial provisions intended to make the position of the persons to whom they apply better than ordinary . . . The other view is with respect much too refined for use in ordinary public administration: it would be quite unintelligible to the persons who are in receipt of the payments named and must be attended by the natural discontent of those who find that the supposed alleviation of their position is a mockery: and that they may be worse off than if they had earned and received only half their pension.'

The Poor Laws, dating from the time of Elizabeth, were the first step in this country towards social insurance; but it was not until the very end of the nineteenth century that the legislature intervened to compensate workment for injury sustained at work, a protection that might be said to rival the relief of poverty in social importance. But the vagrants and beggars of the sixteenth century were a menace to society, and disabled workmen were not. The common law view of employer's liability was that it did not exist. The issue seems first to have arisen in 1837 when a workman who was injured while travelling in his master's defective vehicle, was refused a remedy. Lord Abinger came near to denying that an employee could successfully sue his employer on any ground, and his decision marked the origin of the doctrine of common employment.[15] As the law developed this became one of the major difficulties facing workmen claimants, for if their injury was caused by the carelessness of a fellow-employee, their claim failed. So also did it if the claimant could be shown to have contributed in any degree to the accident by his own carelessness. The underlying idea, characteristic of Victorian thinking, was that an employee accepted the risks incidental to his employment, and that was one of the matters for which he was remunerated. A fortiori, he could not recover compensation if he was at fault himself.

But opinion, and with it judicial opinion, swung in favour of the workman through the second half of the nineteenth century, and

---

15   *Priestley v Fowler* (1837) 3 M & W 1.
   Lord Abinger said: 'But in truth the mere relation of the master and the servant never can imply an obligation on the part of the master to take more care of the servant than he may reasonably be expected to do of himself'.

the Workmen's Compensation Act of 1897 was the first step away from a theory based on fault. Workmen in certain dangerous industries were to be compensated by their employers in amounts of up to half their wages if they were injured in the course of their employment, unless they themselves had committed 'serious and wilful default'. In 1906, the scheme was extended to most employments and to cover some industrial diseases. Thereafter, until the Workmen's Compensation Acts were repealed in 1946 and replaced by a state-funded scheme of insurance, the Acts were progressively extended and changed in favour of the workman.

The Workmen's Compensation Acts are now of no more than historical interest, but during the period of Lord Atkin's career on the Bench, they represented the single largest field for statutory interpretation. They also represented a field of special interest to Atkin himself. Both through the interpretation of these Acts and through the great common law cases, he led the House of Lords in extending the responsibility of employers for the safety and welfare of their men, and in making it inevitable that Parliament would intervene to eliminate the worst anachronisms in that branch of the law. It has been said that Lord Atkin was a plaintiff's judge:[16] whether or not that is generally true, it is certainly true of the Workmen's Compensation cases, and he acknowledged as much in a letter which he wrote to his son, William, in 1942:

> 'Did I tell you that a few years ago they were discussing a Workmen's Compensation Case when the presiding judge said the House of Lords decisions seem to go in cycles, sometimes for the employer, and then for the workman, and one of the counsel said, "When Lord Atkin is riding the cycle there isn't much doubt in what direction it will go". A very pleasant compliment.'

The purpose of the Acts was to compensate workmen who were injured at work, and it was consistent with that purpose to decide cases in the workmen's interest. Consistent also with Lord Atkin's predisposition, and as the successive Acts moved step by step away from a theory of fault, he moved with them giving them as liberal a construction as was possible, without violence to authority or to intellectual honesty.[17] In *Matthews v Robert McClure*[18] a girl working in a textile mill was injured when she carelessly allowed her hair, which was hanging down, to get caught in machinery. The Court of Appeal decided that her own negligence did not disentitle her to compensation, and Atkin said: 'It is the design of the Workmen's

16   Gutteridge 'In Memoriam Lord Atkin of Aberdovey' 60 LQR 332 at 340.
17   See eg *Noble v Southern Rly* (1940) AC 583, where he said of an earlier and binding authority: 'Whether that decision construed the section [viz s 7 of the 1923 Act] as favourably for the workman as the Legislature may have intended is not now a subject for judicial discussion. It is authoritative and as in duty bound I accept it'.
18   (1921) 124 LT 10.

Compensation Act 1906 that a workman is not to be deprived of compensation merely because in doing something he was entitled to do he acted negligently. The actual peril is a part of the employment, a very imminent peril of the employment known to the employers . . .' In 1938, the House of Lords with Lord Atkin presiding, were prepared to say that even extreme carelessness, or rashness, should not prevent a workman from receiving compensation. In reversing a decision of the Court of Appeal, Atkin expressed himself with simplicity:

'I cannot assent to the doctrine that though a man may be doing a piece of work within his employment, and may still be within his employment if he does it carelessly, yet if he does the same piece of work very carelessly he may be found to be doing something outside his employment. Once you have found the work which he is seeking to do to be within his employment, the question of negligence, great or small, is irrelevant . . . With great respect it is not a question of degree . . .'[19]

As he pointed out in the same case, a man's negligence in doing his job is one of the most fruitful sources of injury.

This line of cases was concerned with the interpretation of perhaps the most litigated phrase of the 20s and 30s, 'arising out of and in the course of' the workman's employment. The courts having decided that carelessness in doing a job did not take a workman outside the confines of that phrase, a more obstinate difficulty remained. What if the workman was injured as a consequence of doing something which was actually forbidden? This problem was beyond the reach of interpretation and had to be tackled by Parliament. By the Act of 1923, an accident causing death or disablement was *deemed* to arise out of and in the course of the workman's employment, notwithstanding that at the time the workman was contravening a statutory or other regulation, or an order given to him by his employer, if what he was then doing was for the purposes of the employer's business.[20] Such a metaphysical concept was bound to cause trouble. Atkin prophesied that 'this section may prove to be a gilt-edged section for the legal profession', and remarking that it was not very artistically drawn, said: 'There is a fatality in legislating on workmen's compensation. It seems impossible to legislate in such clear terms as to avoid the possibility of dispute'.[21]

Nothing ever falsified that observation. The Acts went on being refined by hairline distinctions and by gloss[22] until they were repealed after the Second World War. That it was not possible to find a

---

19   *Harris v Associated Portland Cement Manufacturers* [1939] AC 71 at 76.
20   Workmen's Compensation Act 1923, s 7.
21   *Davies v Gwauncaegurwen Colliery* [1924] 2 KB 651 at 661.
22   Examples abound but see eg *Robertson v Anglo-American Oil Co* 26 Ll L Reps 137, a decision against the workman which Atkin reached with reluctance.

straight-forward way through which employers should compensate their injured workmen was a reproach which Lord Atkin felt keenly, but no judge did more than he towards the achievement of that object. As usual he enjoyed dismantling technical obstructions. In a letter of 1940 to his friend in Australia, Herbert Evatt, he said: '. . . we destroyed a technicality which had done injustice for 25 years from a decision of the Court of Appeal that if a workman received any part of an award he could not afterwards appeal for more because the award is one, and he cannot "approbate and reprobate". We have not given our reasons yet, but that decision is going to receive a good hard knock'.[23]

A whole range of new difficulties was introduced when in 1906 disablement by industrial disease was brought into the scheme of the Workmen's Compensation Acts, caused principally by the ineptitude of attempting to assimilate in the drafting of the Acts the behaviour of disease with the sudden effect of an industrial accident. A graphic illustration of these difficulties was given by *Richards v Goskar*[24] and the series of cases which led up to it. The Act of 1925 treated industrial diseases as if they were injuries by accident. A surgeon was required to certify that the workman was suffering from one of a scheduled list of diseases, and that he was thereby disabled from earning full wages; the disablement was to be treated as the happening of the accident; the date of the disablement was to be the date certified by the surgeon, or if he could not certify a date when disablement began, then the date of his certificate. An earlier decision of the House of Lords appeared to establish that certified disablement was to be treated as the accident for all purposes, so that when the disability ceased, compensation ceased as well, even though there might afterwards be a recrudescence of the disease. Such an absurd and unjust result was impossible when the Acts were applied to ordinary accidents, and Lord Atkin, who presided in the House of Lords and gave the only extended speech, set out to establish that it was similarly not correct in relation to diseases.

He began with an analysis of the statutory scheme, demonstrating that disablement was made equivalent to an industrial accident for some limited purposes. But, he said, 'translate disablement into "accident" for all purposes and the scheme falls to pieces'. The Act said in terms that the disease was to be treated as an injury caused by an accident, so how could disablement (caused by the disease) be the accident which caused the injury? He resorted to his favourite Alice. 'The only comparable sequence that occurs to me arose when Alice learned from the White Queen's accident the art of living backwards; first the bandage then the bleeding then the pinprick.'

23   Atkin to Evatt, 15 January 1940. See appendix 4.
24   [1937] AC 304.

Having destroyed the employer's argument on the meaning of the statute, he turned to consider the question upon authority. There the way seemed to be barred by a ten-year-old decision of the House of Lords in the Scots case of *McDougall v Summerlee Iron Co*;[25] but after eight pages of analysis of the decision and the later cases in which it was discussed, he ultimately found a way of removing the obstruction. In so doing he drew a remarkable tribute from Lord Russell.

'My Lords, when the argument on this appeal had concluded my conviction was that the appeal should be allowed if it were possible to adopt that course in the face of what this House had said and decided in the case of *McDougall v Summerlee Iron Co*. I confess that I had thought it impossible to do so. I have, however, had the opportunity of reading and considering the opinion of the noble Lord on the Woolsack. It has opened a way through what I feared was an impasse, and I accordingly am prepared to concur in the motion proposed.'

Lord Atkin's facility with precedents seems to have been at its most formidable when he felt most strongly about the outcome, as he did in *Richards' Case*. He described the question at issue as 'of vital importance in respect of the provision made by the Workmen's Compensation Act for compensation to workmen who suffer from industrial disease'. Richards suffered from miner's nystagmus, a disease with tragic consequences for its victims and a particular tendency to recrudescence. It was apparently caused by the darkness underground, lit only with the concentrated light of the safety lamps. Its physical sympton was a rotary oscillation of the eyeball, but it carried with it a general neurosis associated with the fear of blindness. The disease had engaged the attention of the Medico-Legal Society in 1923 during Atkin's Presidency, and it was characteristic of him to take the compassionate view, as he did then, that there must be accurate knowledge of the disease and full compensation for its effects so that its victims 'should be relieved from the fears which encouraged the disease'.[26] It was therefore not surprising that when, more than ten years afterwards, he was called on to decide a case on the recrudescence of nystagmus, he showed a rare determination to ensure that the workman was fairly compensated.

No subject has illumined the possibilities of judicial techniques of statutory interpretation as has taxation. Taxation is not merely a means of raising revenue to fund government expenditure: it has

25   1927 SC (HL) 72.
26   *Transactions of the Medico-Legal Society* Vol XVIII p 7 (16 October 1923). Atkin is reported as saying: 'The practical position, therefore, was that these nervous disorders must continue to be treated as disorders for which compensation must be given. In that case it was very important from the medical and the social point of view that there should be very full knowledge as to what the disease is, so that persons suffering should be relieved from the fears which encouraged the disease.'

become an instrument for social change, economic stimulus, punishment of the unworthy. And from time to time the judges have reflected in their decisions all these objectives. Moreover, in recent times the House of Lords has invented new concepts in order to develop a highly personal view about the proper purposes of taxation. Although we have no written constitution, it has been judicially declared that the exercise of an administrative discretion by the Inland Revenue Commissioners is 'unconstitutional'.[27] Most radical of all, if a tax avoidance scheme consisting of a number of distinct steps is intended to operate as a combination of those steps, the courts are now entitled to look at the result of the whole rather than of each constituent. The decision which introduced that concept (*Ramsay v IRC*)[28] destroyed at a blow a small but influential industry, the manufacturers and sellers of avoidance schemes, for long regarded by many as socially undesirable.

Lord Atkin's career came too early for the heyday of tax avoidance, and it can only be a speculation what his own attitude to it might have been. He was however party to a number of important decisions in the field of taxation. The earliest of these indicate some predisposition against the revenue authorities, at least when they seemed to be advancing exorbitant claims. Of one such claim, he said in a judgment extending to only five sentences, that it was as clear a case of trying to tax the public twice over as one could expect to find. 'He (his Lordship) thought and had said in the course of the argument that the argument of counsel for the Crown was a pure technicality, or would be so if it was well founded, but the facts disposed of it.'[29] And in *Wankie Colliery v IRC*,[30] a case concerned with excess profits duty and the chargeability of owners of a business for profits earned at an earlier time when there were other owners, he was betrayed for once into extravagant language, saying in a dissenting judgment that the Finance Act in question was 'a piece of confiscatory legislation which is without parallel in the history of Parliamentary government in this country, and which, I should think, would exceed the wildest dreams of the most imaginative high prerogative lawyer in the very worst time of our history'.[31]

Later, in the House of Lords, Atkin's decisions show a tendency against adopting too strict or technical a construction of taxing Acts.

---

27   *Vestey v IRC (Nos 1 and 2)* [1980] AC 1148, eg at 1172–3. All that was necessary to say was that the statute did not warrant the administrative procedure.
28   [1981] 2 WLR 449, eg at 457.
     Lord Wilberforce said (at 459): 'While the techniques of tax avoidance progress and are technically improved, the Courts are not obliged to stand still.'
29   *CIR v Roberts* (1925) 41 TLR 623 at 625.
30   [1921] 3 KB 344.
31   At 365. The majority were narrowly upheld in the House of Lords where Lord Sumner remarked that 'considerations of justice and injustice have not much to do with modern direct taxation: they belong to a different order of ideas. Taxation is concerned with expediency or inexpediency'. [1922] 2 AC 51 at 70.

This often worked in the Revenue's favour. In *Eaton Turner v McKenna*,[32] the taxpayer was employed as a mine manager in West Africa and his salary was paid in England. He argued that because his work was exclusively carried on abroad, he could neither be taxed under Schedule D nor Schedule E. Atkin commented: 'it is said that . . . although you have transferred this employment from Sch. D to Sch. E, you have not found a home for it in Sch. E, and it must wander between earth and heaven because apparently it is not in Sch. D, neither is it in Sch. E. My Lords, in my opinion that is much too technical a view, and an incorrect view of the construction. The rules of Sch. E are intended to be applied so far as they are applicable'.

That was a business-like view of taxation, as was his decision a year later in *Paton v IRC*.[33] There the taxpayer claimed repayment of tax when his bank debited his account with interest on a loan account, contending that he had thereby 'paid' the interest. Lord Atkin responded with a characteristic appeal to common sense. 'The ordinary man would, I think, say that so far from being paid they [the debits] are added to the ordinary indebtedness because they are not paid: and I can see no reason why the law should say anything different. It is obvious that the system adopted by banks, which seems to have been common practice in Lord Eldon's time, is for the purpose of giving them compound interest without perhaps flaunting that fact before their customers.'

Lord Tomlin's memorable statement in *The Duke of Westminster's Case*[34] that: 'Every man is entitled if he can to order his affairs so as that the tax attaching under the appropriate Acts is less than it otherwise would be', was until very recent times regarded as a charter of freedom for the hard pressed taxpayer. Now it is on the authority of Lord Diplock that the statement may in practice mean very little.[35] But what is perhaps less well-known is that the facts of the case are hardly robust enough to bear the weight of such a general assertion, and that Lord Atkin dissented on that ground. The case is not strictly one of statutory interpretation, for there was no difference of view and no argument on the meaning of the legislation. But because of its significance for so many tax cases which followed, it should not be omitted.

The Duke executed a series of deeds of covenant in favour of his employees in recognition of their services, to pay weekly sums to them for the joint lives of himself and the employee with a minimum

32   [1937] AC 162.
33   [1938] AC 341.
34   [1936] AC 1.
35   *CIR v Burmah Oil Co* [1982] STC 30.
Lord Diplock said of the *Ramsay* decision, 'it does involve recognizing that Lord Tomlin's oft-quoted dictum . . . tells us little or nothing as to what method of ordering one's affairs will be recognized by the courts as effective to lessen the tax that would attach to them if business transactions were conducted in a straightforward way'.

period of seven years, regardless of whether the employees remained in his service throughout that period. The test case concerned one of the Duke's gardeners, a Mr Allman, who received (as did all the other employees concerned) a letter from the Duke's solicitors in the following terms which he was invited to sign at the same time as the deed:

PRIVATE
The Grosvenor Office,
53 Davies Street,
Berkeley Square, London, W.1.

To Mr. Frank Allman.   13th August, 1930

Dear Sir,

On Wednesday the 6th instant we read over with you a Deed of Covenant which the Duke of Westminster has signed in your favour under which you will be entitled to a gross sum of £1. 18s. 0d. a week in consideration of your past faithful service and irrespective of any work which you may do for His Grace after the deed comes into effect. The deed will be in force for seven years if you and the Duke should so long live, and His Grace can reconsider the position at the end of that period. We explained that there is nothing in the deed to prevent your being entitled to and claiming full remuneration for such future work as you may do, though it is expected that in practice you will be content with the provision which is being legally made for you for so long as the deed takes effect, with the addition of such sum (if any) as may be necessary to bring the total periodical payment while you are still in the Duke's service up to the amount of the salary or wages which you have lately been receiving.

You said that you accepted this arrangement, and you accordingly executed the deed.

We write, as promised, to confirm the explanation which we gave you on the 6th instant. If you are still quite satisfied we propose to insert the 6th instant as the date of the deed and we shall be obliged by your signing the acknowledgement at the foot of this letter and then returning it to us.

Yours faithfully,
Boodle, Hatfield & Co.

Acknowledgment

To the Duke of Westminster, D.S.O.
And to Messrs. Boodle, Hatfield & Co., his Solicitors.

I have read the above written letter, and I confirm that I accept the provision made for me by the deed. I agree to the deed being dated and treated as delivered by and binding upon the Duke of Westminster and myself.

Frank Allman

In practice, Mr Allman, with all the other employees, fulfilled the expectation expressed in the letter and claimed remuneration only in an amount which, with the covenanted sum, would total the wages which he had been receiving before the deed was executed. The Duke claimed to deduct from his income for surtax purposes the whole amount of the covenanted payment, a tax advantage which would not have been available to him had the money been paid as wages.

The Special Commissioners decided in favour of the Crown on the footing that 'in construing the true effect and substance of the deed . . . we were entitled to consider with these deeds the letters of explanation and form of acknowledgment which were sent to the covenantees'. They continued: 'We held that the payments made under these deeds to persons who remain in the appellant's employ were, in substance, payments for continuing service ejusdem generis with wages or salaries so long as the recipients in fact remain in the appellant's service, and as such were not annual payments which were a proper deduction from his assessment of surtax'. Mr Justice Finlay upheld this decision but it was reversed in the Court of Appeal. The House of Lords held by a majority of four to one, with Lord Atkin dissenting, that the Duke was entitled to the deduction for the covenanted payments.

In the majority speeches in the House much criticism was made of the 'substance of the matter' basis for the Special Commissioners' decision. Lord Tomlin suggested that it was 'a doctrine that the Court may ignore the legal position', and that the sooner it was given its quietus the better. But Lord Atkin saw no difficulty in taking the view that 'the substance of the transaction was that what was being paid was remuneration'.

The essential question, as the Commissioners had appreciated, was what was the effect of the letter? Lords Tomlin, Russell and Wright considered that it had no contractual force, expressing no more than a hope or expectation that the employee would not claim his full wages in addition to the covenanted payments. Lord Macmillan thought the letter was a binding arrangement that the employee would accept the covenanted payments plus the difference between them and his former wages. But, in his opinion, that did not turn the covenanted payments into remuneration.[36]

Lord Atkin's view was that the letter 'was intended to have, and had, far more substantial results than the interchange of unnecessary assurances between master and servant'. Before the deed was executed there was a contract between the two as to the effect of the deed on the existing contract of service. What was its effect? Either, that the employee would take as wages the difference between his former wage and the covenanted payment; or that he would continue to

36   Lord Tomlin at 18; Lord Russell at 23;
     Lord Wright at 30; Lord Macmillan at 26.

serve at the old rate but would take in payment the amount provided for in the deed, and the balance in the old way. In Mr Allman's case, he had been receiving 60s a week; now he was to get 38s under the deed and 22s as ordinary salary.

Lord Atkin asked which of the two arrangements was more likely.

> 'I quite agree', he said, 'that the former is a possible bargain. A servant may agree to work for nothing, or for some sum which is merely a fraction of the current rates of wages. But such agreements are in my experience very exceptional ... The better construction appears to me to be that the servants were never asked to abandon the existing contractual rate.'

When one bears in mind that the arrangements were between a Duke and his employees, many of them in humble positions, and that they were made in 1930, a period of high unemployment, Lord Atkin's view of the arrangements seems at least as credible as that of the majority.

Atkin did not disagree at all with Lord Tomlin's general statement, and on that matter of principle he expressed himself clearly. 'It was not, I think, denied — at any rate it is incontrovertible — that the deeds were brought into existence as a device by which the respondent might avoid some of the burden of surtax. I do not use the word device in any sinister sense, for it has to be recognized that the subject, whether poor and humble or wealthy and noble, has the legal right to dispose of his capital and income as to attract upon himself the least amount of tax. The only function of a Court of Law is to determine the legal result of his dispositions so far as they affect tax.'

Although it might have done, *The Duke of Westminster's Case* tells us nothing about Lord Atkin's own attitude to tax avoidance, and no later case repaired the omission. He never delivered a speech in the House of Lords on the subject. But in 1943, near the end of his career, he concurred (without speaking separately) with Viscount Simon's judgment in *Latilla v IRC*[37] which contained the first generalised attack on ingenious methods of disposing of income 'by which those who were prepared to adopt them might enjoy the benefits of residence in this country while receiving the equivalent of such income without sharing in the appropriate burden of British taxation'. It may be assumed that Lord Atkin's concurrence was not only in the result of the appeal, but also in the social purpose which Lord Simon chose to express and which has been repeated so many times since.

37   [1943] AC 377.

Liversidge v Anderson

Lord Atkin's dissenting speech in *Liversidge v Anderson*[1] was a unique event in his life, for it made him for a short time a public figure. The decision was in any case likely to excite interest because it concerned the meaning and effect of the notorious Emergency Regulation 18B, which gave the wartime Home Secretary the extraordinary power to detain without trial or even charge. Interest was heightened by the extreme language with which Atkin emphasised his disagreement with the other four judges, Lords Maugham, Macmillan, Wright and Romer. That ensured that the decision would become the subject of several leading articles in the press on the following morning. But when, against all convention, Lord Maugham who had presided at the hearing of the appeal, criticised Lord Atkin's speech in a published letter to *The Times*, the case became a sensation.

Liversidge's Case also represented for Lord Atkin the climax of his development of the radical dissenting judgment. Alone among the ten judges who heard the application against Sir John Anderson, the Home Secretary, and his successor Mr Herbert Morrison, for particulars of the grounds for Liversidge's detention in Brixton prison, Lord Atkin upheld his right to have these details. For that the moral courage was necessary which he had commended and defined as the willingness to say 'no', when talking to the boys of his old school.

It is now forty years since the decision was given, and the majority view has finally been interred.[2] Lord Atkin's dissent has finally been vindicated. But it is necessary to recall the context in which the House of Lords heard the case. The argument took place in September 1941 and speeches were delivered on 3 November. It was a low point in the War. The Balkans and Crete had been overrun; the invasion of Russia had carried the Germans close to Leningrad and Moscow; the British summer offensive in the Western Desert had failed; the Japanese menaced the Malayan peninsular and Singapore; Pearl Harbour was to follow in the next month and the United States were not yet in the War. Lord Wright's speech reflected the atmosphere:

1 [1942] AC 206
2 *IRC v Rossminster Ltd* [1980] 1 All ER 80.

132

Mary Elizabeth Ruck, Lord Atkin's mother

Lord Atkin (right) with his brothers Robin (left) and Walter (centre)

Pantlludw, Summer 1895

Lord Atkin with his mother, Mary Elizabeth Steuart (standing) his wife, Lizzie Atkin, and Nain (both seated) and his four eldest children (l to r Grace, Daisy, Dickie (killed 1916) and Gwen)

Laurence Ruck (Taid)

Bernard Darwin, cousin

Berta Ruck, cousin

Lord Atkin of Aberdovey
(as Queen's Counsel,
about 1912)

Sir Thomas Edward
Scrutton (*by courtesy of
the National Portrait
Gallery*)

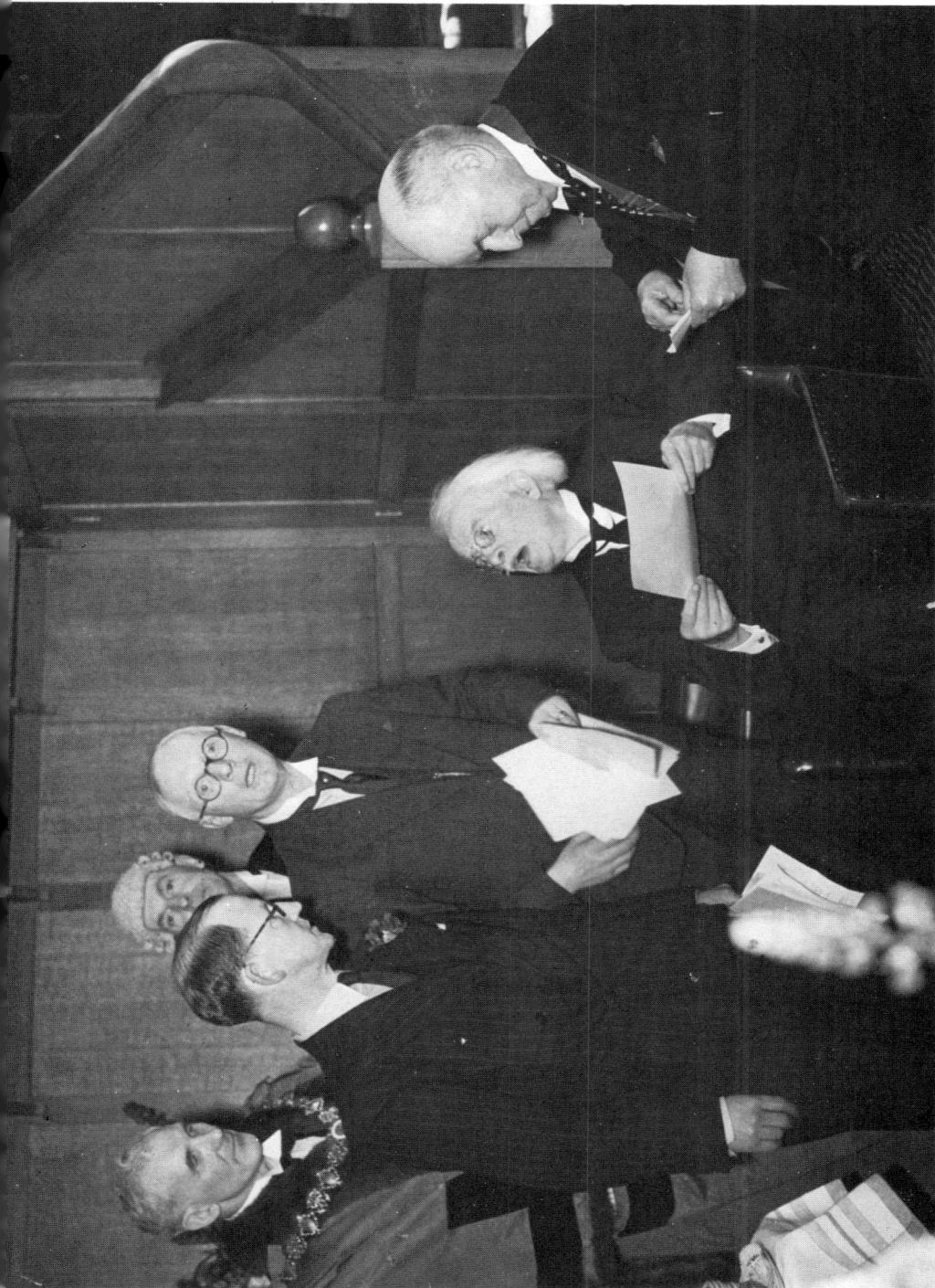

Lord Atkin and David Lloyd George (both seated) at the opening of the Welsh Services Club in 1940

Lord Atkin with eight of his eldest grandchildren at Aberdovey about 1929
L to r (standing) Toby Low (now Lord Aldington), Charles Low;
(centre) Patience Low (now Mrs D.H.R. Martin), Lord Atkin, John David Hope, Christopher Hope;
(front) Peter Macnair (now His Honour Judge Macnair); D. Macnair (now Col. D. Nacnair, retired), J.T.H. Macnair

Lord Atkin of Aberdovey

Lord Atkin on the jetty at Aberdovey

'All the circumstances of national safety to which this House adverted in *Rex v Halliday* are present in this war, only with vastly increased urgency and gravity, because German methods for effecting the poisonous infiltration among British or allied subjects of their purposes and schemes have been immensely more subtle and ingenious than in the last war. Even a judge may be allowed to take notice of the import of words like Fifth Columnists and Quislings and the like.'[3]

Liversidge had been detained under Defence (General) Regulation 18B which provided that:

'If the Secretary of State has reasonable cause to believe any person to be of hostile origin or associations . . . and that by reason thereof it is necessary to exercise control over him, he may make an order against that person directing that he be detained.'

Lord Atkin's dissent resulted in his becoming associated with the opposition to the Regulation itself. But the case was concerned not with the legality of the Regulation, only with its proper meaning. He himself pointed out that no one could doubt that the Emergency Powers legislation was capable of conferring unlimited power on the executive, through the King in Council, over person and property. 'The only question is whether in this regulation His Majesty has done so.'[4] In fact, he was not opposed to the principle of detention without trial in time of emergency. After the decision he wrote to his daughter, Rose:

'I can quite understand the Home Office desire to have the unrestricted power in an emergency: there is a good deal to be said for it. But I cannot understand their explanation that the change of words was just to remind the Home Secretary to be a good boy and apply his mind to the job.'

By his writ Liversidge, who was represented by Mr D. N. Pritt QC and Mr G. O. Slade, claimed that he had been unlawfully detained. The Home Secretary's defence set up his own order which itself gave no particulars of the grounds on which it was made, and merely asserted that he had reasonable cause for his belief. Liversidge applied for particulars of the grounds for Sir John Anderson's belief.[5] The Master who first heard the application refused to order particulars, and that decision was upheld successively by the judge and the Court

---

3 At 265.
4 At 239.
5 In his autobiography, *From Right to Left* (Lawrence and Wishart, 1967), Pritt revealed that the reasons for detaining Liversidge, in addition to: 'You are suspected of having been in touch with persons who are suspected of being enemy agents' were the scarcely credible 'You are suspected of having been engaged in commercial frauds' and 'You are the son of a Jewish Rabbi'. The Home Secretary must be accounted fortunate that particulars were never ordered to be given. Liversidge was apparently released soon after the case in the House of Lords ended.

of Appeal. By a majority of four to one the House of Lords also held that Liversidge was not entitled to the particulars he claimed.

But as Lord Atkin pointed out, the only issue which had been debated in the lower courts was where the burden of proof lay. On this, all were agreed that it was for Liversidge to show that there was no reasonable cause for his detention, and not for the Home Secretary to have to establish that he did have a reasonable basis for his belief.

Until *Greene's Case*, which in the House of Lords was heard with *Liversidge's Case*, came before the Court of Appeal, it had never been suggested or argued by the Crown that in cases of detention under Regulation 18B, the test of reasonable cause was other than an objective one. That is to say either it was for the detainee to show an objective lack of reasonable cause or it was for the Home Secretary to establish it. In fact the Home Secretary (and at least once through the same Counsel who represented him in *Liversidge's Case*, Sir Donald Somervell and Valentine Holmes) had in other cases accepted that positive burden.[6] In *Greene's Case* itself the Home Secretary supplied the detainee with particulars of the grounds for his detention. These were put in evidence by the Crown and accepted by all five Law Lords including Atkin as adequate.

However, when *Greene's Case* reached the Court of Appeal, that tribunal became 'infected with the subjective virus', as Atkin put it. They concluded that the words, 'If the Secretary of State has reasonable cause' were to be given a subjective meaning, that it was for the Home Secretary himself to judge the reasonableness of his own grounds.[7] On this view of what the Regulation meant, questions of onus almost but not quite disappeared. The Home Secretary had merely to assert by affidavit that he had reasonable grounds for his belief, and his assertion could not be challenged unless it could be shown that he did not believe what he said.

This was the effect of the Home Secretary's submissions in the House of Lords. The Attorney-General, Sir Donald Somervell, argued that the Home Secretary's act was an executive act and could not be called in question in a court of law.[8] The reasonableness of the grounds for his belief was a matter for him alone. Of this contention Lord Atkin said:

> 'The result is that the only implied condition is that the Secretary of State acts in good faith. If he does that — and who could dispute it or disputing it prove the opposite? — the Minister has been given complete discretion whether he should detain a subject or not. It is an absolute power which, so far as I know, has never been given before to the executive, and I shall not apologise for taking time to

6   *R v Secretary of State for Home Affairs, ex p Lees* [1941] 1 KB 72; *R v Secretary of State for Home Affairs, ex p Budd* [1941] 2 All ER 749.
7   *R v Secretary of State for Home Affairs, ex p Greene* [1942] 1 KB 87 at 99.
8   At 210.

demonstrate that no such power is in fact given to the Minister by the words in question.'[9]

The case therefore turned on the meaning of the simple words, 'if the Secretary of State has reasonable cause to believe'. Lord Atkin gave a simple answer. 'After all this long discussion the question is whether the words "If a man has" can mean "If a man thinks he has". I am of the opinion that they cannot, and that the case should be decided accordingly.'[10]

The majority declined to allow themselves such a straightforward answer. Lord Maugham was

> 'quite unable to take the view that the words can only have that meaning. It seems to me reasonably clear that, if the thing to be believed is something which is essentially one within the knowledge of A.B. or one for the exercise of his exclusive discretion, the words might well mean if A.B. acting on what he thinks is reasonable cause (and, of course, acting in good faith) believes the thing in question.'[11]

A variety of reasons were collected together to give colour to that view.

Only the Home Secretary could judge the reasonableness of his view that by reason of a person's hostile associations, it was necessary that control should be exercised over him: clearly a matter for executive discretion. The Home Secretary could act on hearsay and did not need legally admissible evidence: it would be strange if that could be questioned in a court. The information would be mostly of an extremely confidential character and it would be prejudicial to the state to have to disclose it in court. The Home Secretary was a member of the Government answerable to Parliament. He was provided with an advisory committee to enquire into cases under the Regulations, and he had to give a monthly report to Parliament including a statement of the number of cases in which he had declined to take the committee's advice.[12] The Regulation was a wartime emergency measure and that context was relevant to the ascertainment of its true meaning. The Home Secretary was an officer whose integrity was entitled to public confidence.[13] The provisions relating to the advisory committee were intended as a substitute for recourse to the courts: the detainee could make his objections to the committee and would be informed by the committee of the reasons for his detention. The word 'reasonable' connotes only that the Home Secretary must not act lightly or arbitrarily.[14] It would be wrong to place the Home Secretary in the dilemma either

---

9   At 226.
10   At 245.
11   At 220.
12   Per Lord Maugham at 220 ff.
13   Per Lord Macmillan at 251 ff.
14   Per Lord Wright at 267 ff.

of making information public which might imperil security, or of withholding the information and risking the release of a dangerous person: to hold proceedings in camera would not reduce the risks.[15]

All these objections to the simple view advanced by Lord Atkin were epitomised by a quotation from *R v Halliday*, a First War case where the issue was whether comparable Regulations were within the powers delegated by the Defence of the Realm Act: 'It seems obvious that no tribunal for investigating the question whether circumstances of suspicion exist warranting some restraint can be imagined less appropriate than a court of law'.[16]

In the most famous passage in the case Lord Atkin dismissed as sophistry the meaning contended for by the majority and their reasons. As to *Halliday's Case* he simply said: 'What that case has to do with the present I cannot see. No one doubts that the Emergency Powers (Defence Act) 1939 empowers His Majesty in Council to vest any minister with unlimited powers over the person and property of the subject. The only question is whether in this regulation His Majesty has done so'.[17]

Lord Atkin's own speech is so well-known that it would be superfluous to mark its originality and power. It has been pointed out that this speech, delivered within three years of his death and at the age of 74, illustrates how radical and adventurous Atkin had become in his later years. But it should not occasion surprise that any man who retains his mental acuity, and who has developed a mastery in his field and a confidence in his style, as Atkin pre-eminently had and did, should at the end of his career become more rather than less innovative. The world of the creative arts has many examples of this phenomenon.

The form of Atkin's speech was this. He first stated the question: what was the meaning of this Regulation, and diverting only to point out that its meaning had never been in question until a few months earlier, he then asserted 'the plain and natural meaning of the words'. Next he showed that this meaning 'has been accepted in innumerable legal decisions for many generations'. He took examples from the common law power of arrest, and corresponding statutory powers, from the action for malicious prosecution, and from such diverse sources as the law relating to the age of consent for sexual intercourse and the Directors' Liability Act. The weight of examples was and was intended to be crushing.

He then subjected the Defence Regulations themselves to analysis, contrasting those cases where it was intended to grant a discretion whose exercise was unchallengeable ('If it appears to the Secretary of State that . . .'; 'If the Secretary of State is satisfied that . . .') with

15   Per Lord Romer at 278 ff.
16   [1917] AC 260 at 269.
17   At 239.

those where the words 'having reasonable cause to believe' import an objective test and a justiciable issue. He gave seventeen examples of the former and twenty-three of the latter, the list in each case being exhaustive. There is nothing in the other speeches in the case which bears comparison with the industry of marshalling this material and the force with which it was deployed.

Having fully developed his own case, Atkin then attacked the arguments of the majority for the 'hitherto unheard of "subjective" construction'. He remarked that the wording of the Regulation had been different in its original form, and had read: 'The Secretary of State if satisfied . . .', but that that wording had been withdrawn and published in November 1939 in its new 'reasonable cause' form. 'What is certain', he said, 'is that the legislators intentionally introduced the well known safeguard by the changed words'. (It will be necessary to return to this point to see whether Atkin was right.) He then pointed out that the Home Secretary had been accustomed to undertake to prove by affidavit the reasonable cause for his belief, and since his speech dealt with *Greene's Case* as well as that of *Liversidge*, he agreed that the burden had in that case been discharged. He dealt also with the arguments for protecting the confidentiality of information about suspected persons, and the powers and responsibilities of the advisory committee.

Finally, he restated his theme, the plain meaning of the words, in three paragraphs which have become famous as literature.

'I view with apprehension the attitude of judges who on a mere question of construction when face to face with claims involving the liberty of the subject show themselves more executive minded than the executive. Their function is to give words their natural meaning, not, perhaps, in war time leaning towards liberty, but following the dictum of Pollock C.B. in *Bowditch v Balchin*, cited with approval by my noble and learned friend Lord Wright in *Barnard v Gorman*: "In a case in which the liberty of the subject is concerned, we cannot go beyond the natural construction of the statute". In this country, amid the clash of arms, the laws are not silent. They may be changed, but they speak the same language in war as in peace. It has always been one of the pillars of freedom, one of the principles of liberty for which on recent authority we are now fighting, that the judges are no respecters of persons and stand between the subject and any attempted encroachments on his liberty by the executive, alert to see that any coercive action is justified in law. In this case I have listened to arguments which might have been addressed acceptably to the Court of King's Bench in the time of Charles I.

I protest, even if I do it alone, against a strained construction put on words with the effect of giving an uncontrolled power of imprisonment to the minister. To recapitulate: The words have only one meaning. They are used with that meaning in statements of the common law and in statutes. They have never been used in the same sense now imputed to them. They are used in Defence Regulations in the natural meaning, and, when it is intended to express the meaning now imputed to them, different and apt words are used in the regulations generally and in this regulation in particular. Even if it were relevant, which it is not, there is no absurdity or no such degree of public mischief as would lead to a non-natural construction.

I know of only one authority which might justify the suggested method of construction: "When I use a word," Humpty Dumpty said in a rather scornful tone, "it means just what I choose it to mean, neither more nor less". "The question is", said Alice, "whether you can make words mean so many different things". "The question is," said Humpty Dumpty, "which is to be master — that's all". (Through the Looking Glass, c. vi.) After all this long discussion the question is whether the words "If a man has" can mean "If a man thinks he has". I am of opinion that they cannot, and that the case should be decided accordingly.'[18]

This passage has been described as 'passionate, almost wild, rhetoric' and to have resulted from some sort of explosion in Lord Atkin's mind.[19] It is beyond doubt that his belief in justice and individual liberty was passionate, and many of his judgments attest this. But the suggestion that he was under the sway of uncontrolled emotion seems quite unjustified. Atkin was capable of feeling, and demonstrating, contempt for the poverty or intellectual dishonesty of arguments to which his own view was opposed. On such occasions, as on this, he thought that 'a dose of ridicule' was apt. Moreover, he was aware that he was hitting unusually hard, for he wrote to his daughter Gwen on 2 November: 'I am giving off my dissenting judgment in the Home Secretary Cases tomorrow: and haven't spared the others. I hope that I shall be on speaking terms afterwards'.

The quotation from *Alice*, a favourite source of Atkin's,[20] provoked a private correspondence with Simon, the Lord Chancellor, with whom Atkin's relations were always less than easy. Simon had decided that he was precluded from presiding at the hearing of the appeal, and had asked Maugham to take his place. On the Friday before Monday, 3 November, when the speeches were to be read in the Chamber, Simon obtained advance copies from Proby, the Clerk to the Lords of Appeal. As a result, he wrote to Atkin the following personal note:

---

18   At 244.
19   R. F. V. Heuston 'Liversidge v. Anderson in Retrospect' 86 LQR 36.
20   See eg *Richards v Goskar* [1937] AC 304 at 312; *The Cap Palos* [1921] P 458 at 470.

31 Oct. 1941
House of Lords. S.W.1.

My Dear Atkin,

I *do* hope you will not resent it if I write this private and friendly note.

I asked Proby this morning to let me see, in confidence, the speeches prepared for the 18B judgments on Monday. They of course call for the closest study and I have not had time for more than a glance.

But my eye catches your very amusing citation from Lewis Carroll. Do you really, on final reflection, think this is necessary? I fear that it may be regarded as wounding to your colleagues who take the view you satirize, and I feel sure you would not willingly seek to hold them up to ridicule. I am all in favour of enlivening judgments with literary allusion but I would venture (greatly daring I know) to ask you whether the paragraph should be retained. Of course it is entirely for you. But I have gained so much from occasional suggestions of yours (mostly, it is true, in cases when we have been sitting together) and I trust you will forgive this query. I at any rate feel that neither the dignity of the House, nor the collaboration of colleagues, nor the force of your reasoning would suffer from the omission.

Yours ever,
John Simon

Atkin replied the following day:

26 Roehampton Close,
S.W. 15.

1 Nov. 1941

My Dear Simon,

I thoroughly understand and appreciate your kind intentions in writing as you do, and I feel sure that you will understand if I write frankly in answer. The present cases as I see them do not merely involve questions of the liberty of the particular persons concerned but involve the duty of the courts to stand impartially between the subject and the executive. I feel strongly about the matter, and I am not dismayed that at present I stand alone.

I have the highest esteem for my colleagues. If I had not I could have used very different language to what I have used. I have not the slightest intent to ridicule them, nor I think does the passage you mention ridicule them. But I did mean to hit the proposed construction as hard as I could and to ridicule the method by which it is reached. I consider that I have destroyed it on every legal ground: and it seems to me fair to conclude with a dose of ridicule. I cannot think therefore that there are sufficient grounds for altering this prepared opinion.

I cannot think that the dignity of the House will suffer: if the House is injured at all it will be in its judicial capacity in missing the opportunity of upholding old traditions of justice: and in placing a strained and ultra-legal construction on words involving personal liberties.

All this will not I know interfere with our own relations.

With many thanks,

Always yours,
A.

The final note from Simon read:

3 Nov. 1941
House of Lords, S.W.1.

My Dear Atkin,

I am most grateful to you for taking my note as you do — I feared you might resent it and I wrote [not] only as an onlooker, but from a friendship which unites me to all my colleagues.

You say, and I readily believe it, that you have no intention of indicating the others: but that *is* the effect of your words. Indeed, you described it as a "dose of ridicule". Suppose I said "The view of my colleagues can only be compared to the dictum of the Mad Hatter"! I am far from saying that I might not have shared your view — but I *wish* you saw your way to omit the jibe. No answer of course.

Yours ever,
John Simon

Today's reader of that correspondence might conclude that Simon's attempt to edit Atkin's speech was deserving of disdain, but that would perhaps be less than fair. Simon's concern, as he said, was to uphold the dignity of the House; and he then had behind him an outstanding record of public service, albeit stained by his association with the policy of appeasement. Nonetheless, the personality which seems to come through the letters helps to show why he continued to bear such a weight of unpopularity.

Lord Simon was not the only judge who was disturbed by the force of Atkin's language. Lord Caldecote, the Lord Chief Justice, was upset by the reference to 'the attitude of judges who . . . show themselves more executive minded than the executive'. He wrote to Atkin on 6 November:

My dear Atkin,

It was rather a shock to me to read your criticism of judges who, you think, have taken the wrong line about Reg. 18B. I can well understand your opinion that a wrong construction has been put upon it, and the undeniable force of your arguments must command respect even from those who have taken a different view.

But what has shocked me has been to be told that when I am face to face with claims affecting the liberty of the subject I am more executive minded than the executive. That is to say that I am no different from the judges who in Stuart days did what the Executive wanted.

I have put myself forward as one of those whom you have criticized in this way, for I have given two judgments in which I came to the same conclusion, in effect, as the majority of the Lords sitting to hear *Liversidge's case*. But of course there are half a dozen others who come under the same condemnation, not counting Lord Justices.

I cannot believe you really meant to say what your language suggests. If you could correct the impression which your words have given, it would be an immense relief to all of us. This sentence from your speech has already been used and twisted by people who wholly misunderstand the nature of the question in *Liversidge's case*, in order to defame the judges.

I beg you won't think I write out of any concern for my own reputation. What I am concerned about is the effect upon the reputation of the Bench for impartiality already produced by your words. I am not appealing to you on grounds of friendship, though you know, I think, how warm towards you my feelings have always been for many kindnesses shown to me.

> Yours ever,
> Caldecote

To this plaintive letter Atkin returned a full and courteous explanation.

> 26 Roehampton Close,
> S.W.15.

> 8 November 1941

My dear Chief,

I am troubled to think that you should have been shocked by expressions of mine in the recent 18B judgment. I cannot think, however, that you have yet had an opportunity of seeing the whole judgment, which would I feel sure make the position plain. May I repeat the offending phrase: "I view with apprehension the attitude of judges who, on a mere question of construction, when face to face with claims involving the liberty of the subject show themselves more executive-minded than the executive". The next sentence begins: "Their function is to give words their natural meaning". The view elaborated just before was that the executive charged with maintaining the defence of the country had deliberately chosen words which in their natural and only meaning gave a safeguard to the subject (i.e., the objective cause), while those of the judges whose judgments were under review, and in particular my colleagues, were impressed with the idea that the interests of the country required that the safeguard should not be there and therefore adopted the non-natural construction (subjective cause). That is what I called and call being more executive-minded than the executive. As to the suggestion that the phrase means that the judges do what the executive wants, I do not think that on consideration you would adhere to that. It cannot and does not mean anything of the sort.

I am rather puzzled to find that you place yourself amongst those who have put the subjective construction on the words. I have in my judgment rather emphasized that the Divisional Court had throughout accepted the objective construction, though with their own views about onus, until they became bound by the Court of Appeal. And I referred to the fact that in *Ex p Lees* counsel for the Home Secretary had accepted the onus. Consideration of the full judgment therefore will reveal:

1. There is no criticism of judges generally but only of those who have adopted this unnatural construction.

2. That there is no imputation of subservience to the Executive.

I would not normally seek to explain any judgment of my own once delivered, but as your letter shows that you are hurt and my own personal feelings towards you are charged with respect and admiration, I have felt bound to write as fully as I could. Make whatever use you please of this letter.

Always yours,
A.

Caldecote replied betraying some relief.

House of Lords,
S.W.1.

10 November 1941

My dear Atkin,

Thank you very much for your letter. I will show it, as you give me permission, to Humphreys who has sat with me in some of these cases and to one or two others for their private perusal. I hope no more will be heard of the comments which I felt sure were based on a misunderstanding of your meaning.

Thank you once more for yet another proof of your kindness to me.

Yours ever,
Caldecote

The speeches were read on Monday, 3 November 1941 in the Lord's temporary Chamber. As he afterwards explained to the House, through mischance Lord Maugham did not receive notice and so could not be there. The scene is recalled by Lord Atkin's daughter, Mrs Robson:

'My father asked me if I would like to come to the House of Lords to hear him deliver his judgment and have lunch with him at the House of Lords afterwards. I sat in a box just above them (Peeresses or Distinguished Strangers?). Macmillan read Maugham's judgment, and nobody seemed to be paying any attention i.e. Counsel might have been asleep or dead. My father began to read his judgment and still nobody seemed to be paying much attention, but suddenly I saw Valentine Holmes sit up and begin to smile and there was a stir from everyone. The whole place became alive.

My father took me with him to the Dining Room and we sat at a table together. Wright, I know, passed us by without a word — as he was a very old friend and a visitor to our house, this was strange but I think perhaps my father knew he was going to be unpopular.

Going home in the Underground that evening, I saw other people's papers with large headlines "Judge likens court to Star Chamber".'

The next morning, 4 November, the Press gave full coverage to the decision, *The Times* and the *Daily Telegraph* publishing temperately worded leading articles supporting the need for the Regulation and the majority view of its meaning. Although the profession knew that with Lord Atkin's strong dissent, the decision must sharply divide opinion, no one could have been prepared for what occurred on Thursday, 6 November, when a letter from Lord Maugham appeared in *The Times* under the heading 'War and Habeas Corpus'.

Sir — Those who took part in the decision of the House of Lords in the case of Liversidge v. Anderson could wish for no better statement of the reasons which guided the House, in affirming the views of so many eminent Judges, than is to be found in your leading article of 4 November, but there is one thing which I would like to add.

Lord Atkin, in his dissentient speech, stated that he had listened 'to arguments which might have been addressed acceptably to the Court of King's Bench in the time of Charles I'. Counsel, according to the traditions of the Bar, cannot reply even to so grave an animadversion as this. I think it only fair to the Attorney-General and Mr. Valentine Holmes, who appeared for the respondents, to say that I presided at the hearing and listened to every word of their arguments, and that I did not hear from them, or anyone else, anything which could justify such a remark.

Yours truly,
Maugham

Atkin's own view was that Maugham must have been unbalanced to publish such a letter. To his daughter Nancy he wrote:

'I suppose you saw Maugham's letter in the Times today. I think he
must be suffering from nervous strain. It is of course quite
unprecedented and quite unpardonable for one judge to attack
another's judgment in the Press, and nothing will induce me to
reply.'

[The letter went on — characteristically — to give details of a
remarkable bridge hand which he had held a few evenings before.]

One such attempted inducement came immediately in the form
of a telegram from Atkin's Inn: 'Grays Inn prays your Lordship to
answer Lord Maugham's letter in Times Stop You are nobly and
incontestably in the right Stop'.

Feelings were running high but Atkin preserved complete silence.
Maugham's letter however met with universal disapproval in the
Press. The *Daily Telegraph* had a leading article on 7 November
headed 'A Judge's Lapse'. It was the more impressive because the
paper had welcomed the view of the majority and disagreed with the
dissent: 'The rebuke to Lord Atkin was in fact superfluous; but even
if the complaint had been never so well justified that could not have
excused the method chosen by Lord Maugham to ventilate it'.

Reynolds News made the same point in more homely language:
'. . . every schoolboy knows that a barrister is no more associated
personally with his brief than a barber with his customer's head'.

Lord Davies put down a question in the House of Lords for
Wednesday, 19 November, asking the Government 'whether they
considered it to be in accordance with the high traditions of the
judiciary and in the public interest that Law Lords should criticize
each other through the medium of a newspaper'. Maugham had
written to Atkin the previous day in terms which could only have
made matters worse:

Private   House of Lords Library
                                        Tuesday

My Dear Atkin,

Lord Davies has put down for tomorrow the 19 a starred
question inviting the Lord Chancellor to reprove me for my
(celebrated) letter to the 'Times'. This may and probably will elicit
an explanation from me. I shall only wish to explain why my
remarks were not made in the House, and why I thought it
necessary to write to the 'Times'.

And I shall end by holding out an olive branch.

I rather think you will wish to be present.

Yours sincerely
Maugham

Atkin replied:

> 6 Roehampton Close
> S.W.15
>
> 20 Nov. 1941

My Dear Maugham,

Thank you for letting me know of the question and your proposed statement yesterday. As a matter of fact your letter only reached me in the afternoon but I should not have been present for I had not and have not any intention publicly to discuss any judgment once it has been delivered.

With best wishes

> Sincerely yours,
> A.

When Lord Davies asked his question, the Lord Chancellor, Simon, not unnaturally disavowed responsibility on the part of the Government for anything judges might say or write, and Lord Maugham then made his personal statement.

'My Lords, arising out of that question, perhaps your Lordships will kindly allow me to explain my position in the matter. In the first place, I should like to point out that I am no longer a Lord of Appeal in Ordinary; I resigned that position last July on grounds of health, and I no longer have the honour to serve His Majesty in any capacity. I sit only, as I did on the Liversidge and the Greene Appeals, when requested to do so by the Lord Chancellor, as a Peer who has held high judicial office. Accordingly, in my view, the Lord Chancellor, apart from the constitutional matter which he has so plainly pointed out, has no more right to reprove me in respect of what I did than he would have to reprove the noble Lord who put down this question if the Lord Chancellor came to the conclusion that it was tendentious and unfair. The only way that I can see that the Lord Chancellor could in any way indicate disapproval of my conduct in the matter would be by declining in the future to ask me to sit on any Appeal here or in the Privy Council, and I will only say that if he thinks fit to take that course I can assure him that I shall in no way complain.

My feeling about the matter is this. I shall not easily forget the kindness that was shown to me by many members of this House when I first appeared here, nor the most generous phrases of congratulation which were addressed to me as to what was described as my patience and courtesy in connection with the Coal Bill, a Bill which was most obnoxious to many of your Lordships in this House. The result is that I do not want, if I may so express it, to spoil my copybook here and I ask your Lordships to listen to me for a few minutes while I explain the circumstances in which my letter was written. In the Liversidge and Greene cases we reserved our judgments. As your Lordships know, in such cases each Lord's speech is printed and circulated, and I was not sitting after the arguments in those Appeals were disposed of and was therefore not coming here day after day. The printed judgments, all of which were written with much care, came in slowly and Lord Atkin's judgment, as it happened, was the last to reach me and it did reach me just at the moment when I was going to the country for a weekend. There were some passages in Lord Atkin's judgment which I wished to discuss with my colleagues, Lord Wright, Lord Macmillan and Lord Romer.

By some mischance the written notice that the judgments would be delivered on Monday, 3 November, did not reach me at all. I heard of the fact in the country on the Sunday afternoon by telephone and too late for me to reach here on the Monday, where my judgment could be and was, in fact, read by Lord Macmillan. And it was thus too late to make any protest about what I took to be an offensive remark in reference to the Attorney-General and his eminent junior, Mr Valentine Holmes, a remark which, as it seemed to me, might cause them pain and perhaps professional injury. It was not likely that the Court — the Court in the House of Lords — would ever be constituted again with Lord Atkin and myself and my other three colleagues, and my instinct was to prevent what I conceived to be an injustice. If one of five Lords sitting here attacks the conduct of Counsel it usually falls to the presiding Peer to protect them. I did not by my letter attempt to criticize my colleague, Lord Atkin, or his statements in other respects, though I confess to my doubts as to the justice of some of his observations. Nor, indeed, did I seek to do anything at all beyond saying that I had heard nothing at the hearing which in my view justified the suggestion that the arguments of Counsel, or some of those arguments, resembled those which State hirelings used to address to removable Judges in the reign of Charles I.

The noble Lord, Lord Davies, thinks that I have lost dignity. I was not thinking about dignity; for I think that when it is one's duty to protect people who are absent or Counsel who cannot protect themselves, a man should do what he thinks is right, whether persons are likely to attack him for so doing, or his method of doing it, or not. Apart from the single question of fact, I was not criticising my colleague, Lord Atkin, at all. He was entitled to his legal views as my other colleagues and I are entitled to ours. Lord Atkin and I have sometimes differed before in judgments, but I should like to say that, speaking for myself, I have never differed from him without much hesitation. All I want to explain to your Lordships is that it seemed to me that the unusual course of writing my letter to *The Times* was the only course open to me after the judgments had been delivered if I wanted to defend Counsel. I have never been one of those lawyers who think they are always right. I may have misunderstood Lord Atkin's meaning. Moreover, "Live and let live" is a pretty good maxim, even in times of war.

The sentence is this: "In this case" — says Lord Atkin — "I have listened to arguments which might have been addressed acceptably to the Court of King's Bench in the time of Charles I."

Of course, it is perfectly clear that no question of the Prerogative of the King or of the power of Parliament or of the Government was in issue on the two Appeals. It was simply a legal question of the true construction of an Order in Council, which could at any time be amended, made under the authority of an Act of Parliament. Lord Atkin's sentence was clearly not written in praise of Counsel, but it may not have been intended to bear the unpleasant signification which I and others thought the words might bear. If Lord Atkin should say or inform me or others that he did not intend to comment adversely on the conduct of Counsel in the matter, I will at once express my regret that I misunderstood him and that I wrote my letter to *The Times*. I thank your Lordships for your courtesy in listening to that explanation.'[21]

Looking back on the entire episode, Lord Maugham's conduct can only be regretted and can only have marshalled support for Lord Atkin. The personal statement remains, as it must then have seemed, both sanctimonious and unconvincing. The last few sentences constituted the 'olive branch' with which Maugham had promised he would end. It was not accepted, and no other Peer thought it appropriate to speak. The House passed on to another topic immediately.

The last parliamentary event in the history of the case came on 26 November, during the debate in the House of Commons on the Address, when Sir Irving Albery moved to add to the Question an expression of regret that 'in view of the recent dissenting judgment given in another place by Lord Atkin', there was no proposal in the Gracious Speech to modify the Defence Regulations so as to provide that detention beyond a specified period should be subject to a right of appeal to an independent tribunal.[22] Far from interesting himself in the debate, Atkin had written to his daughter Daisy two days earlier, saying that he was going to Aberdovey and adding:

'I shall be glad to be away from 18B for a while, especially as there is going to be a debate in the House, though it seems to be on the question whether the Home Secretary should have discretionary powers or not — which has nothing to do with our case in the Lords which was whether the existing regulations gave them to him. As to that I have never been able to see the other point of view . . .'

Much of the debate was concerned with the circumstances in which the wording of Regulation 18B came to be altered in 1939, and it resulted in a victory for the Government. Herbert Morrison, by then Home Secretary, after demonstrating that his own period of administering Regulation 18B had been a period of release rather than detention, challenged those who had moved the amendment to divide the House. Amid scenes of some excitement Sir Irving Albery and his seconder Sir Archibald Southby declined the challenge and Morrison was cheered from the Chamber.

21   121 HL Official Report cols 68-71.
22   376 HC Official Report col 776.

Those who were opposed to the majority view placed in the van of their attack the fact that in November 1939 Regulation 18B had been withdrawn in deference to political pressure, and reissued in a revised form. The original Regulation had contained the words, 'The Secretary of State, if satisfied etc';[23] the revised form ran 'If the Secretary of State has reasonable cause to believe . . .'[24]

Of this alteration, Atkin himself said:

> 'It is not competent to us to investigate what political reasons necessitated this change, but it is at least probable that it was made because objection had been taken to the arbitrary power and it was seen that Parliament might intervene. What is certain is that the legislators intentionally introduced the well-known safeguard by the changed form of words.'[25]

And in a letter to *The Times* a few days after the decision, Mr Gerald Gardiner, then a junior member of the Bar, put the mordant question: 'What is one to think of an Executive whose law officers now argue that the amended regulation means, and must have been intended to mean, precisely the same as the Regulation which was withdrawn?'[26]

---

23   SR & O 1939/978.
24   SR & O 1939/1681.
25   At 237.
26   Lord Gardiner's letter read in full:
   Sir, — The original Regulation 18B conferred on the Home Secretary an absolute discretion to detain persons if he was "satisfied" of certain things. On October 31, 1939, upon a motion in the House of Commons to annul the regulations, grave dissatisfaction with this regulation was expressed in the House on the ground that the regulation left the liberty of the subject to the sole discretion of the Home Secretary. The Government thereupon withdrew the regulations and agreed to amend them to meet this and other objections, and, on November 23, 1939, the amended regulations were made, the new Regulation 18B providing that the Home Secretary could only detain if he "has reasonable cause to believe" those things of which previously he had only to be "satisfied". What is one to think of an Executive whose law officers now argue that the amended regulation means, and must have been intended to mean, precisely the same as the regulation which was withdrawn?
   It may be presumptuous of an ordinary lawyer to express a view upon the decision of the House of Lords, but as so distinguished a lawyer as Lord Maugham has thought your columns an appropriate place in which to comment upon part of the speech of another member of the tribunal, it may be permissible for a humble member of the Bar to follow his example and to say that in places where lawyers meet the view being yesterday expressed by lawyers of all shades of opinion was one of admiration for, and gratitude to, Lord Atkin for his dissenting speech, the contents of which appear to some ordinary lawyers to be unanswerable.
   Yours truly,
   Gerald Gardiner
   3 Hare Court, Temple, E.C.4., Nov. 6.
   Lord Gardiner kindly contributed his personal recollection: 'I was told afterwards that the members of the Bench of my Inn had considered disciplining me for writing the letter, but decided not to, perhaps on the basis that if an ex-Lord Chancellor writes a silly letter to "the Times" he might expect a silly reply'. Lord Gardiner's conclusion (before the decision in *Rossminster* — above) was: 'I think that history has taken the view that in Liversidge v. Anderson the majority were wrong and Lord Atkin right'.

But the circumstances surrounding the change of wording,[27] as far as they can now be discovered, do not reveal any clear intention at all on the part of the 'legislators', nor any cynicism on the part of those arguing the Crown's case. Lord Maugham was nearer the truth when he said that 'Orders in Council making regulations pursuant to an Act of Parliament do not in general receive the same attention and scrutiny as statutes'.[28]

On 31 October 1939, Mr Dingle Foot had moved the annulment of the Defence Regulations, and they had been subjected to heavy and sustained criticism in the House of Commons. Sir John Anderson, the Home Secretary, completely failed to satisfy the critics and lost control of the House. The Government was in danger of defeat and the Lord Privy Seal, Sir Samuel Hoare, was forced to intervene and offer all-party consultations.[29] An informal conference was then arranged and held on 8 November. The Home Office was represented by the Home Secretary, Sir John Anderson, the Parliamentary Under-Secretary, Captain Osbert Peake, the First Parliamentary Counsel, Sir Granville Ram, the Permanent Under-Secretary, Sir Alexander Maxwell, the Secretary to the Home Policy Committee of the War Cabinet, Sir Ernest Holderness, and Anderson's Principal Private Secretary, Mr Norman Brook.

The Conservative Party was represented by Mr H. Holdsworth, Mr K. W. Pickthorn and Commander Sir Archibald Southby; the Labour Party by Sir William Jowitt and the Rt Hon W. Wedgwood Benn; and the Liberal Party by Mr Dingle Foot and Mr Kingsley Griffith.

Brook's note of the meeting lists seven 'specific suggestions' for the amendment of 18B, but they do not include the change from 'the Secretary of State, if satisfied', to 'If the Secretary of State has reasonable cause to believe'. Significantly, one of the suggestions which was put forward was that a detainee ought to be provided with a statement of the grounds on which the order was made 'so that he may know what is the case which he has to meet in any objections which he may make to the Advisory Committee'.

On 13 November, the results of the informal conference, as summarised in Brook's note, were discussed by the War Legislation

---

27 I am indebted to Professor R. F. V. Heuston for drawing to my attention the Home Office papers mentioned in this section and to Mr N. C. Cairncross of the Home Office for making them available to me. Professor Heuston has contributed a full note on the subject in 87 LQR 161: 'Liversidge v. Anderson: Two Footnotes: Footnote 1: The Amendment of 18B'.

28 At 223.

29 352 HC Offical Report cols 1829-1902. During the debate, Herbert Morrison, then in opposition, but who was later as Home Secretary to defend the revised regulations, said (col 1846): 'I am not going to use the argument usually put forward as a matter of courtesy that we do not believe the present Minister would be wicked but that we are afraid his successors might be. I think that any Minister is capable of being wicked when he has a body of regulations like this to administer'.

Sub-Committee of the War Cabinet. Again, nothing is reported as having been said about the change of wording in the Regulation which assumed such importance in *Liversidge's Case.*

Meanwhile, on 11 November, Maxwell had, at the Home Secretary's request, asked the Attorney-General whether there would be any chance of a challenge in the courts to an order which had been made by the Secretary of State in good faith. The Attorney-General (Somervell) replied on 14 November: 'In general the order of the Secretary of State would be conclusive ... Short of some proved fraudulent misuse of power the Court could not look behind the Home Secretary's order'.

In a note of 21 November Maxwell records that he and Sir Granville Ram (who was present with Maxwell at the informal conference on 8 November and who was responsible for drafting both the original and revised forms of 18B) had a telephone conversation with Somervell, in which Somervell confirmed the opinion he had given on the 14th, 'whatever words are used in this Regulation, whether they be "reasonable cause to believe", or "it appears to the Secretary of State" or "the Secretary of State is reasonably satisfied"'. Maxwell's note continues: 'The onus will certainly not be on the Home Secretary to show that his action was reasonable'.

These events suggest anxiety on the part of the Home Office to ensure that an Order could not be challenged in the Courts. It may be that this anxiety stemmed from something which was said at the informal conference on 8 November, though Brook's note is silent on the subject. But Somervell's view that it made no difference what form of wording was used, though itself open to doubt, destroys any charge of cynicism on his part in advancing the Crown's case in *Liversidge's case.*

Nothing else relevant is recorded until the Regulations were reissued with the revised wording: 'If the Secretary of State has reasonable cause to believe ...'

Immediately after the decision was given by the House of Lords in *Liversidge v Anderson* Sir Alexander Maxwell attempted to discover post mortem how it had come about that the wording of Regulation 18B had been changed, and why. As Professor Heuston has said, 'a surprising degree of confusion was revealed'.[30] Ram wrote to Maxwell on 14 November 1941 and gave a long circumstantial account of the informal conference of 8 November 1939. He said that Dingle Foot 'had pressed for the form of words which was always so dear to him "if ... has reasonable cause to believe ..." I whispered to the Home Secretary, on whose right I was sitting, that this might be dangerous as throwing the Home Secretary's action open to challenge in the Courts'. Ram added that Jowitt and Foot denied

---

30　87 LQR 161.

that the words would have that effect, and that they were supported by Spens, 'which made it additionally difficult for the Home Secretary to resist the suggestion'.

Maxwell also asked for Brook's recollection, but his was much vaguer. He did however say, 'I do not believe that any of the Members consulted was left under the impression that changes were to be made in the wording of the Regulations which would have the effect of making the Home Secretary's decisions liable to review, on their merits, by the courts'.

In this recollection, Brook was unequivocally supported by Sir John Anderson in the debate in the House of Commons on 26 November 1941. Speaking of the informal conference Anderson said:

> 'If a request had been pressed during the informal discussions that the reference to the advisory committee should be replaced by a clear provision entitling persons detained under the regulations to bring their case to the courts for review on merits, I should have been bound to make it quite clear that that, in my view, was inconsistent with the requirements of the situation and the executive powers given to the Home Secretary.'[31]

Somervell spoke to the same effect and added in reference to the change in wording, 'That change was not made as a result of any pressure in the Debate or in the subsequent discussions'.[32]

Ram's conclusion was similar. But the difficulty about his apparently detailed recollection is that it was almost certainly wrong about one thing — Spens was not present on 8 November 1939.[33] Moreover, Brook told Maxwell that Sir John Anderson could not 'from his own recollection confirm the account given in Ram's letter', and the Attorney-General reported to Maxwell that Dingle Foot had denied having put forward the suggestion for the new words 'and was surprised when they appeared in a draft produced by the Home Office'.

Under further questioning by Maxwell, Ram conceded that his recollection of events two years before might have been fallible, and accepted that Maxwell's suggested reconstruction of those events might well have been right. This was that there had been some discussion on the possibility of using the phrase 'is reasonably satisfied', but that this was 'repellent to anyone with a sense of language' and that Ram himself had formulated the 'reasonable cause to believe' form of wording. No further degree of certainty is now possible.

The episode has been given in some detail for its intrinsic interest; but also because it demonstrates dramatically what dangers lie in

31   376 HC Official Report Col 790.
32   Ibid, col 807.
33   See Heuston 'Footnote One: The Amendment of 18B' op cit.

wait for courts which seek to look behind the wording of legislation and to discover the intention of the legislators, or — yet more elusive — what legislators think their wording means. Even such an accomplished administrator as Mr Norman Brook (later as Lord Normanbrook, Secretary to the Cabinet) could not be expected to produce a completely comprehensive note of what must have been a diffuse discussion on 8 November 1939.

Atkin received a flood of letters of support and encouragement for his dissenting speech. Some of these betrayed a lack of understanding that the case was simply about the meaning of language used in the Regulation. But many of the writers were distinguished public men and women on whom the implications of the decision were not lost.

Mr Justice Stable, who only a few months earlier had delivered a strong dissenting judgment on Regulation 18B to the effect that it was impossible for a court to decide whether the Home Secretary had 'reasonable cause' without seeing the evidence,[34] wrote immediately after the decision:

'It is a shock to me that the Supreme Appellate Court comes under the influence of war nerves, has decided that the Habeas Corpus Act has been repealed by a Regulation and that only by giving the words of the Regulation a meaning which they don't bear and which could have been very simply expressed if it had been intended.

I venture to think the decision of the House of Lords has reduced the stature of the Judiciary with consequences that the nation will one day bitterly regret. Bacon I think said the Judges were the Lions under the throne, but the House of Lords has reduced us to mice squeaking under a chair in the Home Office . . . '

From Atkin's cousin, Berta Ruck, the novelist, came a characteristically impulsive note:

Pomona, Aberdovey, Merioneth

My dear Cousin Dick,

Will you let me, too, send most sincere congratulations on your protest? We both read with fervent agreement and delight the reports in the *Times* and *Daily Express*. If the utter ignoring of our national rights proceeds to its *logical* conclusion we might as well be under *Hitler*: not one of us is safe.

What a godsend of witty aptings (if I may say so) was your *Alice* quotation: it was a flash of brilliant lightning across all these clouds of confusion and nonsense. Surely 'Lord Atkin's Dissent' will illuminate this page of English history.

You will forgive the gratuitousness of this, a trifle of honouring from the prophet's own country — it truly comes from my heart.

Your affectionate cousin,
Berta.

34   *R v Home Secretary, ex p Budd* [1941] 2 All ER 749 at 763.

Atkin's sister-in-law, Mary Hemmant, wrote more coolly but perceptively: 'You let your fellow judges down lightly when you described them as executive-minded. I am afraid politics is at the back of a lot of it ... I believe future generations will approve your dissenting judgment and condemn that of the majority ...'

Clement Davies described the dissent as 'brilliant masterly and historic'; Maurice Healy reported that when he had met Edward Cave 'he was "leaping" with joy that you should have said what you did, and how you did; and he said he had never read so cogent a piece of logic'; Hartley Shawcross wrote — 'Try as I could, I found your speech quite unanswerable'; the Dean of St Pauls (W. R. Matthews) sent 'a word of congratulation on your stand for the principles of the Common Law of England'; and Cyril Radcliffe who ten years later was to write the advice in the Privy Council in *Nakkunda Ali v Jayaratne*[35] which began the process of burying the majority view in *Liversidge's Case*, wrote:

> 'I only wanted to say how entirely I agreed with every line of your judgment and what a very valuable thing it was that you were there to deliver it — I know how widely the general public responded to the view you took, and I do privately hope that it is the one that will somehow prevail before things go much further.'

Dr C. K. Allen the author of *Law and Orders* which contains a forceful account of the administration of Regulation 18B, and who was always a vehement champion of the individual against the encroachments of executive power, wrote:

> Rhodes House
> Oxford
> 5. xi. 41.

Dear Lord Atkin,

> I expect that this is a very improper letter to be written even by a non-practising member of the Bar, but I cannot refrain from saying that it will be remembered as not the least distinction in your great judicial work that you alone among the Judges have raised your voice against a gross abuse of power. Such cries in the wilderness have strong and long echoes. There is no real answer to the simple point of language on which you took your stand.
>
> This whole business is another warning against bureaucratic 'discretion'. When the facts are known, it will be realized that this terrible power has been used neither wisely nor justly, and that thumping lies have been told about it in Parliament. You were not concerned with that, but what you have said will not be without its effect.

> Yours sincerely,
> C. K. Allen

35   [1951] AC 66.

The pithiest phrase of all came from the Warden of Merton: 'I quite understand the difficulty of Home Secretaries but liberty is more important'.

Academic commentators were divided. Sir William Holdsworth and Professor Goodhart supported the majority view, and the latter engaged in a joust with Dr C. K. Allen in the pages of the *Law Quarterly Review*.[36] Their spirited exchanges deserve to be read in full, as much for their style as for their content. But whatever their views, many critics felt that Lord Atkin had used extravagant language in his peroration. The editor of the *Law Journal* for example concluded that 'it is difficult to answer the cogent reasoning of the dissentient Law Lord'; but 'it is a pity that Lord Atkin saw fit to add to his forcible judgment two matters which were not necessary to his reasoning and therefore added nothing to its strength'.[37] And when Atkin's old friend Professor Gutteridge came to write his obituary notice he gave his opinion that Atkin had expressed himself 'with a freedom which was perhaps unwarranted in the circumstances'.[38] Both writers had in mind the quotation from 'Alice' and the reference to arguments redolent of Charles I's Court of King's Bench.

The fate of Lord Simon's attempt to remove the passage from Lewis Carrol has already been noticed, and it is difficult to understand why satire of this sort should be thought too strong. The line between what is permissible and what is indecorous is no doubt drawn by convention. But ridicule of one's opponent's case is a commonplace: why not by quotation from a classic study of those aspects of human behaviour which cannot survive too close a scrutiny?

To say that the Crown's arguments might have been addressed acceptably to the Court of King's Bench in the time of Charles I was more serious if only because it was not intended humorously. The *Law Journal* thought it must necessarily give offence because it brought to mind 'the venal diligence and prostituted learning' of Noy, Charles I's Attorney-General.[39] Lord Atkin was almost certainly thinking of *Darnel's Case*[40] decided in the King's Bench in 1627 and in which Heath who was then Attorney-General appeared for the Crown. Noy himself was Counsel for Sir Walter Earl, one of the Five Knights who were imprisoned for not paying the King's forced loan. The judges refused to release them on a writ of Habeas Corpus because the return showed that they had been imprisoned *per speciale mandatum Regis*.

---

36   58 LQR.
37   *Law Journal* 14 November 1941.
38   60 LQR 340.
39   Above, note 37.
40   Reported in Howell's *State Trials* (1816) vol 3.

The arguments submitted for the Crown in *Darnel's Case* did indeed resemble those of Sir Donald Somervell, for Attorney-General Heath said:

> 'And, my Lord, unless the Return to you doth open the secrets of the commitment, your Lordship cannot judge whether the party ought by law to be remanded or delivered ... but if there be no cause expressed, this court hath always used to remand them; for it hath been used, and it is to be intended a matter of State, and that it is not ripe nor timely for it to appear.'[41]

Replying to the prisoners' argument that if the return were good they might be imprisoned for ever, Heath said that the security of the state was more important, and advised the judges to take the view that 'we are too wise, nay we are too foolish, in undertaking to examine matters of state, to which we are not born'.[42]

It was Somervell who included in his submissions the quotation from Lord Finlay's speech in *Halliday's Case* which so appealed to the majority: 'it seems obvious that no tribunal for investigating the question whether circumstances of suspicion exist warranting some restraint can be imagined less appropriate than a court of law'.[43]

Darnel's Case, which was concerned with the extent of the royal prerogative, was a wholly different case from that of *Liversidge*, which turned on the meaning of a Regulation admittedly within the power of the executive. But that consideration does not falsify the analogy which Lord Atkin drew. In both cases the Crown argued that a court of law was an unsuitable forum in which to debate matters peculiarly within the discretion of the executive, and it was the acceptance of that view by the majority which led Atkin to attack 'the attitude of judges who on a mere question of construction when face to face with claims involving the liberty of the subject show themselves more executive minded than the executive'.

It may seem gratuitous to offer comment on the merits of the decision in *Liversidge v Anderson*, now that the House of Lords has finally ruled in favour of Lord Atkin's dissenting view, describing the majority decision as 'beyond recall', and saying that its ghost 'need no longer haunt the law'.[44] But even had that not occurred Lord Atkin's speech would have made a more lasting impression on history than those of the majority. And in spite of it there is an abiding interest in the case which neither time nor later pronouncement can altogether erase.

The main ground on which Lord Atkin's speech has been criticised since he delivered it is that it elevated a mere question of language into a proposition of law. The meaning of a phrase in a statute, as

---

41   Howell's *State Trials* (1816) vol 3 at 37.
42   Ibid, at 45.
43   Above; see p 136
44   *IRC v Rossminster Ltd* [1980] 1 All ER 80 at 104.

in a contract, is, it is contended, so much a matter of first impression that an exhaustive analysis of what the phrase means in other contexts is largely beside the point. The task of ascertaining meaning should not be undertaken too literally or too rigidly, but rather more flexibly so as to make room for the true intention of the statute which is to be gathered from a reading of the whole. As Lord Wright put it, the language is to be scrutinised 'in the light of the circumstances and the general policy and object of the measure'.[45] Such an approach will show that decisions made on the meaning of similar phrases in other contexts are no more than pointers. Language in short is not immutable but takes colour from its surroundings.

This argument gains much force from the circumstance that Regulation 18B provided for review by an Advisory Committee whose duties included the giving to the detainee of information about the grounds for his detention, and offering him facilities for a hearing. What purpose could be served by such a Committee if review by the courts was intended all along? It must be admitted that Atkin's answer is less than convincing. He said, referring to the protection afforded by the Advisory Committee:

'These safeguards are nothing compared with those given to a man arrested by a constable who must at once be brought before a judicial tribunal who investigates the case in public. Yet the constable or anyone else empowered to arrest on reasonable cause is liable to an action if he has exceeded his authority'.[46]

This analogy seems not to be in point. The issue is: what was the supposed purpose of the Committee? But, although the argument based on the Advisory Committee is awkward (and Lord Wright afterwards commented that the strength of the Government's case lay largely in the point[47]), Lord Atkin's method of construing the Regulation must ultimately command support. Certainty is not to be sacrificed. If a phrase has a well understood and commonly acted upon meaning, that meaning should prevail. Flexible meanings are well enough if they do not do violence to language: otherwise they deserve the quotation from *Alice Though the Looking Glass*. The point was put tersely by Atkin himself in another case of statutory interpretation: 'In truth, however, when the meaning of words is plain, it is not the duty of the courts to busy themselves with supposed intentions'.[48]

Liversidge's Case and Lord Atkin's great dissenting speech have had a more potent effect on legal than political history. Most people of judgment reluctantly acknowledged that during war time the Home Secretary should have the extraordinary and repugnant power to

45   At 261.
46   At 243.
47   32 Proceedings of the British Academy 307.
48   *Swami v King-Emperor* [1939] 1 All ER 396 at 403.

detain without trial. Atkin himself did not oppose it. Even in the excitement which followed the House of Lords' decision, the amendment to the Loyal Address which was moved in the Commons by Sir Irving Albery asked no more than that a detained person should have after a specified period 'a right of appeal to an independent tribunal'. As has been seen, the Government had little difficulty in beating off even that limited attempt on the Home Secretary's discretion. At no time during the parliamentary debates did anyone suggest that as a matter of principle a detainee should have the right to have the grounds for his detention reviewed by the courts. And Lord Atkin again and again emphasised that the case was concerned only with whether the language of the Regulation did give a power of judicial review, not whether it should.

The legal consequences of the decision cast a longer shadow. If there were ever a danger of forgetting how essential is the judicial task of statutory interpretation where the legislature is omnipotent, *Liversidge's Case* should supply a reminder. It has been objected that underlying Lord Atkin's judgment is the assumption that there is no law other than that pronounced by the courts, and that it follows that acts which are purely executive or administrative, lying outside the law, must be arbitrary. Such an assumption, it is said, inhibits the growth of a body of administrative law. If Lord Atkin did indeed make any such assumption, its virtue has been made clear in the forty years which have passed since the decision. During that period the judges have developed and refined the principle of judicial review of administrative action, on which Professor Goodhart thought that Lord Atkin's speech had placed 'undue emphasis',[49] and it now stands as one of the few precarious bulwarks against increasing encroachment on individual liberty by the executive.

From the rule of law, stated the Petition of the House of Commons to the King of July 1610, 'hath grown the indubitable right of the people of this Kingdom not to be made subject to any punishment that shall extend to their lives, lands, bodies or goods, other than such as are ordained by the common laws of this land or the Statutes made by their common consent in Parliament'.

49   58 LQR 7.

Crime and Insanity,
Legal Education

It is so much a commonplace for English judges to undertake public enquiries into issues of the day that their appointment passes almost without comment. Among the many duties of this kind that Lord Atkin undertook during his long judicial career, two enquiries, concerned with crime and insanity and with legal education, were of special importance.[1] Each touched a subject in which he had an abiding interest.

Atkin's approach to the criminal law derived from his own moral standards, the severity of which is apparent from many of his decisions on civil liability.[2] His views on crime and punishment might nowadays be thought 'right-wing', but they have to be set in the context of their own period when punishment was widely regarded as a wholesome thing, rather than a disagreeable necessity or subordinate to the end of redeeming the wrongdoer. Nonetheless, Atkin was sensitive to the overall humanising trend of the criminal law as he made plain in discussing the offence of manslaughter in *Andrews v DPP*.[3] 'Expressions will be found', he said, 'which indicate that to cause death by any lack of due care will amount to manslaughter; but as manners softened and the law became more humane a narrower criterion appeared. After all, manslaughter is a felony, and was capital, and men shrank from attaching the serious consequences of a conviction for felony to results produced by mere inadvertence.'

At a Gray's Inn House dinner in 1938 he reminded his listeners that 'Lord Hale said somewhere in his "Golden Rules" that, while one's heart prompts one to pity, there is a pity due to the State'. For serious crimes, the outraged conscience of society demanded

---

1   The other appointments of significance were: Chairman of the Munitions Appeal Tribunal (1916); Chairman of the Naturalisation of Aliens Committee (1918); Chairman of the War Cabinet Committee on Women in Industry (1918), whose report was a monumental survey; Chairman of the Irish Deportees Compensation Tribunal (1924).
2   Eg *Re Thellusson* [1919] 2 KB 735 at 764, CA; *Rhodes v Macalister* 29 Com Cas 19, CA; *Solloway v McLoughlin* [1938] AC 247.
3   [1937] AC 576.

158

retributive justice, and he thought and said that no legal or legalistic objection should stand in the way of an international trial of the Nazi War criminals. His own marked copy of Bentham's works attests his approval of the view that penal law should countenance no morbid sentimentality concerning itself more with the welfare of the criminal than with consideration for the victim. The principle that the punishment should fit the crime was part of the Benthamite theory of utility. Implicit in this was the assumption that the commission of crime is a rational process, and that the prospective criminal would weigh the punishment against the fruits of the crime, and so be deterred.

It is not necessary to suppose that Atkin would have accepted literally all of Bentham's reasoning, but it seems clear that his views on punishment were essentially 'utilitarian'. As his daughter Mrs Robson points out, corporal punishment for a child's first offence would often have commended itself to him, 'but very great care and probation if the offender ever came before the Court again'.[4]

This view of the rational nature of crime is well illustrated by Atkin's view about crime and insanity, for when his Committee came to consider the McNaghten's Rules, it had to decide at what point a man who was mentally deranged should be relieved of the legal consequence of his act. The problem had long exercised the Medico-Legal Society of which Atkin was President for seven years between 1920 and 1927. One of the principal objectives of his Presidency was to promote a better understanding between the different points of view of the two professions on subjects where their interests touched each other — compensation of workmen for injury, nervous shock in tort, cruelty and other matrimonial offences, and insanity and criminal liability. He strongly advocated the study of medical jurisprudence for doctors, and the inclusion of the same subject as part of the training for the legal profession.[5]

Unfortunately, the gap between legal and medical points of view was widest on the subject of the criminal liability of the insane. Many doctors believed that lawyers did not understand the nature of insanity, which was an elusive topic not amenable to definition. As emerged from the evidence given to the Atkin Committee, some medical opinion considered that the issue to be put to the jury should simply be: was the accused insane at the time of the crime? That question could be decided on the basis of medical evidence and no further definition would be necessary.

The medical profession increasingly took the view, as the evidence of the British Medical Association to the Atkin Committee put it, that 'Unsoundness of mind is no longer regarded as in essence a disorder of the intellectual or cognitive faculties. The modern view

4 See p 24 above.
5 Transactions of the Medico-Legal Society 1921-2, XV p 8.

is that it is something much more profoundly related to the whole organism — a morbid change in the emotional and instinctive activities, with or without intellectual derangement'.

The predominant legal view was that the rules in *McNaghten's Case*, which had since 1843 formulated the law on the responsibility of those of unsound mind for criminal acts, was still the most reliable test. Essentially, the defence of insanity would succeed under the rules if it were established 'that the accused was labouring under such a defect of reason, from disease of the mind, as not to know the nature and quality of the act he was doing, or, if he did know it, that he did not know he was doing what was wrong'.

Public feeling, long troubled by this intractable problem, was brought to a high pitch in 1922 when Ronald True who had killed a prostitute with elaborate violence after having boasted that he would commit a murder, was convicted and sentenced to death. This was in spite of medical evidence that he was deranged and had acted under uncontrollable impulse, and a direction from the judge that the jury might bring in a special verdict of 'guilty but insane'[6] if they accepted that he had been 'deprived of the power of controlling his actions'. The Court of Criminal Appeal dismissed True's appeal and disapproved of the judge's direction, but True was reprieved by the Home Secretary on the ground of his mental state. Protest about the reprieve inside and outside the House of Commons led to the appointment by the Lord Chancellor (Birkenhead) of the Atkin Committee to consider whether any changes should be made to the law, practice and procedure in criminal trials in which a plea of insanity was raised.[7]

The Committee was composed exclusively of lawyers, with the exception of two representatives of the Home Office, and included the Attorney-General, the Solicitor-General and Sir Edward Marshall-Hall. The composition of the Committee, without a single doctor, supports the view that Birkenhead's aim was to preserve the status quo and to reaffirm the validity of the McNaghten test. The Committee received evidence from the Medico Psychological Association, who recommended simply that the jury should be directed to determine whether the accused was insane at the time of the crime, and if he were, whether his crime was unrelated to his mental disorder. The Committee rejected this proposal as based on a confusion between insanity and criminal irresponsibility. The passage of the Report ends with a characteristic and courteous epigram.

---

6   The Report criticised the illogical and contradictory verdict of 'guilty but insane' which had been prescribed by The Trial of Lunatics Act 1883, passed after an attempt on the Queen's life.

7   Cmd 2005, 1923.

'When once it is appreciated that the question is a legal question, and that the present law is that a person of unsound mind may be criminally responsible, the criticism based upon a supposed clash between legal and medical conceptions of insanity disappears. It is not that the law has ignorantly invaded the realm of medicine; but that medicine, with perfectly correct motives, enters the realm of law.'

The British Medical Association also submitted a report. They recommended the retention of the existing rules but with the addition of a further ground of defence that the accused was acting under an uncontrollable impulse. This the Committee accepted and adopted. Atkin himself was much impressed by the many cases of mothers seized with the impulse to do away with their babies,[8] and impressed also by the experience of the additional defence in Queensland and South Africa. He did not think that the additional defence of uncontrollable impulse was a big step, for he commented on the Report at a meeting of the Medico-Legal Society:

'In deference to medical opinion, as to which the Committee was entirely unanimous; they recommended one change — if it was a change — a very small change, but it was one which he was not sure was going to be received with universal favour by the legal profession . . . in view of the fact that it was accepted unanimously by the Committee, by the Medico-Legal Society, by the Prosecuting Counsel to the Treasury at the Central Criminal Court, and by others, he thought the public might feel satisfied that the proposal was not likely to result in the criminal law not being properly administered'.[9]

The doubt whether the profession would welcome the proposal was well-founded. Hewart, the Lord Chief Justice, described the idea as 'fantastic'.[10] Opposition was widespread and the Report had a bad press. Birkenhead had hoped for a conservative paper from the Committee and opinion was that the recommendation was radical. Kleptomaniacs, it was said, would escape conviction for shop-lifting, forgetting perhaps that it was unlikely that shoplifters would voluntarily accept detention during royal pleasure. The Government did not act, and a Private Members' Bill introduced by Lord Darling, failed.

Atkin's feeling that the proposed change was hardly a change at all was prompted not only by judicial directions to juries, as in True's case, suggesting that irresistible impulse was already a ground for a special verdict, but also, it seems, an increasing tendency of juries

8   See also Atkin's contribution to the debates on the Preservation of Infant Life Bill where he said it was very difficult to get juries to convict mothers who had killed their babies at the time of birth: 72 HL Official Report Col 271.
9   Transactions of the Medico-Legal Society, XVIII p 24.
10 *Kopsch* (1925) 19 Cr App R 50 at 51. Hewart said: 'It is the fantastic theory of uncontrollable impulse which, if it were to become part of our criminal law, would be merely subversive. It is not yet part of the criminal law and it is to be hoped that the time is far distant when it will be made so'.

to look at the mental condition of the accused more broadly than the McNaghten Rules would permit. Irresistible impulse was recommended again in 1953, but again no action was taken.

The Report on Insanity and Crime was a model of conciseness, extending only to seven pages on the issue of criminal responsibility. It illustrated well the clarity and decision of the author's mind. To him insanity was difficult to define and the medical view of it was in flux. But criminal responsibility was a different thing which must remain constant and readily understandable by a jury. This view was memorably put by Lord Devlin much later:

'So my conclusion in the end would be that I would not be prepared to alter the M'Naghten Rule. As it is a matter of theory, I think there is something logical — it may be astringently logical, but it is logical — in selecting as the test of responsibility to the law, reason and reason alone. It is reason which makes a man responsible to the law. It is reason which gives him sovereignty over animate and inanimate things. It is what distinguishes him from the animals, which emotional disorder does not; it is what makes him man; it is what makes him subject to the law. So it is fitting that nothing other than a defect of reason should give complete absolution.'[11]

The Report of the Atkin Committee demonstrated another quality in his thinking: a willingness to move forward if the ground was firm, to align the law more nearly with informed public opinion. The pure application of the McNaghten Rules no longer satisfied juries in all cases. Uncontrollable impulse could not be fitted into the scheme, and there was a growing number of instances where there was a refusal to convict men whose mental state had deprived them of the power to resist. Atkin thought he had proposed only a little step: Hewart thought it fantastic. But Atkin's instinct was surely right. History was not on the side of the unqualified logic of the McNaghten Rule and Lord Devlin. Public concern about the difficulty of defining insanity continued, and juries, it seems, more and more asked themselves simply whether or not the accused was mad. McNaghten eventually faded into disuse and was supplanted by the compromise solution, imported from Scotland, of diminished responsibility and reduced sentence.

The progress of legal education in England has had to contend with a long history of scepticism and complacency. Until the reforms of the nineteenth century there was little formal education and those entering the profession depended almost entirely for their training on the haphazard apprenticeships which the Bar and solicitors provided. Even now there is within the profession strong support for the view that in the training of a lawyer, the value of practical

11   Devlin *Changing Legal Objectives* (ed MacDonald, Toronto, 1963) p 85.

experience far outweighs anything which can be gained from formal education in legal principles.

Lord Atkin had a lifelong belief in the value of legal education, and in this and in the advancement of proposals for improvement, his was almost a solitary voice from the Bench. These beliefs derived from his consciousness of the permeating influence of law in society: 'almost the most powerful and the most pervasive force which influences the life of a citizen from its very beginning to its end', he described it, '. . . these rules of civic conduct enforced by the State are of the very essence of civilized society. They are not merely the framework of Society, but they supply the very force by which Society exists at all. Without law there can be no such thing as Society'.[12]

He deeply regretted that the ordinary man was inclined to look upon law as either a dishonest game or a piece of medieval magic.[13] The way of dispelling such notions was through legal education. He considered that everyone should have some knowledge of our legal system, and that law should be taught as a sixth form subject. 'I commend to your consideration as the eventual moral of my address' he said, in his Presidential speech to the Holdsworth Club, 'the question whether we cannot all do a little more towards making a knowledge of our English law and its administration part of the ordinary equipment of the good and efficient citizen.' Elsewhere he pointed out that it seemed inexcusable that law had ceased to play the part in higher education that it did in the days of Fortescue, and that Locke and Blackstone desired for it in their time.[14] With Sir William Beveridge, Atkin established a Chair of English Law at the London School of Economics. Part of the Professor's duties was to give an annual course of lectures on 'The Elements of English law' for laymen. Dr Edward Jenks who had previously been Director of Legal Studies of the Law Society was the first holder of the Chair, and in the preface to his *Book of English Law* which resulted from the lecture course, he paid Atkin a warm tribute, describing him as a joint author of the plan on which it was based.

Lord Atkin's conception of the place of law in University education was a modern one. He told an audience of law teachers that he would like to see it forming part of a degree in 'civics' which might include also history and economics. That he thought would be one of the most valuable courses that a man who is going to play a part in public life could possibly take.[15] It is worth remembering that this was said in 1932 when mixed degree courses were almost unknown

12 'Law and Civic Life', Presidential Address to The Holdsworth Club of Birmingham University, 9 May 1930.
13 'The Place of Law in University Education', Lecture at the London School of Economics, 5 October 1923.
14 Foreword to Jenks *The Book of English Law* (Murray, 1927).
15 'The Future Development of English Law' (1932) Journal of the Society of Public Teachers of Law 28 at 31.

and when it was widely held that the proper training for public life was a degree in classics.

His friend, Professor Gutteridge, once wrote to him quoting another University law teacher as saying that Atkin was 'the one person to whom one can unbosom oneself on this matter'. 'This matter' was one of the main obstacles to reform. Gutteridge described it (in 1932) as 'the almost complete lack of contact between the practitioner and the academic lawyer in England' which he attributed to the fact that the Universities were late in the field, and to an inferiority complex on the part of the teacher which was 'bad for the teaching of law and also inimical to the future of English law'. Atkin agreed: one thing which was doing harm, he thought, was 'the absence of public criticism by men who know: and the abundance of criticism by the ill-informed'. This was not necessarily flattering to law teachers — although Gutteridge himself was an honourable exception — since Atkin went on to say that practising barristers were excluded from any form of self-advertising, and judges were not permitted to write at all, leaving published comment as the exclusive province of teachers. He thought that 'It would help the position of teachers very much if some of them showed up at times as discriminating champions of the profession'. Nonetheless Atkin agreed with Gutteridge's main thesis that there was much more academics could do if the practitioners would only give encouragement.[16]

The opportunity to do something to improve co-operation between the Universities and the profession came in 1932 when Atkin was appointed by the Lord Chancellor (Sankey) as Chairman of a committee on Legal Education whose task was to consider 'the organisation of legal education in England with a view to (a) closer co-ordination between the work done by the Universities and the professional bodies and (b) further provision of advanced research in legal studies'.[17] The Committee included Beveridge, then Director of the London School of Economics, Harold Laski, who had been agitating for a review of legal education in this country, Gutteridge and Mr Gavin Simonds KC.

The Committee made two recommendations. In order to avoid overlapping in teaching and examinations, it proposed the setting up of a standing Advisory Committee consisting of members nominated by the Council of Legal Education and the Law Society, on the one hand, and by the Society of Public Teachers of Law on

16   See appendix 5 for text of letters.
17   Report of the Legal Education Committee: Cmd 4663, 1934. Laski, although signing the Report, submitted an addendum in which he pointed out with justice that there was no provision for practical training for barristers comparable with that for solicitors' articled clerks, and in arguing the case for an advanced research institute, he said, 'The public does not realise that, among the great professions in this country, the law stands alone in not having developed either systematic methods or definite institutions for the encouragement of research into its own subject-matter'.

the other. Secondly, it recommended the establishment of an 'Institute of Advanced Legal Studies' to promote research in all branches of the law, not least in comparative legal research, where 'we lag behind many Continental countries', and to act as a centre of study for those coming from overseas Dominions and Colonies.

As so often, the Government did nothing to implement its own Committee's proposals. Fifteen years later in 1947 a question in the House of Commons asked what action was proposed: the Attorney-General's answer exactly reflected the complacency of the Inns. The functions of the proposed committee, he said, were already being satisfactorily performed by the professional bodies who were 'in a position' to provide co-ordination with the Universities. Another Committee had been appointed (in 1938) to look into the question of a research institute, but its proceedings had been suspended. There were other, more urgent, demands on legislative time.[18] Eventually, the Institute of Advanced Legal Studies was established by the University of London in 1946 and an Advisory Committee on the lines proposed by Atkin and his colleagues was set up in 1972 following a similar recommendation of the Ormrod Committee.[19]

The proposals which the Atkin Committee made were neither comprehensive nor profound, and although the Report was on the whole well received, later criticisms were trenchant.[20] But it would be wrong to ignore the difficulties which indifference and inertia placed in the way of reform; and the Institute of Advanced Legal Studies serves as a memorial to the work of the Committee. The Report however did not fairly reflect Lord Atkin's fervent advocacy of legal education both within and outside the profession, because it inculcated clear and accurate thinking, because it was necessary for an understanding of the force which animated civilised society, and because the result of teaching law is to ascertain truth 'for the highest end, namely, justice'.[21]

18   437 HC Official Report cols 189–190.
19   Cmd 4595, 1971.
20   Particularly by Gower 'English Legal Training' (1950) 13 MLR 147.
21   'The Future Development of English Law' (1932) Journal of the Society of Public Teachers of Law 28 at 30.

Lord Atkin's Legacy

On 27 June 1944 tributes were paid to the memory of Lord Atkin in the Chamber of the House of Lords. The Lord Chancellor, Viscount Simon, said:

'Lord Atkin in point of service as a Judge, was the doyen of the Judiciary. He served as a Judge for no less than 31 years. To find any parallel one would have to go back, I think, to the eighteenth century, and remember that Lord Mansfield was Lord Chief Justice for 32 years ... Lord Atkin, I think, would be classed as what is called a "strong" Judge. He listened with courtesy, patience, and respect to the arguments as they were stated, but it must very seldom have happened that the arguments came to a conclusion without Lord Atkin having in substance made up his mind. I think that he relied less than many members of these two supreme tribunals do on the conference and discussion which takes place after the arguments are over. He was, therefore, a strong Judge, and his strength largely consisted in his conviction that English law is at bottom a sensible thing, and that, when he had grasped the facts and applied his great knowledge of the law to those facts, the conclusion would emerge.'

The Solicitor-General, Sir David Maxwell Fyfe, paid a different, and rarer, tribute.

'Among us he will be remembered as bringing to legal problems that rare gift, seen only once or twice in a legal generation, of constructive intuition, which operates after learning and analysis are exhausted. To the corporate life of the law he gave his kindness, energy and true understanding in many fields.'[1]

Atkin's strength as a judge, which Simon had selected as his leading characteristic, lay in his ability to come to a clear conclusion and adhere to it. He never once acknowledged in a judgment that his mind had fluctuated in the course of the case, and he himself said that he found the hearing part of a case more difficult than the determining. He was a decisive man with a compelling sense of right and wrong which he was able to carry over into judicial decision making generally, whether or not the issue had a moral content.

---

1 *The Times*, 28 June 1944.

Atkin rarely changed his mind on any question. An interesting example of this was his attitude to the value to be attached to a witness' demeanour. As a judge of first instance he had tried Ball and Elltoft for murder at the Liverpool Assizes in 1914, a notorious case which became known as 'the Sack Murder'. Ball's calm and untroubled manner, although guilty (as he afterwards confessed) and convicted, had deeply impressed Atkin. He twice made observations many years later in the Court of Appeal about the unsafe character of demeanour as a guide to truth, and on the second occasion, in an insurance case in which the underwriters alleged fraud, he referred to 'the Sack Murder': 'The lynx-eyed Judge who can discern the truthteller from the liar by looking at him', he said, 'is more often found in fiction or in appellate judgments than on the Bench'.[2]

Atkin saw issues in terms of clear and definite dividing lines. He exemplified this by his strong belief in the separation of powers between executive, legislature and judiciary. The history of the seventeenth century, which he thought of as the worst period of our history,[3] showed what could happen if judges truckled to the executive. That the maintenance of freedom depended on the rule of law administered by an independent Bench needed reiteration not only in *Liversidge v Anderson*, but also in the *Wiltshire United Dairies Case*,[4] where money was sought to be levied without parliamentary sanction, and in *Ford v Blurton*, where Atkin said 'Anyone who knows the history of our law knows that many of the liberties of the subject were originally established and are maintained by the verdicts of juries in civil cases. Many will think that at the present time [1922] the dangers of attack by powerful private organizations or by encroachments of the executive is not diminishing.'[5]

But it was as important, although not so well accepted, that the judges should not stray into the ground of the executive. For this reason Atkin said in *The Arantzazu Mendi*, 'The non-belligerent State which recognizes two Governments, one de jure and one de facto, will not allow them to transfer their quarrels to the area of the jurisdiction of its municipal Courts'.[6] And in *Secretary of State for*

---

2   An account of the Sack Murder Case is given in R. Storry Deans *Notable Trials: Difficult Cases* (Chapman & Hall, 1932). The two Court of Appeal cases are *Soc d'Avances Commerciales v Merchants Marine Insurance Co* (1924) 20 Ll L Rep 140 at 152 where Atkin said, 'I think that an ounce of intrinsic merit or demerit in the evidence, that is to say, the value of the comparison of evidence with known facts, is worth pounds of demeanour'; and *Lek v Matthews* (1926) 25 Ll L Rep 525 at 543 (the passage quoted in the text). Scrutton took a contrary view and attached importance to demeanour (at 535). In the House of Lords (29 Ll L Rep 141) neither Lord Sumner nor Lord Carson was much impressed by Atkin's observations. By 1935 Atkin seems to have modified his view somewhat: see *Powell v Streatham Manor* [1935] AC 243 at 254, although that case did not involve fraud or moral turpitude.

3   See *Wankie Colliery v CIR* [1921] 3 KB 344 at 365.

4   *A-G v Wiltshire United Dairies Ltd* (1921) 37 TLR 884, CA.

5   *Ford v Blurton* (1922) 38 TLR 801 at 805, CA.

6   [1939] AC 256 at 265.

India v Sardar Rustam Khan,[7] in giving the opinion of the Board of the Judicial Committee, Atkin declined Counsel's invitation to regard a treaty between the Khan of Kalat and the Government of India as ' "a commercial contract" intended only to effect a more convenient method of collecting revenue', and held that the exercise of powers under the treaty were acts of state for which the Government could not be impleaded.

In 1931, the Judicial Committee heard an application by a British Indian subject who contended that the Commissioner of Lands in Kenya had no power to impose conditions on the sale of plots of land, that only Europeans should bid, and that the purchasers should not permit Asiatics or Africans to live in the houses to be built on the plots except as domestic servants.

> 'It is desirable to point out', Atkin said, 'that the Courts are concerned only with the bare question of law — namely, the powers of the Commissioner under the Ordinance. Questions of policy, or, in other words, how the legal powers shall be exercised, are not matters for the legal tribunal, but have to be determined by the appropriate constitutional authority . . . If any restriction be allowed the question whether the restriction should be based on racial distinctions is obviously not one of law, but of policy.'[8]

It is tempting to say that the Board there missed an opportunity to uphold the dignity of the coloured races, but that would be to fall into anachronism. There was no race relations legislation in 1931, and no basis on which it could be said that the power of disposal was restricted. As Atkin said, 'there does not exist, and never has existed, any legal right of any particular member of the public to take part'. The only way in which the court could decide against the Commissioner was on the ground of policy. That the Board refused to do, for it would have meant invading the territory of the executive.

To Atkin's mind, there was an eqully clear line between the proper concerns of Church and state. In Wales, the position of the Church as an English state Church had led to its alienation and rejection, and he supported disestablishment because it would compulsorily set the Church free from the entanglements of the state. Again, when the Church was unable to come to terms with the reform of divorce law in 1937 because in its eyes the marriage bond was indissoluble, Atkin unhesitatingly took the part of reform. The tragedy of an unwanted marriage was for him more serious by far than the maintenance of doctrine and he supported A. P. Herbert's Bill with all the considerable force at his command. In his view, dogma had to give way to the individual conscience and the imperatives of human unhappiness. That view, with its implied restriction on the

---

7   [1941] AC 356.
8   *Commissioner for Local Government Lands v Kaderbhai* (1931) AC 652 at 654, 659.

preserve of the Church, led him into serious dispute with the Welsh Bishops, the nature of which is important for an understanding of Lord Atkin's beliefs. But it is not necessary to think that he would have agreed with Lord Melbourne that things had come to a pretty pass when religion is allowed to invade the sphere of private life. Such cynicism was no part of his thinking; but as the needs of society changed, the Church — as the law — had to avoid becoming stranded on the beaches of the past. It was not merely permissible, but necessary, if compassion required it, for the state to legislate in the field which had historically belonged to the Church.

In describing Atkin as a strong judge, Lord Simon had remarked that he relied little on the discussion between members of an appellate court after the completion of the hearing. He may have been hinting at the difficulty which some of Atkin's colleagues apparently felt in debating with him the determination of a case. It has already been noticed that Dunedin had described him as 'obstinate if he has taken a view and quite unpersuadable'.[9] Lord Dunedin was not alone in that opinion, and Lord Denning thought that Atkin was inclined to reach a conclusion early. He recollects a case in which he appeared as a silk in the House of Lords when Atkin was sitting. 'It was in the Chamber. Ld. Atkin was on one of the side benches. He had also read the papers beforehand — and I am afraid that he had often made up his mind beforehand — so the argument of Counsel did not influence him much. He seemed always concerned to get the others round to his way of thought.' Lord Radcliffe went so far as to write that Atkin (and Blanesburgh), although 'themselves the nicest of men, seemed positively to prefer that a case should go on for ever to the possibility of an argument of which they disapproved remaining on its legs'.[10] He would form a view, Lord Radcliffe said, 'and he was going to use whatever odds he possessed . . . to try to see that that succeeded'.[11]

So many witnesses, including Lord Simon in his tribute, have attested to Atkin's kindness and consideration during the hearing, and to the frugality of his questioning, that Lord Radcliffe's strictures seem hardly credible. But what happened after the hearing is another matter, and one upon which it is not now possible to be definite. Atkin certainly attached great importance to 'bringing his brothers round', and, if the rarity of his dissent in the House of Lords is a guide, seems to have had a large measure of success in doing so. He did not himself experience much difficulty in reaching a conclusion or, it appears, in maintaining it in face of the opposition of his fellow-judges. He could no doubt be formidable, in common with all great judges. This was especially so in the work of clearing away the debris

9 Heuston *Lives of the Lord Chancellors* p 481.
10 36 MLR 559 at 562: review of Blom-Cooper and Drewry *Final Appeal* (OUP, 1972).
11 Paterson *The Law Lords* (Macmillan, 1982) p 71.

of history, as in the *United Australia Case, Fibrosa* or *Richards v Goskar*.[12] Here be brought a sort of passion to the handling of precedent in order to achieve justice. He was profoundly impatient of that melancholy satisfaction which the more conservative judges experience in declining a common-sense or business-like solution, and he may have betrayed that impatience behind the scenes. For this reason, perhaps more than any other, he thought of the Chancery viewpoint as the antagonist of 'business'.

Strength was the judicial quality for which Lord Simon had commended the memory of Lord Atkin, and there is a profusion of his decisions which bear that out. First things first was a theme of his contribution to the law: sanctity of contract in *Bell v Lever Brothers*, certainty in the commercial code in *Re Wait*, the cutting down of unholy doctrine in *Radcliffe v Ribble* or *Caswell v Powell Duffryn*.[13]

Lord Simon was perceptive in linking Atkin's strength with the conviction that 'English law was at bottom a sensible thing'. The just solution was not an abstraction but something which could be tested against a plain man's idea of fairness. In the *Fibrosa Case*,[14] he described the conclusion that a man who has paid money and received nothing for it, should be able to recover his money, as an 'answer that I venture to think would occur to most people, whether laymen or lawyers'; and of debits made by a bank to its customer's account, he said, 'The ordinary man would, I think, say that so far from being paid, they are added to the ordinary indebtedness because they are not paid: and I can see no reason why the law should say anything different.'[15] Atkin constantly tested the law against the expectations of ordinary men and would not permit the two to diverge. *Donoghue v Stevenson* may have had a revolutionary effect on the law of tort, but the decision itself was no more than common fairness. 'I do not think so ill of our jurisprudence', Atkin said, 'as to suppose that its principles are so remote from the ordinary needs of civilized society and the ordinary claims it makes upon its members as to deny a legal remedy where there is so obviously a social wrong'.

It was sensible also to give legal sanction to a promise of marriage made after decree nisi but before it had become absolute. Indeed, Atkin's speech in *Fender v Mildmay*[16] is a sermon on the text that 'English law is at bottom a sensible thing'. And for similar reasons he was opposed to the idea that certain classes of document, as wills, should have their own technical rules remote from common sense. To his mind a will was a business document and judges should not permit precedents to 'constrain them to give a meaning to wills

12 [1941] AC 1; [1943] AC 32; [1937] AC 304.
13 [1932] AC 161; [1927] 1 Ch 606, CA; [1939] AC 215; [1940] AC 152.
14 *Fibrosa Spolka v Fairbairn Lawson* [1943] AC 32 at 50.
15 *Paton v IRC* [1938] AC 341 at 347.
16 [1938] AC 1.

which they know to be contrary to the testator's intention';[17] again, leases were a species of contract and he saw no reason why the doctrine of frustration should not apply to them as to all other contracts.[18]

In honouring Lord Atkin's memory, Sir David Maxwell-Fyffe chose another quality and called it 'constructive intuition', an elusive quality which he said operates only after learning and analysis are exhausted. He referred to the imaginative leap which enables the law to move forward and occupy new ground, and he might have added that in Atkin's cases what was achieved was done without damage to the existing fabric. For Atkin, conscious that without the force of precedent, justice would be at the caprice of the individual mind, had an invariable respect for decided cases. He often admitted with reluctance that he had no choice but to follow. In *Ford v Blurton*[19] he declined to distort the unpalatable words of the Administration of Justice Act, 1920 abrogating a litigant's right to a jury, and in the Court of Appeal in a case on whether a requisitioned ship was engaged in a 'warlike operation', he said in reference to an earlier decision, 'If that could be distinguished, it must be done by some other Court. It is very important to avoid finely-drawn distinctions which interfere with the effect and authority of decisions of the Court'.[20] Even in the court of final appeal, the authority of the House of Lords was paramount, and he said in *Rose v Ford*, of the rule that the law did not recognise the death of a person as giving rise in itself to a claim for damages: 'The reasons given, whether historical or otherwise, may seem unsatisfactory; but it is of little purpose in a legal decision to criticise them, for the rule has the authority of this House'.[21]

In *Donoghue v Stevenson*, by use of the learning and analysis to which the Solicitor-General referred, Atkin beat a path through the old authorities to the point at which 'constructive intuition' was free to operate. He and his colleagues of the majority created a new unifying tort whose importance came to overshadow all others, and marked out for a limitless future the principle on which courts could decide whether one man should be responsible to another for an act of carelessness. Many feared that the decision would bring after it an unmanageable flood of claims, but history has justified the intuitive judgment of Lords Atkin, Macmillan and Thankerton. The unique authority which the decision possesses derives partly at least from the moral ground on which it is placed, an improbable basis for a case on the liability of a manufacturer of bottled drinks. The

17 *Perrin v Morgan* [1943] AC 399 at 415.
18 *Matthey v Curling* [1922] 2 AC 180 at 199, CA.
   In *National Carriers v Panalpina* [1981] 2 WLR 45 at 77 Lord Roskill acknowledged that 'the genesis of the suggestion' was in Atkin LJ's dissenting judgment.
19 (1922) 38 TLR 801.
20 *Adelaide Steamship Co v The Crown* (1922) 12 Ll L Rep 305 at 309.
21 [1937] AC 826 at 833.

responsibility for the moral content of the decision was Atkin's alone, and in giving impetus to the development of the law of negligence it was Atkin particularly who was engaged in the task which Lord Radcliffe described as a necessity for every system of jurisprudence, that of 'relating its rules and principles to the fundamental moral assumptions of the society to which it belongs'.[22]

Atkin's dissenting judgment in *East Suffolk Rivers Catchment Board v Kent*[23] is an important, and perhaps insufficiently recognised, example of his ability to illuminate the future. The Catchment Board had power but no positive duty under the statute by which it was constituted to maintain and repair walls and banks along the tidal section of the River Deben. Henry Kent occupied a dairy farm whose boundaries ran along the river. As a result of exceptional tides and gales 50 acres of the farm were flooded. The Catchment Board attempted to repair the breaches in the ancient bank, but were so incompetent that, although the gap should have been closed within 14 days, the flooding was in fact not cured for 164 days. The House of Lords decided by a majority of four to one over the solitary dissent of Lord Atkin that, as the Board were under no duty to repair the wall, or to complete the work having once begun it, they were under no liability to Kent, the damage suffered having been caused by natural events.

Atkin began his speech by saying:

> 'I cannot help thinking that the argument did not sufficiently distinguish between two kinds of duties: (1) A statutory duty to do or abstain from doing something. (2) A common law duty to conduct yourself with reasonable care so as not to injure persons liable to be affected by your conduct.'

The first duty, he said, was primarily a duty owed to the state and was not necessarily owed to a private citizen; but as to the second, 'every person whether discharging a public duty or not is under a common law obligation to some persons in some circumstances to conduct himself with reasonable care so as not to injure those persons likely to be affected by his want of care'.

When, nearly forty years later, the *East Suffolk Case* was first comprehensively discussed by the House of Lords in *Anns v Merton London Borough*, Lord Wilberforce remarked that only one Law Lord in the earlier case had considered it in relation to a common law duty of care. 'It need cause no surprise', he said, 'that this was Lord Atkin'.[24] It is surprising that none of the four judges of the majority even considered the possibility that the Catchment Board might have a common law duty in addition to its statutory duty, a

22   *The Law and its Compass* (1960 Rosenthal Lectures, Faber and Faber, 1960) p 63.
23   [1941] AC 74.
24   [1978] AC 728 at 757.

duty in private law as well as in public law. Even more remarkable is the fact that the significance of Lord Atkin's dissent in the *East Suffolk Case* was not grasped until Lord Wilberforce formulated the issue in Atkin's own terms in *Anns' Case* by saying: 'The problem which this type of action creates, is to define the circumstances in which the law should impose, over and above, or perhaps alongside, these public law powers and duties, a duty in private law towards individuals such that they may sue for damages in a civil court'.[25]

The decisions in *Anns' Case* and its predecessor in the Court of Appeal, *Dutton v Bognor Regis UDC*[26] have been credited with achieving a change in the direction of the law by opening up the possibility of common law negligence suits against local government authorities for acts or omissions of their officers.But the true point of departure was, as Lord Wilberforce acknowledged, the dissenting speech of Lord Atkin in the *East Suffolk Case*.

The intuitive and farseeing judgment which Sir David Maxwell-Fyffe attributed to Atkin was employed in his great decisions extending private civil liability. In *Donoghue v Stevenson* and the *East Suffolk Case* he fixed responsibility for carelessness regardless of contractual nexus or public accountability. In *Hambrook v Stokes*,[27] he and Sir John Bankes removed some of the worst anomalies affecting the recovery of compensation for injury by shock. They disposed finally of the suggestion that, in order to succeed, the plaintiff must establish that the shock derived from fear for his own safety rather than the safety of others, an anomaly which Atkin said, would be 'discreditable to any system of jurisprudence'. In *Banque Belge v Hambrouck*[28] he would have permitted ill gotten gains to be traced and recovered in all circumstances so long as the means of ascertainment were available; and in *Everett v Griffiths*[29] he would have made liable those who were responsible for wrongly incarcerating a man as a lunatic, whoever they might be. It was no coincidence that all these judgments related the law more closely to moral principle and social need.

An appraisal of Lord Atkin's judicial style, that curiously individual but essential thing, leads to the difficulty enountered in any discussion of style, that any general description will prove to be no more than a 'sieve through which the particular achievement of genius is so apt

25 [1978] AC 728 at 754.
26 [1972] 1 QB 373. The Court of Appeal decided that if an Inspector employed by a local authority failed to make a proper inspection, the authority might be liable under the principle of *Donoghue v Stevenson*, but no reference was made to Lord Atkin's dissent in the *East Suffolk Case*, except by Sachs LJ at 402 who oddly described the case as 'one in which the failure to proceed with the building work sufficiently quickly was held to be in essence a case of non-feasance — though Lord Atkin's dissenting speech shows how close it came to that borderline'.
27 [1925] 1 KB 141, CA.
28 [1921] 1 KB 321, CA.
29 [1920] 3 KB 163, CA.

to slip'. This is especially so in Atkin's case for his own style had many forms. He could adopt the style merciless, as in the *Portuguese Bank Note Case*;[30] or dismissive, as in a case about a notice to quit 'at the earliest possible moment', which he described as 'short, simple and wrong';[31] or passionate as in *Everett v Griffiths*;[32] or rhetorical as in *Ambard's Case*;[33] or tersely lucid as in *Ariadne Steamship Co v McKelvie*; [34] or graphic as in *Glasbrook v Glamorgan Country Council*;[35] or ironic as in *Canadian Transport v Court Line* where he congratulated an arbitrator whose Special Case was niggardly of facts for 'having achieved a degree of abstraction which is certainly rare and perhaps admirable'.[36] The varieties might be further multiplied.

The English legal judgment is a species of essay for which an unusual freedom of expression is permitted, at least by comparison with other legal traditions. It lends itself naturally to metaphor, epigram or literary allusion. Yet the judge is constrained by circumstances peculiar to his task. He must ensure that what he writes will later be accorded the exact meaning he intended, and that after detailed, and possibly hostile, scrutiny by minds trained in the same way as his own. He must be not only accurate but impregnable. Some of the words he uses have a specialised secondary meaning. These considerations lead to caution and conventionality, two qualities which are not easily compatible with literary elegance. It must be accepted that much of the content of the law reports bears the mark of these constrictions, with prose made heavy by subjunctives, conditionals and the passive voice. In most recent times only Lord Denning has consistently triumphed over these difficulties.

The first thing to be said about Lord Atkin's style is that, like his style as an advocate and his manner as a judge, it always avoided the flamboyant or showy. Even when he employed a rare flourish, as in the passage about the ghosts of the past in the *United Australia Case*, it was free of exhibition. Sir Arthur Quiller Couch remarked that, 'Though personality pervades Style and cannot be escaped, the first sin again Style as against good Manners is to obtrude or exploit personality',[37] and that is as true of a legal judgment as of a piece of literary criticism. Atkin's writing was literary. He was widely read, and quoted from his favourite works. The passage from *Alice Through the Looking Glass* in *Liversidge v Anderson* is the best-known example, but he had other favourites. He once described a plaintiff's

---

30   [1932] AC 452.
31   *Phipps v Rogers* [1925] 1 KB 14 at 29, CA.
32   [1920] 3 KB 163.
33   [1936] AC 322.
34   [1922] 1 KB 518, CA.
35   [1924] 1 KB 879, CA.
36   [1940] AC 934 at 937.
37   *The Art of Writing* (Guild Book edn, 1946) p 165.

case as being 'as destitute of merits as Dr Johnson's leg of mutton which he said was ill-fed, ill-killed, ill-hung and ill-dressed; the only difference being that this case has been admirably dressed before us as any rate, it having been very well put'.[38]

But what stamped Atkin's individual style more than anything else was his gift for aphorism, with which he summed up his argument. At their best these epigrams were unforgettable and ended the debate with a conclusive snap. Thus he said 'there is no caste in contracts'; 'A rule is not proved by exceptions unless the exceptions themselves lead one to infer a rule' (an entirely satisfying explanation of that puzzling saying); 'convenience and justice are often not on speaking terms'; 'legal fictions have a tendency to pass beyond their appointed bounds and to harden into dangerous facts'; 'the habit of making unfounded generalizations is ingrained in ill-educated or vulgar minds'; and 'finality is a good thing, but justice is a better'.[39]

Atkin's prose as an appellate judge was rarely less than compelling, particularly so in those cases in which he expressed himself with his characteristic terseness. The judgments after *Liversidge v Anderson*, itself a speech necessarily comprehensive and long, were in general short and concise, even where the decisions were of high importance as in the *Fibrosa Case* or *Perrin v Morgan*.[40] And although there is much that is memorable in his judgments in the Court of Appeal, the power and originality of his expression seemed to gain on his promotion to the House of Lords. *Hyman v Hyman*,[41] for example, was only just over a year after he became a Lord of Appeal. In general his personal style became more effective with time.

The presentation of Atkin's argument seems occasionally to have been so forceful as to carry his colleagues with him to acceptance of a questionable proposition. The leading judgment in the controversial series of Canadian constitutional appeals, about which Lord Wright, although a participant, later experienced doubt, ended with the memorable 'watertight compartment' metaphor.[42] And Atkin's speech in *Rose v Ford*, commended in Lord Wright's obituary tribute as 'masterly', contained the short assertion, pregnant with difficulty for the future: 'I am satisfied that the injured person is damnified by having cut short the period during which he had a normal expectation of enjoying life: and that the loss, damnum, is capable of being

---

38 *Montgomerie & Workman Ltd v Ramchander* 16 Ll L Rep 75 at 77, CA.
39 *Hyman v Hyman* [1929] AC 601 at 625.
    Fender v Mildmay [1938] AC 1 at 14.
    General Medical Council v Spackman [1943] AC 627 at 638.
    Chung Chi Cheung v R [1939] AC 160 at 174.
    Knupffer v London Express [1944] AC 116 at 122.
    Ras Behari Lal v King Emperor (1933) 60 LRIA 354 at 361.
40 [1943] AC 32; [1943] AC 399.
41 [1929] AC 601.
42 *A-G for Canada v A-G for Ontario* [1937] AC 326 at 354. See above, p 110.

estimated in terms of money: and that the calculation should be made'.[43]

Atkin was an advocate of multiple judgments and the separate expression of each judge's views. 'It is a help', he said in 1927, 'to know the different reasons that are given, and my own experience leads me to believe that law very often grows out of the excrescences and different variations that are found in judgments. Law as a science would be weakened if we could not resort to the judgment of each judge, and there have been times when dissenting judgments in the ultimate tribunal have been of the greatest value, though tending to throw doubt upon the actual proposition of law that has been decided'.[44]

His own work bears that out. He dissented only rarely in the House of Lords, and then with dramatic effect, but whether as a warning against heresy, as in *Liversidge v Anderson*, or as prophetic indication of the future, as in the *East Suffolk Case*, his own dissenting judgments, as well as his separate concurring judgments, always threw the law into relief so that the issue could be the more clearly appreciated.

The period between the Wars, which coincided with Lord Atkin's career on the Bench, has been thought of as a period of quiescence in Britain, at least by contrast with the social upheavals which followed the Second World War. The work of administering the law, it has been suggested, has reflected this, so that the 30s were a decade of relative inactivity for the judiciary when compared with the heady 60s or 70s. What great issues arose between the Wars which could bear comparison with the new-found power of trade unions, race relations or the development of women's rights, all of which have occupied the English courts since the War? Such generalisations are not entirely to be trusted. Social revolutions have their consequences in the courts, but the development of the law depends on the greatness of its judges as well as on the press of events. Moreover, the judges do their work, if not by stealth, then unnoticed. There is little awareness by people of the major shifts in the rules which govern their lives. Atkin made a similar point himself in a letter to Sir Herbert Evatt written in 1940: 'How little the public realise how dependent they are for their happiness on an impartial administration of justice. I have often thought it is like oxygen in the air: they know and care nothing about it until it is withdrawn'.[45]

Although the development of judge-made law for the most part goes publicly unnoticed, and although in England the judges do not, as does the Supreme Court of the United States, have power to outlaw the work of the legislature and so directly affect social policy,

43   60 LQR 332. [1937] AC 826 at 834.
44   'Appeal in English Law' 3 CLJ 1 at 9.
45   See appendix 4 for text of letter.

much can be and is achieved by the English Bench. The development of a strong and certain commercial code must be credited to the judges along, and many fundamental liberties of the English subject derive from decisions of judge and jury. During the 1930s and in the early years of the Second War, Atkin led the House of Lords by frequently presiding and by the force and subtlety of his own intellect. He was more than anyone else responsible for the direction, style and purpose of judge-made law in the period. During that time, the reputation of the House both for the quality of its decisions and for its integrity was enhanced, and on the rare occasions when, as in *Liversidge v Anderson*, its intellectual honesty came into question, Atkin's own dissent protected its reputation. That speech alone had profound consequences for the credit of the judiciary.

Atkin's leadership was supported by Lord Wright and the Scots, Macmillan and Thankerton. Their achievements lay in the generalised extension of civil responsibility, epitomised by the decision in *Donoghue v Stevenson*, and most strongly marked in the development of the right of workmen to safe working conditions under statute and at common law. The unifying of principles of civil liability for fault or carelessness carried with it the task of clearing away the debris of the past for which Atkin had a special enthusiasm and outstanding gifts. His success as a reformer owed most to his profound knowledge and respect for the law. But it also owed much to the indefinable quality of judgment, his feeling for the time when a branch of the law was ripe for a general statement, and his vision of the consequences which would follow.

There remains the liberal spirit which gave impulse to his work. Law to him suffused itself throughout the complex structure of society, quickened by the idea of man's responsibility to man. The profound movements which took place during the years of Atkin's ascendancy to extend civil liability so as more closely to reflect the moral and social assumptions of contemporary England were to a high degree his personal achievement. Compassion and freedom from narrow prejudice were the qualities which in Lord Wright's words 'animated his work', the mark of his rare greatness as a judge, and the things for which he himself would have wished to be remembered.

Appendices

1. Autobiographical Fragment

AUTOBIOGRAPHY J.R.A.

I was born in Brisbane, Queensland on Nov. 28., 1867. My father, Robert Travers Atkin, was an Irishman whose father and grandfather owned some landed property in County Cork. It descended to him and by settlement to my Mother and I suppose I had an interest so that I might have belonged to that unfortunate class, the Irish landlord. It was, however, held on a not unusual Irish tenure, a lease for three lives perpetually renewable. There was never much margin between the rents paid by tenants and the headrents: by the time my Mother became interested the margin was minute: and land troubles and a suit against a negligent Trustee caused the property to be sold; and since my boyhood it is but a vague memory. I still retain some of the delightful names: Castle Treasure and Fernhill: and there is a name which to me smacks rather of Irish middleclass — Atkinville. Owing to my Father's early death and my Mother's occupation with her young children in Wales, I lost the opportunity of knowing much of my Irish relations, Warrens, Travers, Hungerfords. A former Judge of the Irish Probate Court, Mr. Justice Warren was a cousin and I believe that I once as a boy on a fleeting visit to Dublin saw him in Court. There were two well known characters, also cousins, twin brothers Roberts, both fellows of Trinity College, Dublin, who will live in the memory of old T.C.D. men.

One story of a member of our family I recall. He was a solicitor in County Cork in the early years of last century and, troubled with the care of his practice and a large family, decided to quit. He set sail for Australia in a sailing ship leaving a note for his wife that when he had made good he would send for her and the family. But he had misestimated the character of his Irish wife. When he arrived at Sydney he found her and the children all drawn up in a row on the quay, having come by one of the early steamboats. He accepted the situation, made good, and ended in some judicial position.

My Father, soon after marrying my Mother, went out with her to Queensland, then a very young Colony, about 1863 or 1864. They were to make their fortune on a pastoral station: in a year or two that failed and the only souvenir of that period I possess is a collection of aboriginal weapons, boomerangs, spears and clubs captured by the combined station owners after defeating a raid in force by the natives. My Father then turned to what was obviously his natural bent — politics and journalism. He was appointed Editor of a Daily paper run in the Liberal interest in Queensland: he became Member of the Legislative Assembly for East Moreton and in a year or so led his party in the House. My Mother used to correct proofs, write social articles and reviews, though she cannot have had much time for she had three sons, born in 1867, 1869 and 1870. The promising career ended all too soon. His health had never been strong and he died in 1873 after unremitting care had been spent on him by his friend and my future father-in-law, Mr. William Hemmant, then a prosperous merchant in Queensland and also a Member of the Legislative Assembly. My father must have been a man of exceptional gifts, if one may judge from an inscription upon a public memorial set up to his memory in Queensland, which I cannot forbear to quote:

> "Erected by the members of the Hibernian Society in memory of their late Vice-President,

> ROBERT TRAVERS ATKIN

> born at Fern Hill, County Cork, Ireland, November 25, 1841; died at Sandgate, May 25, 1872. His days were few but his labours and attainments bore the stamp of a wise maturity."

On another face of the pedestal are the lines:–

> "This broken column symbolises the irreparable loss of a man who well represented some of the finest characteristics of the Celtic race — its rich humour and subtle wit, its fervid passion and genial warmth of heart. Distinguished alike in the Press and Parliament of Queensland by large and elevated views, remarkable powers of organization, and unswerving advocacy of the popular cause, his rare abilities were especially devoted to the promotion of a patriotic union among his countrymen, irrespective of class or creed, combined with a loyal allegiance to the land of their adoption."

Meanwhile at the end of 1870 my Mother and the children had come home. The baby was ill and the only hope, so she was advised, was to take him home at once. There were no liners, so my Mother, an Irish nurse, the three babies (eldest three years old) and a goat embarked on a sailing ship of about 800 tons, "The Chartyce", and sailed home round Cape Horn. Together with other products of the Victorian age I laugh at the notions some of our novelists and journalists seem to entertain on the Victorian women. We know enough about them to realise that enterprise and endurance are not gifts given in the age of Edward and George and that women were much the same then as now.

But this voyage seems to have been undertaken as a matter of course. I can remember nothing of it except that we started with pigs, sheep and poultry behind bars beside the bulwarks. What I do remember is arriving at Pantlludw, my Grandmother's house in Wales, all decorated for the occasion, and seeing for the first time our dear rosy-cheeked little nurse, Jane Jones, standing on the steps in the hall ready for us.

It would be impossible for me to give any accurate statement of influences that moulded my life without giving some sort of picture of my Grandmother, Mrs. Ruck, with whom my brothers and I spent the next ten years of our life. The picture has been drawn by a much more competent pen than mine in my cousin, Bernard Darwin's book* but I may fill in some lines. She was Mary Anne Matthews, daughter of Richard Matthews of Esgair Foeleirin in the County of Merioneth, and was descended by lines of Welsh ancestors, who owned estates, mostly small, in Merioneth and the neighbouring county, Montgomeryshire. They were freeholders and, I imagine, cultivated their own lands, with small fortunes and much pride of race. I have seen pedigrees which run up to Bleddyn ap Cynfryn, Prince of Powys, who died in 1073, and trace through Baron Lewys Owen, who was murdered by robbers from Mawddy in 1555. Welsh names ran in past days, as I was taught they did in Greece, the son took his grandfather's name and so in succession. Thus Oliver Morris of Esgair was succeeded by Morris Oliver, who was succeeded by Oliver Morris and so for six or seven generations.

My Grandmother had two brothers but they both died before she married, one, Richard, when wandering on travels abroad, the other, Oliver, drowned as a boy while bathing in the Dovey with the curate of Pennal. Judging by a water-colour drawing of her when about eighteen, she must have been a beautiful girl, tall, dark, a perfect figure and regular features. She was an heiress in a small way and was educated by her widowed mother as it was thought an heiress should. Before she was twenty she was married to my grandfather, Laurence Ruck, a young Englishman who had just come into his fortune. His people came from Kent; he had been adopted in his youth by an uncle who had made money as an army contractor in the French wars, and left his property to young Laurence, who became Laurence Ruck of Cranbrook Manor House, Newington in the County of Kent. He went to Magdalen College, Oxford in the days of Dr. Routh. I did not gather from his accounts of his college life that he did any work there. He kept horses and hunted, and on attaining his majority came down and married his Welsh wife, to whom he had been introduced by her brother, Richard. They had six children: two daughters (of whom the eldest was my mother) and four sons.

Eventually they settled down at Pantlludw, a small country house nestling under the hills surrounded by trees; in the front was a verandah — a novelty in those days. I don't think there are more than four bedrooms and two sitting rooms, with of course accomodation for maids. There they brought up the family. It would have been impossible to get them in if they had not taken from Lady Londonderry a small cottage, Votty, at the bottom of the grounds.

* *The World that Fred Made.*

This consisted of two rooms and an attic at the front and two rooms at the back, fitted up with camp beds, where the uncles used to sleep when home on leave. Neither house had a bathroom, there was of course no water laid on and, as they say, the sanitation was external. It is perhaps as well to remember that many well-to-do refined people lived in those conditions in those times and found them endurable. My grandfather devoted a good deal of his money and his leisure to beautifying the grounds. He made a drive of about a quarter of a mile through the woods from the high road, supporting it on a retaining wall. He cut innumerable paths, planting the slopes with rhododendrons; there were three gardens — they were both keen gardeners. He cut out a bog at the top of the hill about 800 feet up and made a lake of about 3 acres, and a short distance from the lake he built a three-roomed cottage with two or three outbuildings.

Into this home my Mother and her three children were fitted. The three children, nurse and nursemaid were given the front part of Votty to live in: and we came up to the house for our mid-day dinner. In the summer time we lived in the cottage at the top of the hill. At the beginning of May Kerry, the mare, was harnessed to a large sledge on runners: our beds and other belongings were loaded up, and the sledge dragged up the rough mountain road. It was an ideal life for children: we ran about the hills, rolled down the mossy slopes, dragged withered branches from the wood below for firewood, and had our moments of excitement when an uncle brought in rabbit for the pot, or our grandfather came to spend the night in the only bedroom which, selfishly as some thought, he had reserved for himself.

In the mornings, after a year or two, my Mother toiled up the hill to give us lessons: there I began English history with "Little Arthur", followed as a more advanced course by "Mrs. Markham". On Sundays we went down the hill to dine with our grandparents. With varying conditions it is the life that Welsh children in the country have lived and are still living. It results in fixing in every fibre the feelings that culminate in that passionate love of hill and gorge and trees and brooks and bracken that fills the heart of every Welshman, and I have no doubt is one of the elements of nationalism.

When the summer life in the cottage on the hill was first suggested my anxious Mother demurred. Suppose the children fell into the lake. "My dear", replied my grandmother, "if the children are so stupid as to fall into the lake, it is much better that they should be drowned young". This characteristic saying had its intended effect. There was no further demur and we did not fall into the lake. It is difficult to give an impression of this grandmother of ours whom we called by the Welsh name "Nain" (pronounced Nine). When I first was able to appreciate her she was over middle-age and very stately. Both she and my Mother had the appearance of sailing into a room; you cannot now "sail" in short skirts. She had the widest range of interests, literary, social, political, family, gardening. She was well-read and corresponded with literary personages such as George Eliot and Bret Harte. She seemed to love letter-writing and kept in constant touch with her children in different parts of the world, including her grandchildren. She had a store of good stories, mainly of Welsh life, which she knew profoundly. Benevolent and wise, she was consulted by young and old; and no one sought sympathy in vain. She was too warm-hearted to be impartial. Her friends were invariably right, intelligent and well-meaning; their opponents were wrong, stupid and malicious. She was quite a good hater — in theory: but an enemy in distress would immediately have received assistance. All the lame dogs of the neighbourhood found their way to Pantlludw.

For some reason or other she was not on good terms at one time with the clergy of her own parish of Pennal or the neighbouring parish of Machynlleth. In consequence, every Sunday wet or fine she or my grandfather drove us in the wagonette to the little church at Corris, a slate-quarry village five miles away. We passed two turnpikes, a small naptha works — wood naptha — and drove down the beautiful valley of the Dulas. I know every yard of that road and look out for the rocks from which hung the icicles in the winter mornings. The choice of church was probably not unconnected with the merits of the successive incumbents of Corris. The first, when I was a boy, was Dr. Daniel Evans, a fervid preacher and speaker, a protagonist of Church Defence on public platforms. He received for his services from the Archbishop of Canterbury the Lambeth degree of D.D. He was an authority on Church music and edited the Welsh Hymnal which is the foundation of our present Welsh Church Hymnal. Greatly as Nain admired him, he was not allowed liberties. When in the Pantlludw drawing-room, still thinking of his hymn tunes, he was suddenly pulled up. "Mr. Evans, you are humming:" He died Vicar of Caernarvon. His successor was a saintly man, John Morgan, afterwards Rector of Llandudno and Archdeacon of Bangor. There never was a better-loved priest. His son, the present Bishop of Swansea and Brecon, follows in his footsteps. The third was Robert Edwards, a most successful parish priest. His is an interesting case for at one period he had fits of intemperance, and was, I think, suspended for a time. But by struggle and will and the help of a good wife he entirely recovered. I do not think he ever lost the confidence of his parishioners. We in Wales are very indulgent to men whose shortcomings bring them under the notice of the law if otherwise they are popular.

I remember years ago the case of a country solicitor who held all the offices in his district and was suspended by the Court for suppressing a will. It made no difference to his popularity: I am not sure that it permanently lost him his appointments. Mr. Edwards died the very respected incumbent of an important living in Anglesey.

In 1876, when I was not yet nine, I went to the Friar School, Bangor, as a boarder. I had already had experience of a scholarship examination. A benevolent Welshman, having a presentation to Christs Hospital School, arranged to give it by competition. I think the limit of age was nine: I do not remember the subjects but they were a mixed lot, including Latin and Huxley's Principles of Physiology. I know I stumbled in my viva over the word "oesophagus", rather a mouthful for a boy of eight. My Latin I had sought to acquire from the curate at Machynlleth and I used to walk to his lodgings three times a week. The winner was a choir-boy from a Welsh Vicarage, whose name I cannot now remember but who may possibly see this reminiscence.

Friars, to which I was sent, was one of the oldest Grammar Schools in Wales. It was founded in 1568 on a site which had been occupied by a community of Black Friars, who had been expropriated by Henry VIII. I have before me the statutes as drawn by Dean Nowell of St. Paul's in 1568. The schoolmaster and usher were to "instruct their Scholars as well with good nurture and civil manners, as with good literature with exercise to speak Latin and other honest discipline". "They shall not be too sharp nor too remiss in due correction of their Scholars but shall to the best of their powers teach as well the poorest man's child as the richest without partiality." The key to the education is found in this article, "Nothing shall be taught in the said School but only Grammar and such Authors as concern the Latin and Greek tongues." The scholars were to "use to speak Latin as well without the school as within". Well-meaning, optimistic Dean! There was a syllabus attached for the different forms. For the second form the pretty proverbs and short sentences Publican annexed to Cato's works, Colloquia familiaria Erasmi, Aesop's fables and for the third form the work of Erasmus de civitate, part of Ovid's Tristia and some of the comedies of Plautus or Terence, such as be most chast and least meddled with wantonness. And also the Alphabet and Greek letters. For the fourth form the Georgics, Greek dramas, Aesopi apologus graeci, Erasmus de copia verborum and some part of Horace. For the fifth and highest form Erasmus de conscribendis epistolis together with some of Cicero's letters, Sallust's histories, Cicero de officiis, some books of the "Aeneid", some of Caesar's commentaries and some of Isocrates in Greek. There is here a good assortment of Latin, though Livy and Tacitus are absent, but there is very little Greek. One has, however, to consider what Greek and Latin texts were in 1568 available for schools, a topic with which I am not familiar.

There is one other form of instruction that I find interesting. "Besides the said ordinary lectures, the Schoolmaster or Usher by the Schoolmaster's appointment shall every night teach their Scholars three Latin words with the English signification which every one of the Scholars shall render without the books openly in the midst of the School so that the Schoolmaster may hear and reform them every morning at their first coming to the school". They were to begin with words concerning the head, following with every part of the body and proceeding to the names of "sickness, diseases, virtues, vices, fishes, fowls, birds, beasts, herbs, shrubs, trees and so forth they shall proceed in good order to such thing as may be most frequented and daily used". I should think that this was a good way of acquiring a vocabulary. I know that when I was at Oxford my I.C.S. friends who were acquiring native languages used to go about with lists of oriental words in their pockets which they learned by heart.

But this is all antiquarian. In 1876 of course these statutes were obsolete. The school had had fluctuating fortunes. In 1789 the school had been rebuilt. For fifty years it flourished exceedingly, then its fortune diminished, and in 1866 after the death of the then headmaster it was closed until 1872, when the Governors determined to reopen it under a new scheme with the Rev. D. Lewis Lloyd as the young and energetic Headmaster. Lloyd was one of the most eminent Welshmen of his day: a born teacher and administrator. He had been Headmaster of the small Grammar School at Dolgelley for a few years, and had raised it to the standard at which boys took open scholarships at the Universities. He came to Friars in 1872 after it had been closed for six years; he left it in 1879 with 130 day boys and 30 boarders and with a yearly record of scholarships at Oxford and Cambridge. He went to Brecon in 1879, where for one cause or another the school had consisted of about 20 boys; he left it in 1890 a school of about 160 boys, mostly boarders, whose three or four open scholarships a year were the usual tale. He was then appointed Bishop of Bangor, but his health had begun to fail and he resigned in 1898 without having made the mark as Bishop which in normal circumstances he would have done. I owe to him more than I can measure of such success as I have been blessed with.

In 1876, therefore, I went to this old School of boys of all ages from eight to eighteen. I went in August, conforming to the old practice of two terms a year. Next term, however, we adopted the present system of three terms, so that I lost my share of a long Christmas holiday. When I first went we played a nondescript game of football, according to the rules of which you could run with the ball if you caught it on the first bounce. We soon adopted the new Association rules. The last year we were in the semi-final for the Welsh cup. I remember the Headmaster flinging his mortar-board into the air when we got the final goal that put out Wrexham, our opponents. I cannot help thinking that the growth of the laws in games in our own time presents an analogy to the growth of the civil law. There are the varying local customs which gradually become fixed with judges to interpret the code and a legislature to alter it. Many of the games have had their rules formulated by a club consisting of players of repute deriving no authority from any direct representation. Some rules are a necessity and once formulated they obtain a ready acceptance. The leading club corresponds to a leading chief, for I am convinced that much of the traditional law in native communities which the historian attributes to custom must be the result of decisions — often repeated decisions — of the powerful head of the local community: decisions which no doubt would be followed by his successors. The rules in one seem to be customary, but would emanate not from tendencies or superstitions of the community but from the tendencies or superstitions — and often the reasoned determination — of the most powerful individual — a different matter likely to defy scientific analysis.

One half-holiday I spent with a friend collecting mussels on the shore of the Menai Straits. They were brought home for the seed pearls contained in them and were dissected in the school lavatory basins. I suppose that they were minor cousins of the Conway mussels which in old time were famous for pearls.

We used to attend service at the Cathedral, where the Bishop, Bishop Campbell, was not inspiring and the Canons all seemed incredibly old. But the dominating figure was the Dean, Henry Edwards, an elder brother of the late Archbishop of Wales, a man of commanding personality and forcible eloquence. He was a powerful defender of the Welsh Church but wore himself out and in a state of mental derangement took his own life. It was a loss which the Welsh Church could ill bear either at that time or any other. I only remember one biting phrase of his alluding to the practice common in those days but abandoned now by which non-conformist divines could purchase without more the degree of D.D. from certain small American Universities. "They doctor their vanity without examining their ignorance".

I was happy at Friars; got on fairly well with my work; began Greek when I was nine and won a prize in my second year. At the end of 1878, however, Mr. Lloyd was appointed Headmaster of Christ College, Brecon. Incidentally, a letter from my Mother asking him to take me there crossed one from him asking her to send me there. So I left Friars. Lloyd was succeeded there by an excellent scholar, Mr. Glynn Williams, who maintained the standards of the school, and its numbers, until misfortune fell upon Bangor when in 1886 a severe epidemic of typhoid attacked the town and the school had temporarily to be withdrawn to Penmaenmawr. Naturally parents feared Bangor for a time and the numbers dropped. Then came the Welsh Intermediate Education Act of 1889; a few schools were exempted from its operation — Brecon and Llandovery in South Wales, Ruthin in North Wales. A powerful attempt was made to secure exemption for Friars in view of its great traditions and high position in Welsh education. I was asked as a more or less recent old boy to attend a deputation which Lloyd headed to the Board of

Education. We were received by a crabbed person, Sir George Young, who intimated that we had quite misunderstood the new proposal; that the same high standard of education as had been given in the old schools would be maintained and strengthened; that boys would still go direct to Oxford and Cambridge; and that a classical education would still be available for all classes.

That the schools have been very popular and given a secondary education to thousands who would otherwise have gone without is indisputable. But two or three years ago I asked a boy of fifteen who was attending a large school of over 300 boys and girls whether he did any Latin. No: there was only one boy in the school who did it. He was the son of a retired English Public School teacher. However, the children in this school are very well taught science subjects and a modern language.

Friars is now an Intermediate School; it has beautiful new buildings and a fine healthy site but I gather that it has become increasingly "modern".

Brecon I can only write of with the glowing heart of a grateful old pupil. It is a foundation of Henry VII founded on an old monastic situation; the school chapel occupies the site of the choir of the old church. The beautiful buildings are situated near the banks of the Usk in a lovely district of Wales. The school had dwindled to a form of about 15 boys before Lloyd went there; he left it a flourishing public school of about 160 boys, mostly boarders, which had made a name for itself both in teaching and sport. When I left, for two or three years the head boys in Classics, Mathematics and Science had always taken an open scholarship at Oxford or Cambridge, and often there were one or two more. I do not know how Lloyd maintained this high standard. He had not, of course, the competition of the Intermediate schools to take away promising boys; moreover he knew most of the Welsh clergy, and had other means of learning of boys likely to profit by the education he could give them.

I had a very happy time at Brecon, doing well at work and winding up by gaining a classical demyship at Magdalen before I was quite seventeen. For three years I was in the cricket eleven and for my last year in the football fifteen, where I played full back, the least attractive place in the field, for when your side is winning you have little to do, while if it is losing you have everything to do, and must put up with many failures. The success of a child's education must depend more upon the teacher than the curriculum or tradition or environment or any other single factor. There are two of our Brecon masters to whom I owe special gratitude. The first is Stepney Rawson, one of the most brilliant all-round men I ever met. He was Westminster and Christ Church, had a first in Mathematical Moderations, had been captain of the Oxford Association XI and an English International; for two years he had been twelfth man for the University cricket XI, was an exceptionally good skater, and a shot. He was an expert musician, acted as our organist, and organised a class in which he taught the choir, including myself, the elements of music. I used to be able to convert from one key to another without much trouble. He eventually left us to join his brother's firm of Woodhouse and Rawson, who were pioneers in electric lighting. The two partners had together either won or been runners up in the Lawn Tennis Doubles championship at Wimbledon. He returned for a visit a year or two afterwards to give the town a demonstration of the new form of domestic and public lighting. I suppose that this was in 1883 or 1884. He made mathematics an attractive subject and thanks to him I passed the Oxford and Cambridge certificate examination in Higher Mathematics — a magniloquent term — when I was fifteen. That sufficed for a Cambridge matriculation, and I was then taken off mathematics and concentrated on classics. It was probably a mistake; but in any case such elementary training as I had convinced me of the importance of some such mental training as an ingredient in the complete system of education.

The second man I have to mention, F.S.N. Bousfield, supplied a different ingredient and to him I am more indebted than any one individual for my own mental equipment such as it is. He was an acute looking man, a complete sportsman in every sense; a classical scholar of Lincoln, Oxford, with a first in Greats. He took the fifth form but he had special charge of English essays for the fifth and sixth. We read with him books that required accurate thinking. Mill on Liberty was one; but I think the most valuable was Sir George Cornewall Lewis on "The Use and Abuse of Political Terms". I do not know to what extent it is in use now but I should deem it one of the very best instruments of education available. As many people well know, it contains discussions on terms in general use, liberty, rights, people, democracy, popular, nation and the like, with accurate analyses of the various meanings with which they are used; and instances of fallacious arguments based upon using them in different meanings, sometimes in the same sentence. I have often thought what an admirable thing it would be for every politician to have to face an examination in such a book before he was allowed to speak or write on public affairs. It would cramp the style of a good many of us.

Our essays would be set on a general subject, such as Ambition, Patriotism, Greatness; and the one forbidden form of approach was to write frothy sentimentalities about them. We had to define our terms, extracting the definition from the varying uses of the terms, and then illustrating. It may be that this method is more generally used than I suppose; but if a main object of education is to train the young mind to think for itself and think correctly this was an admirably adapted means. It certainly was an invaluable help in legal work.

Bousfield was a most popular companion. He was in charge of one of the school houses, where he kept open house for Old Boys, with whom at their earliest visit he established the most friendly relations. Later he took up a scholastic appointment in Queensland, where he married and was still living when I began these memoirs. No doubt the State has realised what a valuable import he was.

I suppose that my schooldays resembled closely those of other boys in like circumstances; and I will not dwell on them. I recall three experiences which were exciting at the time. The first year I was in the cricket XI I was fifteen and we played the Swansea club on their fine ground. Their batsmen were too good for us and they began hitting up a big score. I was in the long field, very far out, and one of their men made a tremendous hit in my direction. Surely no ball ever went so high before. I seemed to be waiting minutes for it and then held it to the generous applause of the gallery. At that time the rule as to declarations had not been passed, and if the team who won the toss were doing well they had all to get out if they wanted a chance to put their opponents out. As a last hope for our side I was put on to bowl slows: the Swansea batsmen took their opportunity and I got five wickets for about thirty runs. I do not think, however, that they had time to get us out. The next experience is also a cricket one. In our last year we played our chief rivals, Llandovery, on their ground. I made 95 and against our score of about 240 they made 35. I had been bowled by D.W. Evans (afterwards an international Welsh forward and late manager of the great Davies anti-tuberculosis organisation) by what I am certain was the best ball he ever bowled in his life. On returning to Brecon Budworth, who made 60, and I were carried through the town by the boys. The third experience was in December 1884. I had been for a walk with one or two fellow prefects and with G.T. Johnson, an old boy who was then a science demy of Magdalen. We were late for tea and as we walked up the hall to High Table there was a storm of cheering, which I thought was a welcome to Johnson. When we sat down someone congratulated me. I said, "What for?", and I was told I had got a classical demyship at Magdalen. As this was my grandfather's old college, the news seemed too good to be true. Telegrams fled in every direction. Lloyd's chief comment was, "I ought to have kept you for Balliol next year." It was fortunate for me that he did not, for I never was a classical scholar of Balliol scholarship standard. Later, however, a year after Lloyd had left, we won a Balliol classical scholarship through C.T. Davis who, when I left, was a small boy in the first form. But Lloyd with his unerring eye for an able boy had spotted him, for I remember his gibing at us in the sixth when dissatisfied with us by saying "I have got a little boy in the lowest form who is going to beat the whole lot of you." He became Sir Charles Davis, K.C.M.G., Permanent Under-Secretary of State for Dominion Affairs.

My home life when I was at Brecon was in new surroundings. At the end of 1880 my mother had married Lt. Col. Thomas Ruddiman Steuart, formerly of the Honourable East India Company's Service. He and his first wife had been tenants of my grandmother at Esgair, her other house about three miles away from Pantlludw. They had been great friends of the family and about two or three years after his first wife's death he and my Mother were married. He was about thirty years older than she but there never was a happier marriage. There is a natural tendency to extol those one loves but if I tried to be impartial I should arrive at the same result. He was the most perfect example of a soldier and a gentleman that I ever met. Tall and commanding-looking, he had a gentle courtesy and unassuming disposition which endeared him to everyone with whom he came in contact. He had occupied important positions in civil government in India, to which he had been transferred from the army. He ended as Collector for Upper Scinde, under Sir Bartle Frere, the Commissioner, and as such had had control over the district during the Mutiny. My Mother induced him to write his reminiscences, which were privately published and, if I wished, I have only to fill these memoirs with extracts to make them really interesting. I will content myself with one. He had been married but a few months and was a subaltern though temporarily in command of the light company of his regiment, when an execution took place of eight dacoits. There were threats of a rescue and the whole regiment was ordered to keep the barrack square, where the gibbet had been erected. The light company were ordered to guard the gibbet. On the execution taking place the ropes of four men broke and the victims were left struggling on the ground. The Brigadier galloped up to young Mr. Steuart and shouted "Tell your men to shoot them, sir, shoot them." After a moment's pause the young officer lowered his sword and said that he respectfully declined to carry out that order: the men had been sentenced to be hanged not shot. He was not the executioner. He was ordered under arrest and retired sorrowfully to his quarters, for the fortunes of himself and his young wife were perhaps crashing. His colonel and brother officers, however, came and congratulated him and after a few days he was released. The Brigadier had been severely reprimanded by the Government and the Commander-in-Chief. My step-father was only twenty-one at the time: and this has always seemed to me a remarkable instance of courage and initiative in an emergency. He belonged to a well known family of Writers to the Signet in Edinburgh: the business is still carried on there.

My Mother and I received a warm welcome from our new Scots relations one of whom, Francis Steuart, Advocate, is a well known historical and antiquarian writer. Soon after their marriage my step-father and Mother settled down at Penmaenmawr, which was my home until my marriage in 1893, and continued to be their home until 1896 when he died, aged eighty-eight, one of his last words being, "I have had a very happy life". I am thankful for every remembrance of him.

Part of my holidays were still spent at Pantlludw. My grandfather had lent me an old 16 bore single-barrelled muzzled-loading gun; and equipped with powder-horn, shotcase, wads and a box of percussion caps I used to wander through the woods. There was no dog and rabbits were stalked. Later I was promoted to the use of my step-father's double-barrelled pinfire gun, and occasionally travelled over the upland farms where, in those days, there were partridges for those who could shoot them. Now I understand they have disappeared from the district. I remember walking for some hours with an 8 lb. hare in the game bag. I little knew what I had let myself in for. I think my most exciting sporting moment was when I was out under the auspices of Evan, Nain's righthand man, gardener and woodman, but above all things in his own time, poacher. Suddenly he stopped me. "Look, look!" I could see nothing until his pointed finger directed me to a woodcock lying couched beneath a hedge, and so wonderfully camouflaged in the surrounding bracken, dead leaves and twigs that only Evan's experienced eye could see it. "Shoot, shoot", he whispered. But sitting rabbits were one thing — a sitting woodcock was another. I walked it up and its swerving flight was too much for both my barrels. Poor Evan. During my visits I used generally to sleep down at Votty and used to go down at night in the dark, no lantern and of course no torches. I knew the way so well that I found I could see in the dark. A few yards down the drive, then at a big rhododendron a dive down a steep garden path, two gates and then the cottage. If you deviated you were brought into the right track by a slap from a wet rhododendron branch. How often did I patrol the drive in a soaking Welsh rain trying to secure a woodpigeon with birds signalling on every side and eventually breaking always away on the far side of a tree several yards from that from which they appeared to be sounding. Your woodpigeon is a natural ventriloquist. But to walk through dripping woods adequately protected gave me, as I daresay it has to others, a sense of freedom and independence of nature which is exhilarating.

In October 1885, still in my eighteenth year, I went up to Magdalen. It was too young, at any rate it was too young for me, and I should have profited more by having another year at school. Magdalen was then a markedly well-to-do college; most of the men came from the larger public schools; and I, young and sensitive with a small allowance within which I was resolved to keep, took time to find my bearings. Not unnaturally I fraternised with the Brecon and other Welsh boys I found there. There is always a tendency for Welsh people out of Wales to draw together. "You Brecon boys are so gregarious," complained our Headmaster. I made one good friend in John Sankey, then a Scholar of Jesus, afterwards a fellow-member of the South Wales Circuit, a brother Judge, and a Lord Chancellor under and with whom I had the pleasure of sitting in judicial work.

I lived for the first three years in ground floor rooms in the Cloisters. In my fourth year I lodged out and had the advantage, with a recently acquired friend, A.J. Grant, of taking rooms at the house of Greenstone, our Junior Common Room Steward, well known to generations of Magdalen men. Grant was a striking figure. Tall and strong, he was the most mature, looking ten years older than his age. He was an I.C.S. man, spending his two years at Oxford before he went out. A man of great ability and decided character he met with rapid success in India and was winning a deserved reputation when he died after seven or eight years' service from some tropical disease. He played for two years in the University Lawn Tennis team. In the last year I also played in every match, until the Cambridge match, when I was quite properly dropped. I had played with Grant in the final of the College competition the day after the last paper in Greats, and I had failed to hit a ball; and the captain quite rightly would not take the risk.

My other Magdalen friend was Hugh Spencer, also an I.C.S. man of very quick parts, who served his full time in India with success. He lived with his widowed mother in Clifton where on a visit to them he and I walked over to Weston-super-Mare to lunch with his mother's sister, Mrs. Macready. There we met her son, then a young subaltern in the Gordon Highlanders, afterwards famous as General Sir C.J. Macready, Adjutant-General for part of the war and afterwards Commissioner of Metropolitan Police. His mother had married the great actor as his second wife. The direct link with the drama in the early part of this century was fascinating; but Mrs. Macready, like her sister, belonged to the body of Plymouth Brethren, and we did not hear or seek to acquire any theatrical reminiscences. It happens that on going to Bristol for that visit I travelled on the G.W.R. broad gauge, which was removed shortly after. I suppose it was too expensive, and in the battle of the gauges fought in Parliamentary Committees, the present gauge rightly won; but how luxurious railway travelling would have become if Brunel's decision had been universally adopted.

I came down from Oxford with two seconds in Classical Moderations and Greats and had at the time the mortification of hearing as to both class lists that one more first in any paper would have given me my first. I suppose I should have worked harder; but the absence of a first does not appear to have done me any harm except perhaps in the estimation of people, and there are many, who judge a man solely by the ability he exercised at school or college or hospital when he was twenty-two. To men who know that a man's career develops in accordance with the education he gives himself after that period, mere school or academic success will seem relatively unimportant. Nevertheless I should have liked to have had those two firsts.

In those days, as I now look back, I think that the college authorities did not exercise adequate guardianship over their undergraduates. After all, eighteen and nineteen is not an age at which youth should be left entirely to itself, especially when subject to the influence of small coteries of older men. Freshmen come up from schools where they have been subject to a perhaps silent but all-pervading tutelary guidance. The vast majority come to no harm, and therefore benefit, but there have always been instances in every year of boys who have lost values, and indeed have been harmed, when tactful guidance could have kept them in the right path. To avoid good-natured friends construing these words as a confession, I may say that I am not referring to myself, who on the whole kept to the straight and narrow path. In my first term there was a freshman who possessed a name associated with both a bank and a brewery. He lodged out, entertained lavishly, and in the last week of term gave a "wine" to the freshmen of his year in which champagne and other drinks flowed very freely. He did not appear next term, and it appeared that his father was a poor incumbent, who had doubtless scraped and borrowed to give the boy a University education. He was next heard of from the police who wanted him for pretending to be one of his Magdalen contemporaries. This is an extreme case: but I have known of several where boys of slender means have in associating with others of much larger fortunes, which in itself is entirely harmless, emulated their expenditure and incurred liabilities which would be a burden to themselves or their parents. In such cases a word to the improvident or, still more wisely, to his rich friends might have been life-saving.

In my time our Dean was A.D. Godley, a scholar and a wit beyond compare. He was in those days apparently very shy, and it appeared to embarrass him as much as the wrong-doer when a rebuke had to be administered. He had a gift of quiet sarcasm, which is in general an irritant to the young, but in his case was expected and indeed welcome. His gift of parody was unrivalled; some of his Platonic dialogues read like Jowett translations from the original; and his verse was as good. It was only when a complete edition of his writings was produced, edited by his friend, C.M.C. Fletcher, our Modern History Tutor, that I became acquainted with his verses on the Motor Bus, which (with permission) I repeat:

> What is this that roareth thus?
> Can it be a Motor Bus?
> Yes, the smell and hideous hum
> Indicat Motorem Bum:
> Implet in the Corn and High
> Terror me Motoris Bi:
> Bo Motori clamitabo

Ne Motore caeder a Bo-
Dative be or Ablative
So thou only let us live:
Whither shall thy victims flee?
Spare us, spare us, Motor Be!
Thus I sang; and still anigh
Came in hordes Motores Bi,
Et complebat omne forum
Copia Motorum Borum.
How shall wretches live like us
Cincti Bis Motoribus?
Domine, defende nos
Contra hos Motores Bos!

Our President, Warren, was the founder of modern Magdalen. He came there as a young tutor from Balliol in 1877, aged twenty-four, when the College had no particular reputation except as the resort of a well-connected and dilettante set. From his first years somehow or other the College began to be conspicuous in the Schools or on the river and in sports generally. He became President in 1885 and reigned till 1928, when the College had acquired its present position, which I need not glorify. I doubt whether in his earlier days he was popular; he was not effusive; and popular opinion condemned him a snob. I have no doubt that he derived pleasure from associating with the influential and titled people whose sons flocked to the College. He did not conceal his satisfaction when Prince Christian Victor, and afterwards the Prince of Wales, came under his charge; but is there any Head of any College who did not envy him? He was in fact a good administrator, and had the schoolmaster's eye for the right man both in studies and in sport. Later generations learned fully his worth; and at the College dinners towards the end of his term one could see how popular he had become. He was a distinguished scholar, Hertford, Craven, Gainford Prize, and a man of exquisite literary taste. I had the advantage of reading Virgil with him; probably his favourite author. At any rate he never failed to give effect to Virgil's curiosa felicitas by the same studied aptitude and charm of words which the phrase connotes. It was the same choice gift of words which attracted him to Tennyson, whose acquaintance he was proud to possess. To read Virgil with Warren, Sophocles with Arthur Sidgwick, Tacitus with Haig, was a literary education in itself. One other tutor at Magdalen I must mention, Aubrey Moore. He was our philosophy tutor. There were probably men better adapted to training their men for firsts. He did not trouble to consider what the examiners were likely to ask. He believed in "divine philosophy" as scientia scrutiarum, and set himself to realise and expound the unification of knowledge. He was in Holy Orders and a frequent preacher in the University Church; and had done much before his untimely death to reconcile science and the Christian religion. He had physical disadvantages: a very pronounced hunchback, he was almost a dwarf; but physical appearance was transcended by the lofty spiritual expression of a mobile beautiful face. It was a privilege to take an essay to him and after a few words of criticism hear him discourse for the remainder of the time on eternal verities often little related to the particular subject-matter. I owe him much.

And so having finished my "education" I passed into the world to educate myself. I do not pose as an "educationalist", heaven forbid, though I have been on the government bodies or courts of about a dozen educational establishments. One is reminded of the definition of a jurist as a man who knows a little of the laws of every country but his own. To my mind the best thing said about education is the saying of Sir Robert Morant when a Chief Inspector of Schools in a report to the Education Department:

"We may assume that university teaching is teaching suited to adults: that it is scientific, detached and impartial in character: that it aims not so much at filling the mind of the student with facts or theories as at calling forth his own individuality and stimulating him to mental effort: that it accustoms him to the critical study of the leading authorities with perhaps occasional references to first hand sources of information, and that it implants in his mind a standard of thoroughness, and gives him a sense of the difficulty as well as of the value of truth. The student so trained learns to distinguish between what may fairly be called matter of fact and what is certainly matter of opinion, between the white light and the coloured. He becomes accustomed to distinguish issues, and to look at separate questions each on its own merits and without an eye to their bearing on some cherished theory. He learns to state fairly and even sympathetically the position of those to whose practical conclusions he is most stoutly opposed. He becomes able to examine a suggested idea, and see what becomes of it before accepting or rejecting it. Finally without necessarily becoming an original student gains an insight into the conditions under which original research is carried on. He is able to weigh evidence, to follow and criticise argument and put his own value on authorities."

I suppose the sum of it all is that the education of the young is an attempt to equip each individual mind with intellectual tools adequate to cope with such problems as he encounters or challenges in his path through life; and to mould his character so that he is not overthrown. The prayer to give us a right judgment in all things covers the intellectual side; but we must add Kant's good will.

I came to the Bar because a cousin of my grandfather, Edwyn Jones, was a barrister in substantial practice and had promised to guide my first steps. We had no connection with the English law and I do not think my people knew a single solicitor except two or three local solicitors and a family solicitor ensconced amongst his deed boxes somewhere in Bedford Row. No acquaintance of that kind brought me any work. But Edwyn Jones was to be a tower of strength. He was a Bencher of Gray's Inn, and to Gray's Inn, therefore, I was admitted in 1887. When I came up to eat dinners I would go to his chambers in Fountain Court and stay at his house at Wallington. He examined me for the Bar Final and took me in viva voce, and whether because my papers had been satisfactory or whether he was prejudiced I know not but the only question I was asked was what were the provisions of s. 4 of the Statute of Frauds. He was large, sensible and genial, very popular, and one of those men who seem never to tire in helping a friend.

Gray's Inn, when I joined it, had not yet recovered its early prestige as it has now. There were several old Benchers whose connection with the law was shadowy; and there was no one in big practice at the bar. There were our two judges, Manisty and Huddleston, but they were old and took little part in the management of the Inn. Our numbers were small; few students came from the Universities, with the result that our company at dinner was varied and interesting. I would sit in a "mess" consisting besides myself of a consular officer from Japan, a native of Barbados and an Irish Nationalist. Harold Cox wore a red tie and promulgated Socialism. Sidney Webb was all for law and order. Two of the brightest spirits were Sinclair Cox and Bowen Rowlands, son of the King's Counsel who was one of our Benchers. Both have fallen out of the profession but might have reached any heights. At that time we all sat in "messes" of four according to seniority, an excellent plan in a small community for it encouraged comradeship; each mess talked amongst its own members. Now the seniority rule only obtains amongst the bar. We used to have a good dinner, soup or fish, joint, sweet, cheese and two or sometimes three bottles of wine. In those days each mess had its own joint placed on the table, which the senior carved for himself and then passed across the table to the second senior and I have seen some strange carving. It must have led to appalling waste, and the system was abolished when the new regime of efficiency was inaugurated under the auspices of Lewis Coward and Mattinson, to whom the present happy financial position of the Inn is largely due. Mattinson is now our Senior Bencher, having been appointed in 1891. I have been his colleague there since 1906 and during most of the time he was Chairman of our Finance Committee. Soon after taking silk he left the Bar for the City and to mammon gave up what was meant for mankind. His great success there as the head of flourishing financial enterprises is well known. He is a financial administrator of the very first order, far-seeing and yet with a microscopic eye for detail. There never was a man who to a greater degree combined enterprise with economy, possessing with these qualities remarkable powers of exposition. I am satisfied that if during

the 1914–18 war he had had an effective voice at the British Treasury
we should now be paying probably 1/- less income tax.

We then dined at six; quite a convenient time, as men could come
to the Inn straight from chambers; and the music halls and theatres
opened at 6.30 or 7.0. The dinner hour is now 7.0. During the
1914–18 war we had occasion to review the various changes of the
dinner hour from about 1750, when it was 1.30; changed twenty or
thirty years after to 3.0 "because of the habit of the Judges to sit
later"; then moved to 4.0. There it remained for a good many years,
until per saltim it reached 6.0. The occasion was the necessity to
reconcile the Government view that there should be no unnecessary
evening dinners with the regulations which prescribed keeping terms
by attending so many dinners in term. The regulations did not
prescribe any time for dinner, and we easily got over the difficulty
by fixing the dinner hour at 1.15. The same course has been adopted
in the present war. What is the use of management by lawyers if
they cannot get over a small difficulty like that. People have sneered
at the regulations for keeping term by eating dinners. I can only
speak from experience of my own time; but from that experience I
would say that it is a very important part of legal education. It serves
the University purpose of bringing young men together in the
comradeship of a profession and at a time when they are often living
in London with no special cultural ties. From Hall have sprung our
Moot Society, Debating Society, Common Room, Golf Club, Field
Club and last but not least "Graya" the Society's terminal magazine.

I must say a few words about the Moot Society. Mooting, or the
arguing of a legal point before senior members of the profession,
used to be the principal form of organised legal instruction and there
is a full account of it in a report of Sir Nicholas Bacon to Henry
VIII about 1540, from which it appears that mooting took place in
Hall every night after supper in the vacations, which would mean
outside the legal term of about three weeks. The practice became
neglected and was not revived till at Gray's Inn in 1875 Judge J.A.
Russell Q.C., father of our well beloved C.A. Russell, K.C., and like
him a bencher of the Inn, founded the Moot Society, under whose
auspices moots have been held continuously every term in Hall
except in wartime. The practice is for the President for the evening
to set a question, which is published in advance; he dines with the
Bench and after dinner comes into Hall with some of the Benchers,
and hears the point argued by counsel drawn from the younger
barristers and the students, who sit at a table just below high table.
The practice is almost identical with that described by Sir Nicholas
Bacon. "On a forme sitteth down two Inner-Barristers and on the
other side of them on the same forme two Utter-Barristers." He goes
on to say that the Inner Barristers do "in French openly declare
some kind of action after which the Utter Barristers argue such
points as be disputable within the Case." He explains that Utter

Barristers are so called "for that they when they argue the said Courts they sit uttermost on the formes which they call the Barr". "All the residue of learners are called Inner Barristers which are the youngest men that for lack of learning and continuance are not able to argue and reason in these Motes." Except that the juniors do not now open the pleadings but follow their leader, and that the arguments are not as they were then conducted in Law French, the procedure is practically unchanged. The procedure is prescribed to be that of the Court of Appeal, which is taken to mean that counsel are subject to a "certain amount of interruption" from the Bench. These interruptions are more valuable at this time than they are even in Court, for students have to lose their debating society form of speech and have to think and think quickly while on their legs. I had the advantage of arguing in several moots; my first before Crump K.C., who had set a question on restraint of trade. Later I had the privilege of presiding more than once. When a Bencher, I took my turn at being Master of the Moots, i.e. the President of the Moot Society, and while holding that office prepared a publication, "The Moot Book of Gray's Inn", in which we published a selected number of moots with the subjects, the presidents of the evenings, "counsel" and the decisions, with short notes of the legal distinction of presidents and "counsel". We have owed our success as a Moot Society to the fact that the institution was not, as it were, imposed on "Hall" from above but is managed almost entirely by a Committee of students and barristers presided over by a Bencher, whose chief duty is to secure the leaders of the profession as presidents for the evening. In times past there are few Judges, Lords Justices or Lord Chancellors who have not at one time or another officiated to the great advantage of the younger men.

In the first autumn after I had come down from Oxford it was desired by my mentor, Edwyn Jones, that I should enter for the Arden Scholarship at the Inn, which was at that time worth £60 a year for three years — it is now £100. The subject is always two set books and on this occasion the subjects were Landlord and Tenant and Bills of Exchange, the books being Woodfall on Landlord and Tenant and Byles on Bills of Exchange. Two less exhilarating books could hardly be found. I had read no law at all and my first introduction was in the pages of Woodfall. To me, who did not know the elements of contract or tort, what an indenture or a mortgage or a devisee or an assignee were, much of my reading made clear; and it did not surprise me that the award went to Ernest Bowen Rowlands. The next year the position had cleared. The subjects were Partnership and Trusts and the books Lindley on Partnership and Lewin on Trusts. I cannot recommend Lewin for general reading, but Lindley was a revelation. I owe more to the intensive study of that book than to any other legal teacher. The clear arrangement, the grasp of principle, the pellucid exposition, place it in a class by itself. It contains a statement of practically the whole law of agency besides discussions on the principles of equity, of bankruptcy, of joint and several property and of joint property. I read it under the guidance of my good friend, Charles Herbert Smith, afterwards a well known County Court Judge and a brother Bencher, who at that time did some coaching. There could be no better guide; a sound and learned lawyer (he was an LL.D. of London) and an enthusiast, he could hardly fail to turn out a winner. At any rate I was awarded the scholarship and a great boon it was.

I am bound to say that I did not myself receive much benefit from the instruction provided by the Council of Legal Education. The system was not elaborated as it has been later; the readers (lecturers) were accomplished lawyers, but I think the principal object before all students was to qualify as soon and perhaps as easily, as possible; and the necessary matter could be readily and more quickly obtained from text books. Of course this recourse sometimes proved deceitful. I have heard Lord Summer, a great scholar and fellow of his College at the time, recount that having to pass in Roman Law he was told that he could learn enough to pass from the small Hunter on Roman Law by reading it in the train on his way to the examination. "I tried it," he said, "coming up from Liverpool but unfortunately it was an express train." I should be the last to throw doubt upon the expediency of giving systematic instruction to bar students (I was the Chairman of the Council of Legal Education for several years) but it cannot be denied that so far as the bar is concerned the quality of lawyers, both at the bar and on the Bench, was at least as high in the days before lectures were established and a pass compulsory as in the present time. Abbott, Maule, Parke, John T. Coleridge, Alderson, Shand Willes, Blackburn, Bowen, Brett, Vaughan Williams and, to name but a few great equity lawyers, Sugden, Bethell and Fry, passed no examination. The fact is that every barrister is under daily compulsion to educate himself; he has to study intensively new subjects day by day; his academic knowledge has to be constantly refreshed and matured by study of recent cases to such an extent that the original foundation affords very insufficient support. The practice of reading in chambers with an experienced lawyer, which was the one form of external instruction that the lawyers I have named received is still the effective stimulus to professional knowledge of the law. The conditions are different in every other profession; doctors and solicitors deal directly with the layman; their mistakes, if any, have immediate results; and there is no controlling hand, such as the judge, to correct and redeem them before they are irremediable. Barristers have as their clients lawyers and the inefficient are soon detected.

After call I took for my chambers half a room on the first floor of 3 Pump Court from F.C. Moncrieff, a son of the well-known Lord Justice Clerk of Scotland. He had for some years devilled for Robert Finlay but at this time was chiefly engaged in journalism and only resorted to his room to take examinations of witnesses ordered by the Scots Courts. I thus became acquainted with Scots procedural terms, which therefore did not take me unawares when it became my duty to hear Scots Appeals. The set of chambers, belonged to the then Recorder of London, Sir Thomas Chambers, whose clerk was in attendance on the Recorder in the City. Our chambers, therefore, were in charge of the boy, Alfred Harrison, who continued to be my clerk until he died just before I went on the Bench. No one could have had a more loyal friend and servant; he used to prescribe regular hours for business and if I were late I found him opening the door with his watch in his hand. He was a bachelor, secretary of the Liberal Association in his North London constituency; and, like most barristers' clerks, was treated as a valuable legal authority by his own circle. Work was slow at first. Before I was called I had became engaged to my dear wife, Lizzie Hemmant, the eldest of a family of thirteen of William Hemmant, who had in the early days of Queensland established himself in business in Brisbane with a partner, Mr. Stewart. The business had flourished and at this time Mr. Hemmant was the resident partner in England, controlling the goods exported to the firm from England and all over the continent. He had been in politics in Queensland, where he had been assisted politically by my father, and had held office as Colonial Treasurer. He was very well-read in politics and economics, had a complete knowledge of business methods, and a power of rapid decision. It was a commercial education to me to discuss commercial points with him; undoubtedly I profited by this early learning to understand and appreciate the business man's attitude towards business problems. He then lived at Blackheath and had given almost his first work to Norman Herbert Smith, the son of a Blackheath neighbour, who had just started in business on his own account as a solicitor in the City. He had promised to give me my first brief and a few weeks after call it was delivered; a case for opinion, with a sovereign a shilling and half-a-crown for the clerk. I cannot remember the details but I know that it was one of the most difficult cases I ever had to advise upon in my whole career, for it concerned the powers of the executors of a testator domiciled in France under a will in English form dealing with personal property in Constantinople. Perhaps it was well to be tried high at the beginning, for Smith continued to be my client throughout the whole of my time as barrister and in the first years almost my only one. He was one of the ablest business advisers in the City; from his youth up he inspired confidence; and the present position of his firm reflects the success which had attended it at the time of his death. It may be an encouragement to young lawyers, whom I am chiefly seeking to interest in this part of these memoirs to have a record of my fees for my first years at the bar: 1891: £35; 1892: £37; 1893: £59; 1894: £100; 1895: £110; 1896: £345; 1897: £346. After that they kept increasing and the corner was turned.

2. *Lord Atkin on his grandmother*

APPRECIATION BY HER GRANDSON LORD ATKIN OF ABERDOVEY.

My recollections of Nain date from early in 1871. When aged 3½ with two younger brothers we came with my Mother to live at Pantlludw.

My impressions of the first arrival do not include Nain: they vaguely recall the gates and the town decorated with evergreens: and Jane, the Uncle's ex-nurse, and our nurse-elect standing at the bottom step of the stairs in the front hall.

Nain figures in one's early days as a creature of awe She-who-must-be-obeyed. This is partly due to the fact that it was she who was requisitioned when chastisement was to be inflicted. We children and nurses lived at Votty, 2 rooms and an attic in Winter; and the lake cottage 2 rooms in the summer. I remember more than one painful occasion when Nain came sailing over from Pantlludw to execute judgment. My Mother must have been considered insufficiently firm in our treatment. When it was first suggested that we should spend the summer months on the hill by the lake maternal anxiety expressed the fear that the young children might come to harm. "Really Tilly if they are so weak minded as to fall into the lake it would be much better that they should be drowned early." There were no more protests, and no one did fall into the lake. Even to a child it was apparent that she was a dominating figure. By the way she was not Nain when I first met her. She was Grandmama and he was Grandpapa. My Mother used to call them Papa-Mama, until a time when I remember she made the revolutionary change into Father and Mother. Nain and Taid were introduced I think from Berta & Co. Taid was to us even more awe inspiring: it was wonderful that any of his opinions should ever be dissented from. He was very kind and joked with us. For some reason he would not let us have the use of the third room at the cottage on the hill. He sometimes came and slept there and one of the delights of the small boy who slept in the next room was to be given a cup of early morning tea without milk or sugar made on a spirit kettle resting on an old lifebuoy which had come from a wreck at Aberdovey. When we got older I remember his producing from his treasure store in the room at the back of the laundry a cricket bat and ball. Both I should think were fifty years old. He played with us in the field the other side of the high road, bowling round of course. He had tales of single wicket encounters of which Alfred Mynn was the hero. I remember the Sunday Drives to Corris Church. Taid generally drove Kerry the mare in the wagonette; if not he then Nain. We went in all weathers; one recalls the stones by the way; I know the places now. Nain frequently drove on week days by herself. She invariably gave a wayfarer a lift. Kerry, knowing her Mistress's habit, on one occasion stopped on overtaking a solitary traveller. It turned out to be Mr Price the Rector of Pennal with whom Nain had not been on speaking terms for years. Every instinct compelled an invitation and the rift was to some extent healed. I don't think that in those days she rode but she was very active; and did much gardening. I remember croquet parties but don't know whether she played. There was an annual expedition up Cader Idris; and I went up with her first when I was five. Others may have told the tale which to me is hearsay that, when she was younger, when the party arrived at the top one of the men broke away from the picnic having become suddenly deranged and started to run to throw himself over the precipice. She alone had the presence of mind to seize him round the waist and hold him till the slower witted males of the party came to the rescue. She played round games of cards with us —"commerce" "cheating" and "snap". Does anyone play commerce now? I think they played it in Horace Walpole's time.

There comes a break in our association while we boys were living with our stepfather and Mother at Penmaenmawr. We of course saw her from time to time and were invited to stay at Pantlludw. Delightful visits: one was getting old enough to appreciate her wit and wisdom, the outstanding character. It was bracing. "Of course my dear" she once said to me "You must always remember that you are not nearly as clever as your brother Walter". This was perfectly true: but unexpected: and I don't remember that it had been earned. I remember the walks over to Votty in the dark. One knew every inch of the way: if you did err from the path you were recalled by the swish of a wet rhododendron bush on your face.

I resume more acute memories at the time when she established herself at Pantlludw alone except at first for Uncle Ithel: and when I used to spend substantial parts of the vacation with her at first by myself and afterwards, when I became engaged, with Lizzie. One could then discern the wonder of her. There never was a more interesting companion whether for young or old. The interest was not derived from books. Native wit, large sympathy, great experience of life cultivated by association with all classes of people, an active memory stocked with folk tales and countryside traditions made her conversations inimitable. She had strong likes and dislikes. She detested pretence either in rank or religion: and she was not sparing in her denunciation of her pet aversion, the sanctimonious Calvinist. Her sympathies were with people: not so much politically as in their ordinary life. We were never allowed to speak of the "common" people. I am afraid she liked a Poacher: she used to say that in her young days when the Dovey was not preserved it teemed with fish. One of the happiest adventures of her life was when she went to the Assizes at Dolgelly to give evidence as she said "for the river" in a case which involved the existence of a public right of way over

Llwyngwern bridge and its approaches. She used to narrate with gusto how she baffled cross examining counsel (I believe Sir John Eldon Bankes then a junior on the circuit) and how popular the verdict was. She maintained almost feudal relations with her tenants. I remember for instance the charming relations between old Edward Jones of Hendrewallog and herself when he came with the rent. A long conversation in Welsh: "Mistress" was how he addressed her: and had I suppose ever since her Mother's death. They were all on yearly tenancies and had been so for generations. Fixity of tenure did not require to be given by law. She would as soon have burned a tenant at the stake as give him notice. Her vivid interest in life reflected itself in the extent of her correspondence. She spent a great part of her days writing to friends of her youth, to strangers on topics she was interested in such as genealogy, to her children and grandchildren. Another absorbing occupation was needlework. When not writing or reading she spent hours sitting near the French windows at Pantlludw reproducing in silks the flowers and leaves that she found in her garden. She worked them on pieces of silk that happened to give her the background she required. She never drew a pattern. A pansy lay before her on the table: and she transferred its manifold colours to the material on which she worked. Lizzie and I have about a dozen specimens, each a collection of flowers on material about a foot square, pansies, sweet peas, copper beech leaves, anemones, polyanthus and the lilac. We have had them framed in a screen and treasure them. Her other recreation was patience of which she played many varieties chiefly the one with two packs which is known in the family as the Engineers. Is that its name to the public? I have always thought she named it for herself as being introduced by her R.E. sons. By this time she did not go far out of doors. But she retained the stately movement which always impressed her visitors. Perfectly erect she sailed into the room. "Vera incessu patuit Dea." But the wonder of this latter life was that all the beautiful manifestation of it was displayed amidst almost continuous physical pain which at times appeared torture. She was racked by neuralgia day by day and hour by hour. I have never heard her complain though I have seen the beautiful face flush and quiver with pain for which there appeared to be no relief. That in these conditions she could give the joy she did to those about her is in itself one of the most remarkable proofs of those remarkable qualities which I find myself so inadequately recalling. The greatest woman I have ever met, I thank God for every memory of her.

3. *Letters from the Lord Chancellor, Lord Hailsham, and his Permanent Secretary, Sir Claud Schuster*

HOUSE OF LORDS,

S.W.1.

2nd November 1936.

My dear Lord Atkin,

Your letter of the 1st November causes me the greatest embarrassment and anxiety. Naturally, coming as it does from you, it would command my immediate obedience, but the matter is not in my hands. The composition of the House of Lords and of the Judicial Committee has always, during my tenure of office, been settled upon the express instructions of the Lord Chancellor of the day, subject only to those rare occasions when sudden illness or some sudden emergency forces either the Registrar or the Clerk of the Parliaments and myself to take a sudden decision.

The proposed composition of the Boards on this particular occasion was not settled in an emergency, but by the Lord Chancellor himself after the very fullest consideration of the nature of the cases to be heard and of the work of both Tribunals. He dicussed it with me at great length. No man is more conscious than he is of the importance of the Dominion Appeals and he gave particular attention to the nature of the Canadian Appeals now to be heard.

I must admit, however, that he does not share your view about the Indian Appeals. It would be hyperbole to say that he regarded the ordinary Indian Appeal as of an importance equal to that of a Dominion Appeal. It is difficult to state the shade of differentiation in his mind between the two, but it corresponds very closely to the view which all his predecessors have taken on the matter. Recent events in India, and events which are about to happen, particularly the establishment of the Federal Court, render it in his view most desirable that there should be no appearance of giving to the Indian a less measure of judicial strength than is approriate to the Dominions, though, as there are two persons holding highly paid offices in respect of their Indian experience and two or three others available who also have Indian training, it is not necessary to observe exactly the same principles in constituting an Indian Board as in constituting a Dominion Board. The fact remains that he regards it as essential that there should be not less than one non-Indian presiding over that Board, and that that president should be, not necessarily a Law Lord, but a Privy Counsellor, who commands respect not only by his holding that office but by seniority in it.

The Lord Chancellor has been throughout both his terms of office exceedingly anxious that the Indian cases should not fall into arrear, and it has been his habit to look at the Indian list as jealously as at the Dominion List, and to pay almost a closer attention to it, because there is a slight — and perhaps pardonable — tendency in the minds of those in charge in Downing Street to give way rather to the importunities of the Dominion Counsel than to Indian necessities.

In fact, on this particular occasion the Lord Chancellor settled that Roche and not Thankerton should sit on the Dominion Board. The reason for this was that Thankerton by frequently sitting and presiding on the Indian Board has acquired a peculiar experience of the Indian cases, and experience has shown that he can get through them, not indeed in indecent haste, but with advantageous celerity. Also he is senior to Roche and, as such, he seemed to the Lord Chancellor, so far as such matters can be looked at, to have a reasonable claim to preside on one of the Boards.

When, however, I learned that Thankerton was anxious to sit in the Canadians, I asked Colin Smith to arrange that this should be so, so far as Roche was willing to consent to the arrangement. I thought that this exercise of discretion on my part was within the kind of liberty which I might assume after my conversation with the Lord Chancellor, and I am fairly confident that in doing so I was doing what he would have done in my place. I did not trouble him personally with the matter because the time when it came to my knowledge coincided exactly with his visit to London and a fresh examination by the doctors, and it was, therefore, a peculiarly inappropriate moment to trouble him with business.

There is a further point which is of some importance. It is impossible with the present staff available always to constitute a Dominions Board of five Law Lords, even when Wright is available and is reckoned as a Law Lord. The work of this House must go on, and the Indian or Crown Colony cases must go on also. We are, therefore, dependent on outside help. The Lord Chancellor cannot allow a state of things to arise in which ex-Judges of the English High Court or ex-Lords Justices of the Courts of Appeal are to be put in a separate category and regarded as fit to sit in one class of case but not equal to another. For one thing, I do not suppose that a man of Rowlatt's experience and standing would consent to occupy such a position. For another, we should, by acknowledging the principle, gravely weaken the authority of any man so placed when he sits on an Indian or Colonial Board. It is, of course, a most disagreeable task to attempt to estimate the fitness of the eminent lawyers who alone are qualified to sit on the Judicial Committee. From our point of view, they are all equally fit, though no doubt in a particular class of case a member of the Court who has had a particular experience seems peculiarly suitable, e.g. in old days Phillimore for an Admiralty case, or Moulton for a Patent; and it is, of course, necessary when we take Scottish cases here that we should have a strong Scottish element and when we take equity cases a strong equity element.

I hope you will not think this letter too argumentative in tone. It is an honest and greatly embarrassed endeavour to explain to you exactly what has happened, and to recall to your mind difficulties of which you are no doubt well aware but which you possibly may not have seen exactly in the light in which my successive masters, and particularly my present master, saw and sees them.

If, after having read this letter, you think that I ought again to communicate with the Lord Chancellor, I will at once send him your letter.

Yours sincerely,
Claud Schuster

Pardon the length of this letter, necessarily written in great haste
C.S.

The Right Hon.
Lord Atkin.

HOUSE OF LORDS,
S.W.1.
3rd November, 1936.

My dear Atkin,

Claud Schuster has shown me your two letters of the 1st and 2nd November,* with regard to the constitution of the Board to hear the Canadian Appeals on Thursday next. I am very much concerned to realise that you and some of my other colleagues take the view that the composition of the Board will not command sufficient authority in the Dominions. I have, myself, always taken the view that it is essential to have the strongest possible Board for Dominion Appeals; and I personally have presided as Lord Chancellor in every Appeal from the Dominions during the last time that I held that office, and I proposed to do so during this tenure of office, if my health had permitted. As it was, in view of the fact that the Dominion Appeals were due to commence on Thursday next, and that the Canadian cases were obviously of grave constitutional importance, I caused Schuster to write to Sankey, as the only available ex-Lord Chancellor, to explain to him the position and to ask him if he would be good enough to take my place as President of the Board. Unfortunately, Sankey

---

* These letters cannot unfortunately be traced.

was unable to see his way to render me that assistance. In these circumstances, I had chosen what I thought was as strong a Board as it is possible to compose, in yourself, Macmillan and Roche and Wright, who had kindly consented to come up from the Court of

Appeal and Sidney Rowlatt, whose merits I regard as second to none. Since then, I gather that Thankerton has expressed a desire to sit and his recent visit to/Canada renders him a very suitable member of the Board, and I have no hesitation in agreeing to his exchanging with Roche. But I cannot agree to regard the Judicial Committee as composed of two grades of Judges, one, the Law Lords, and the other, the ex-Judges and Lords Justices who give us help from time to time. To do this would be to render it practically impossible to obtain the help of retired Judges and Lords Justices and it would render the authority of any Board which was constituted with them for Indian or Colonial Appeals very questionable. Actually, in the present case, Rowlatt has already been asked and has agreed to sit and any change would involve my telling him that he was not now regarded as a strong enough member, which would be a very grave reflection on himself and a very poor return for his willingness to help. No doubt, the judgment of the Board will be delivered by one of the senior members in cases of such importance as those which are coming for hearing on and after Thursday, and I do not imagine that the Board would contemplate any other course. But I do not think that it is possible to improve upon the constitution of theBoard in fact and I cannot believe that the legal authorities in the Dominions are so little aware of the merits of our Judges that they seriously think that because a man has not been a Law Lord, he is not as well qualified as any other member of the Judicial Committee. I am very sorry to differ on a matter of this kind from yourself and the other Law Lords, especially as I am not able to come and talk it over with you or with them; but I feel that it would be an intolerable position to accept that only Law Lords were good enough to hear Dominion Appeals. I hope very much that the judgment of the Board in these cases will be such as to command respect by its merits and to convince the public in Canada of the correctness and strength of the Judicial Committee's view.

I am very sorry to be unable to be with you myself.

Yours ever,
Hailsham

HOUSE OF LORDS,
S.W.1.
17th November, 1936.

My dear Atkin,

I was glad to get your very kind letter. I think that you and I are agreed as to the paramount importance of retaining the appeal to the Privy Council from the Dominions of the Crown and as to the importance of constituting a Board which will inspire confidence by its decisions in all parts of the Empire. I am glad to tell you that I have recently heard indirectly that no less than four of the Canadian counsel who were engaged in the recent Privy Council appeals have severally expressed the greatest possible satisfaction at the constitution of the Board, so that obviously you are all impressing, as I felt sure that you would do. The truth is that we both miss Buckmaster more than ever from the Supreme Tribunal, but, none the less, I expect the decisions, when given, will carry conviction, which, after all, is the best test of the strength of the tribunal. I can only say again how sorry I am that I should leave my colleagues to carry the burden of the judicial work unassisted by their official head.

Yours ever,
Hailsham

4. *Letter from Lord Atkin to Sir Herbert Evatt*

74 Ashley Gardens,
London SW1.

Jan. 15 1940

My dear Evatt,

It is always a pleasure to hear from you, but I had to delay answering your letter of Dec 4th until I came back to town from Wales where I had been spending Christmas with one of my daughters. I have now been able to look at the cases you mention. Perkins v. Stevenson[1] is reported at length in the Law Times. On reading the full report I am not quite clear that the Court of Appeal went as far as you think. They were dealing with the case where a man had received compensation for a time, and then sued at Common Law, and applying former decisions upon the Act, they came to the conclusion that since compensation had been received no Common Law claim could be entertained. I think they were probably right on construction though the Act in this respect seems to me oppressive. Then they seem to seek to reinforce their view by the consideration that the Act allows compensation after an abortive damage claim but in that case expressly provides that costs of the damage claim may be deducted from compensation. There is no converse right given to deduct compensation from damages, they say, hence we are confirmed in the view that after compensation is received you cannot get damages. It is a poor argument for they seem to forget that in assessing damages you could take into account compensation, in which respect you are surely clearly right. But they only speak of a right to take compensation from damages and say they know of no such right. This is probably correct: if an employer had a judgment for damages given against him for £X, I don't see that he could deduct from the judgment sums which he had paid in compensation: but of course that is not what would be done. The damages would be assessed as in the cases in your Court after taking into account compensation or any other payment made by the employer by reason of the accident. In any case I don't see that you need be affected in any way by the judgment. It is purely obiter, unnecessary for the decision and deals with an hypothesis which in this country cannot arise at present viz. that compensation should be paid and damages afterwards awarded.

We had a couple of interesting W.C.A. cases in the Lords last term. In one the seaman had died from yellow fever contracted from the bites of mosquitoes in ports of Senegal to which his ship had been sent. Half the crew were infected and a quarter died. Said that it was an ordinary risk of the locality, which we wouldn't

1 *Perkins v Stevenson* [1939] 3 All ER 697, 161 LT 149

have.[2] In the other we destroyed a technicality which had done injustice for 25 years from a decision of the Court of Appeal that if a workman received any part of an award he could not afterwards appeal for more because the award is one, and he cannot 'approbate and reprobate'. We have not given our reasons yet, but that decision is going to receive a good hard knock.[3]

I hope that you are continuing from time to time your literary efforts. I read with greatest interest your story of Governor Bligh. How little the public realise how dependent they are for their happiness on an impartial administration of justice. I have often thought it is like oxygen in the air: they know and care nothing about it until it is withdrawn. We have had a change of Chancellor,[4] but the new one hasn't sat in the Lords yet, though he had in the Privy Council. He is a very sensible good fellow and ought to do well. But I suppose it is disrespectful to say that the judicial job like any other has to be learned. I am left solitary now for I lost my dear wife in February after 46 years. Fortunately I have married daughters in London and they are very good in looking after me. We hear no war news that you do not get: and that seems to me precious little. However we are determined to put an end to the gangsters as you all are.

With every good wish for the New Year.

Always sincerely yours,

Atkin.

---

2 *Dover Navigation v Craig* [1940] AC 190.
3 *Lissenden v Bosch* [1940] AC 412, overruling *Johnson v Newton Fire Extinguisher* [1913] 2 KB 111.
4 The new Chancellor was Mr Thomas Inskip appointed Lord Chancellor 4 September 1939 and became Viscount Caldecote 7 September. He resigned on 12 May 1940 when Sir John Simon was appointed.

5. *Correspondence between Lord Atkin and Professor Gutteridge*

Confidential

> The Rydings,
> Sylvester Road,
> Cambridge.
>
> 27th Nov. 1932

Dear Lord Atkin

I enclose M's letter. I agree with most of his statements, but I think that he is unduly pessimistic.

He is troubled by a state of affairs which I have always regarded as a great misfortune, namely, the almost complete lack of contact between the practitioner and the academic lawyer in England. The gulf between the two is very wide — much wider than it is in America or on the Continent. The reason for this is no doubt the historical development of the teaching of English law and the fact that the Universities were late in the field, but it has led to the development of an inferiority complex on the part of the teacher which is bad for the teaching of law and also inimical to the future of English law. There is so much that the Judge and the practitioner cannot do because they have not got the time to spare, but which ought to be done and can only be done by the academic lawyer. I mean such tasks as the production of legal treatises; the study and development of certain departments of the law which are unremunerative to a practitioner e.g. Public and Private International Law and Comparative Law and Legal History. It is a matter of grave concern to us at the present time that we have so few International Lawyers. There are only five in the Institute of International Law: Brierly, Pearce, Higgins, McNair and Fischer Williams. The result is that we cannot make our weight felt in any of the discussions which are constantly taking place, and the French have dug themselves in so thoroughly that it will be difficult to turn them out. English law is losing ground on the Continent because we cannot conduct the necessary propaganda: the Germans are hard at work trying to push it out of the Corn Trade and the other bulk trades as they pushed it out of Japan. I regard this movement as being somewhat serious for us now that we are no longer in a position of economic predominance.

It cannot be disputed that the University lawyer is regarded with benevolent contempt in England. This seems to be due to the following causes:–

(a) The difficulty of recruiting first rate men as law teachers
(b) The absence of contact between the teacher and the practitioner

(c) The prevalence of the erroneous idea that there is something
which is to be termed "practical" as opposed to theoretical law.

As regards (a) and (b) the situation is improving. The law faculties
at Oxford and Cambridge are growing in strength and have great
influence in their Universities. London is also on the upgrade. I
doubt if much can be done at the provincial Universities for
financial reasons. The teaching staffs are very small and they are
constantly losing their best men because the stipends only provide
a base livelihood. We have nearly a thousand students at Oxford
and Cambridge doing law in some form or other, which is several
times more than all the other Universities combined, if one leaves
out the articled clerks. We can give a man a good prospect of
making £1,000 a year or so before he is too old. But even with us
it is difficult to hold the right type of man. The reason is not
money but the lack of prestige attaching to law reading. The
remedy seems to me to be a wider recognition of the importance
of the work which is being done by teachers. Several of us
"*quorum pars minima fui*" have received the honour of silk and
this has helped a very great deal. I often wonder if it would not be
a good thing if each Inn of Court appointed a teacher to the Bench
if the right kind of man of sufficient standing were available. This
should be an exception to the convention that only persons
actively engaged in practice are eligible, and would only be
adopted in the case of a very small number of teachers of real
eminence. This would bring teachers and practitioners into contact
and would much improve the status of the law teacher without
causing any serious dislocation of existing traditions.

I also feel that the moribund rule that the works of legal authors
must not be cited in argument unless they are defunct is rather
derogatory to academic lawyers. It is more honoured in the breach
than otherwise but its formal abrogation would be a step towards
the recognition of the work of academic lawyers.

Academic lawyers might also be made more use of by
Government Departments than at present. As Committee men
and investigators they have the advantage of being able to devote
more time to their duties, and they are independent of vested
interests such as Trade Organisations and the like. But above all,
the recognition of some part of University examinations as
exempting from the professional tests would do more than
anything else to close the gulf, and this brings me to point (c)

(c) It is true that law can and should be taught as a living thing
and not as an abstraction. This does not mean however that there
is such a thing as practical law, unless one applies the term as one
of reproach to certain topics where the law is entirely a matter of
detail without any principle behind it. The law teacher, whether he

be a practitioner or a don, must teach principles and given the right type of teacher the result will be the same in both cases, except perhaps in the case of certain technical subjects which are not taught by the Universities. I think that every law teacher should have practical experience as early in his career and as much of it as possible, but I do not think that it is necessary for him to be actually in practice when he teaches. I am convinced of this as the result of my experience in London University where some of the teachers devoted the majority of their time to practice, whilst others made teaching their chief duty. It is not difficult for a teacher to find out what is going on, and sometimes he is more up to date than a busy advocate who cannot spare the time to investigate certain movements in the law.

Some subjects are best taught by practitioners e.g. Procedure Probate and Divorce, certain branches of Commercial law etc. I feel that such subjects are the peculiar province of the professional law schools and should not be attempted except in bare outline by the Universities. But Contract, Tort, Property, Criminal Law etc. can really be dealt with best by an experienced teacher who knows how to present the matter. The Council of Legal Education have recognised this in appointing Holdsworth for instance as one of their readers. If we could only get rid of this idea that University lecturers teach something which is different in kind from what the legal apprentice ought to know, a very great step in advance will have been made. It may have been true in the past that University teaching was unsuitable but it is certainly not so now.

Lastly if something could be done to bring judges, practitioners and teachers together in a body charged with proposals for the reform and improvement of the law, we should have still further bridged over the gulf. Next to increased recognition of University examinations this seems to me to be the most likely method of counteracting the present — very unfortunate — isolation of the University teacher from the rest of the legal community.

I hope I have not bored you, but as M. very truly says you the one person to whom one can unbosom oneself on this matter.

Yours very sincerely,
H. C. Gutteridge

4 Verulam Buildings,
Grays Inn,
W.C.1.

Dec. 4 1932

My dear Gutteridge,

   It was kind of you to write to me fully on the subject of
['s] letter. I agree with both of you in a good many respects.
I think with you that the position is improving. One thing that is
doing English law harm is the absence of public criticism by men
who know: and the abundance of criticism by the ill-informed. It
is largely due to the rule which prevents practising barristers from
efforts which appear to be self-advertising, and prevents judges
from writing at all. It seems to me to be particularly within the
province of law teachers. I would include suggestions on and
criticisms of the existing body of the law, the administration of the
law from time to time, refutation of all ill-informed criticism and
suggestions for reform based on comparative law.

   It would help the position of teachers very much if some of
them showed up at times as discriminating champions of the
profession.

   As to the difference between academic teaching and practice I
quite agree that ideally there should be none. In fact there is. You
with your own experience don't feel it; but one only has to look at
some articles and notes in the law magazines to see how
impractical the writers are. Personally I am inclined to think that
[   ] is one of them. However I quite agree that many or
perhaps I should say some teachers with only academic experience
have a lively enough imagination or sympathy to be admirable
guides in the appreciation of principles.

   We can more fully discuss these and other topics at another
time. I only sat down to thank you for your valuable letter.

   With best wishes.

Always yours,
Atkin

6. *Correspondence between Lord Atkin and the Archbishop of Wales*

3c Morpeth Terrace,
Westminster, S.W.1.

Feb. 15. 1938

Dear Archbishop,

I see in this week's, County Times a copy of a letter addressed
by the Bishops of the Welsh Church to their churches which has
caused me the greatest concern. Their attitude to marriage and
divorce is one from which I together with I think many others
totally dissent; and I fear that it will completely alter my relations
with the Welsh Church. Before coming to any final decision
however I should be helped if you would kindly let me know
whence the bishops derive the authority to give the directions
contained in the letter. My difficulty is this. A parishioner as a
member of the Church I always thought had two rights enforceable
at law.

1. To be married in his Parish Church.

2. To be admitted to Holy Communion unless repelled by the
incumbent in possession for his nature as a notorious evil liver.
This point was modified by the recent Divorce Act which allows
an incumbent to refuse the use of his Church for the marriage of
divorced persons.

In respect of both rights the objection of the incumbent and his
right to repel are questions that arise between his parishioner and
the individual incumbent and depend upon the individual
discretion of the latter. I do not think that either right can be
lawfully refused by an incumbent not exercising his own discretion
but acting upon a general direction given to him by superior
authority. I am quite clear that the discretion granted by the
Divorce Act was intended as a convenience to tender consciences
of incumbents and not of Bishops and that it was never
contemplated that the Bishops could take advantage of it to give
general directions. If I had thought this possible I should not have
dreamt of taking the step I did in the House of Lords to extend
this convenience to the Welsh Church. If the law be as I consider it
to be how can it be altered under our constitution by the letter in
question?

Always your sincerely,
Atkin

18th February 1938

From the Most Reverend
The Lord Archbishop of Wales,
Bishopscourt,
Bangor,
North Wales.

My Dear Lord Atkin,

I thank you for your frank letter, expressing disapproval of at least one portion of the recent letter issued by the Bishops. I am sorry, but suppose that the difference of view rests on a priori grounds.

You ask me some questions, which I hope may be answered thus:–

1. The "Parishioner" in the old sense of the term disappeared on the 31st March 1920: and with him any legal rights which he may have had before that date.

2. No Parishioner has ever had the right to be married in Church except under the conditions of the Ecclesiastical Law: if excommunicate he was not even allowed to enter the building [Canon LXXXV of 1603/4].

3. The Churches in Wales since 31st March 1920 belong not to the Incumbent nor to the Parish, but only to the Bishops Clergy and Laity of the Church in Wales "for any of their uses and purposes" [Welsh Church Act 1914 s. 13(2)]. Residents in an Ecclesiastical District (even though still called a Parish) use the Churches situate therein by permission of the Bishops Clergy and Laity of the Church in Wales acting through the Governing Body.

4. The Bishops have the right, within the limits of the Ecclesiastical Law, to issue orders to their Clergy, on the basis of the oath of Canonical Obedience taken by every Clergyman at his ordination or appointment. Metropolitical and Diocesan Visitations rest on that basis.

In conclusion I have only two remarks to make. I have not hastily formed the opinions which I have expressed in this letter: my study of them began in boyhood. Next, although I do not feel at liberty to say why, I think 1938 will show that we have only done in Wales what the Church will do in England, only more promptly, so that everyone knows how the matter stands.

Believe me

Yours sincerely
C. A. Cambrensis

3c Morpeth Terrace,
Westminster, S.W.1.

Feb. 20. 1938

Dear Archbishop,

I am very much obliged to you for your answer to my letter but I regret to say that it fails to remove the difficulties I tried to express. It would serve our purpose to put an argument down in detail. I will content myself in this.

1. As to the right to be married in Church, given the term parishioner in relation to parish as it is to be found in a hundred places in our constitution with an express definition in Chapter VI, a parishioner is taken to be a person recorded as such in the parish and on the electoral role of each parish. Such a person had in my opinion before the Divorce Act of 1857 a right to be married in his parish church and by the incumbent of the parish. The Divorce Act relieved the incumbent of his legal duty to perform the ceremony and this recent Act has now relieved him of his legal obligation to allow the Church to be used. That there was such an obligation before the recent Act is I think made manifest by the fact that it was thought necessary to insert a clause removing it. Why otherwise did the Welsh Bishops move the insertion of an amendment making this clause apply to them? The legal right in England still subsists in Wales but is of course now contractual. My objection is that the statutory relief is given to individual incumbents and is out of order if the incumbent is acting only on general orders from his bishop. If the fact be that the Churches are now the property of the Bishops Clergy and Laity of the whole Church and therefore the rights are subject to their licence, I think it is they and not the Bishops alone or the clergy that can refuse the licence. As the law now stands I submit that this matter is entirely covered by the recent Act.

2. Right to repel from Communion.

As in the former matter so in this. I cannot find the answer to my question by what authority the Bishops gave the directions in question. With great respect the right to give and order and the duty to obey are two different things. I do not think that their oath of canonical obedience goes beyond obedience to a lawful order: but whether it does or not, the order must surely be capable of being justified within the ecclesiastical law. I suggest that the sole right to repel is in the first instance in the incumbent, and on the ground stated — the [rubric] or possibly the additional ground of [illegible].

I am strongly of opinion that at any rate the innocent party to a divorce has a legal claim against any clergyman who repelled him and sheltered under his Bishop's directions.

I cannot expect you and the Bishops to withdraw your directions much as I should desire it. In my opinion formed in much distress they are contrary to the law regulating members of the Welsh Church and violate the constitution. I find it impossible to continue to hold office in the Church in these circumstances and I am proposing to resign from any of the bodies of which I am a member. I shall have to give reasons for this step and I should be glad to have your permission to use this correspondence if I find it desirable. If however you have any objection as of course is quite possible I shall of course refrain from using it.

Always yours sincerely,
A.

23 Feb. 1938

From The Most Reverend
The Lord Archbishop of Wales,
Bishopscourt,
Bangor,
North Wales.

My Dear Lord Atkin,

I am very sorry to learn from your letter of the 20th inst. that you intend (as your previous letter foreshadowed) to resign every "body" of the Church in Wales of which you are a member, because the Bishops of the Province on 29th January 1938 gave certain directions to their Clergy. I repudiate utterly your allegation that the directions of the Bishops violate the Constitution of the Church in Wales.

I say this emphatically because you wish to publish your letters to me, and my replies: I raise no objection to publication.

I express the earnest hope, however, that, before deciding to resign or to publish, you will wait to learn how the Church in England will act. You will then have the more or the less reason for objecting to our Directions.

You have done me the kindness or writing at length; if this reply is brief, it is because a letter will not suffice to cover the ground of controversy which, as no one knows better than you, is very wide.

In conclusion I can only repeat my expression of sorrow at the course proposed.

Believe me, dear Lord Atkin.

Yours very sincerely,
C. A. Cambrensis

INDEX